I0823023

TRANSACTION DENIED

TRANSACTION DENIED

Big Finance's Power to Punish Speech

RAINEY REITMAN

Beacon Press, Boston

Beacon Press
24 Farnsworth Street
Boston, Massachusetts
www.beacon.org

Beacon Press books
are published under the auspices of
the Unitarian Universalist Association of Congregations.

Printed in the United States of America

29 28 27 26 | 8 7 6 5 4 3 2 1

AUTHOR'S NOTE

Fifty percent of the author's profits from this book are going to support the Freedom of the Press Foundation, a nonprofit that protects the rights of an uncompromising, independent press. Learn more about Freedom of the Press Foundation's mission and become a member at https://freedom.press. For more information about this book, including supporting materials, policy suggestions, updates, and discussion guides, and to schedule a book event in your local area or online, visit https://financialcensorship.org.

This book is printed on acid-free paper that meets the uncoated paper ANSI/NISO specifications for permanence as revised in 1992.

Text design by BookMatters, Berkeley

Library of Congress Cataloguing-in-Publication Data is available for this title.

Hardcover ISBN: 978-0-8070-1911-5
E-book ISBN: 978-0-8070-1913-9
Audiobook: 978-0-8070-2323-5

The authorized representative in the EU for product safety and compliance is Easy Access System Europe 16879218, Mustamäe tee 50, 10621 Tallinn, Estonia: https://beacon.org/eu-contact.

For my partner and steadfast supporter, Anton

And in the memory of

JP Barlow, Daniel Ellsberg, Michael Ratner, and Martin Stolar

CONTENTS

TRANSACTION DENIED

INTRODUCTION

FINANCIAL EXCLUSION AS PUNISHMENT

"I believe this was resolved today and they will be reaching out to you or the account holder shortly. Cheers."

It was such a reassuring message. It was an email sent to me from an associate general counsel at PayPal, someone who ought to be able to figure out what was going on with our organization's PayPal account.

But the situation was not resolved.

I'd spent seven months on a campaign to try to free Chelsea Manning, the whistleblower accused of sending files to WikiLeaks. Jeff Paterson, an ex-Marine of towering height and a droll sense of humor, was my closest colleague on the campaign. He and I were on yet another call trying to deal with the newest challenge: PayPal had frozen our campaign account. We were speaking with Vanessa, from PayPal's Office of Executive Escalations. She had just told us that we could verify our account with them by starting a line of credit with PayPal, and Jeff was explaining that we had already done that. Even as I listened to Jeff explain the situation yet again, I kept rereading that pointless email I'd received from PayPal's associate general counsel—"I believe this was resolved today and they will be reaching out to you or the account holder shortly."

After weeks of emails and calls, we kept hitting dead ends at PayPal. Nobody at the company would unfreeze our account or even give us straight answers as to why our account had been frozen in the first place.

Of course, we had our suspicions. We believed we were singled out because Chelsea Manning was controversial, her leaks were polarizing, and there was a media storm around anything related to WikiLeaks. And while we hadn't done anything wrong, PayPal was apparently under no obligation to let us keep our account.

I'd moved to San Francisco a few months earlier to take a job at the Electronic Frontier Foundation (EFF), a civil liberties nonprofit that was mostly lawyers and software developers. I led their three-person activism team. In the evenings and in the mornings before work, I was volunteering my time to work on Chelsea Manning's campaign. It consumed me; it was what I did instead of trying to make friends in this expensive new city I was suddenly living in.

And things were dire. Chelsea was being held in a brig in solitary confinement in Quantico, Virginia, awaiting her pretrial hearing. She had already been in solitary confinement for more than six months. It was hard to get details about her situation, but what I'd heard was deeply disturbing. She wasn't allowed to have her prescription glasses, and she was denied reading material and nearly all communication with the outside world. Once a day, she was escorted to a different room in the prison where she was allowed to shuffle in a circle for an hour before being returned to her tiny cell.

My apartment at the time had a wall of windows that faced the windows of the matching apartment next door, with a small airway between the two. I have this theory that all housing options in San Francisco that aren't outrageously priced have a fatal flaw. My apartment's fatal flaw was the complete lack of privacy. Because our windows faced each other directly with less than six feet of space between us, I always knew whether the couple next door was home and exactly what they were doing. The only privacy I could get was closing my blinds—blocking out the small amount of indirect sunlight I could get—and putting on headphones. It was an awkward, tense way to live, as if I were living in an aquarium under constant observation.

How much worse was Chelsea's situation, I often wondered as I lay in bed trying not to listen to the conversations of the couple in the apartment next to me. Chelsea spent all day every day under the constant observation of guards who were ostensibly assigned to her as some sort of suicide watch but whose incessant, wordless observation must itself have been a form of torture.

Worry over Chelsea's situation was this constant, burning discomfort in my body. It was a physical sense that I wasn't doing enough. On some level, I always felt like if I were a better activist or had better connections, she'd already be free by now—or at least out of solitary confinement. I kept hoping we'd reach some turning point in the campaign and she'd be heralded as a hero, her wrongful imprisonment a centerpiece of the nightly news.

Talking to Jeff was normally a balm to my restless discontent. Maybe it was something about serving five years in the Marines, or maybe it was the hard-fought calm from working with the chaotic and passionate peace community, but Jeff just managed to take everything in stride. A conscientious objector who sat down on the tarmac and refused to be redeployed after the United States started to send troops to the Gulf War, Jeff now ran Courage to Resist, an organization that advocated for war resisters and raised funds for their legal defense. He knew all about dealing with the military court systems and often walked me through what we could expect in Chelsea's trial.

Courage to Resist was acting as the organizational home for our support efforts, a necessary infrastructure for our campaign. Helpfully, Courage to Resist was itself sponsored by the 501(c)(3) organization Alliance for Global Justice—which meant people could make tax-deductible donations to the support efforts. Donations that were currently being frozen by PayPal.

Courage to Resist had used PayPal for five years without any problems. Since becoming the hub of the Chelsea Manning Support Network, the PayPal account had been used for Chelsea's legal defense and advocacy. While not the only way to donate to the campaign, it was a major way that international supporters contributed.

But in December 2010, the credit card companies had moved to cut off financial services to the whistleblower website WikiLeaks. That same month, PayPal contacted Courage to Resist to ask for additional verification about our account. Jeff had answered all the questions, provided Social Security numbers for himself and others involved in the campaign, and even agreed to open a line of credit with PayPal—something we had no need of—to meet their new requirements to maintain the account.

A month later, PayPal froze our account.

Jeff was our expert in all things related to military trials, but this was my opportunity to shine. I'd been working as a consumer advocate in San Diego before taking the job with EFF; I had spent countless hours intervening on company policies on behalf of innocent consumers. This included weighing in with financial institutions on issues like account verification and compliance. I had great contacts at PayPal, and I'd resolved suspended accounts before.

"Don't worry," I'd told Jeff. "I'm sure we can get this sorted right away."

I began reaching out to PayPal, bringing Jeff in for phone calls and emails with the PayPal Office of Executive Escalations and their associate general counsel for global privacy. I didn't worry when we didn't get everything resolved in the first call; I knew these things sometimes took time. But we were hitting dead ends. PayPal now said they could only reconsider our account if we gave them access to our organizational bank account and the authority to withdraw funds.

For Jeff, that was a complete nonstarter, as this was the account with all the donations made for Chelsea's defense. He didn't trust them not to take funds out of the account. Plus, why did they even need this now?

In that final call with Vanessa from PayPal, she tried to argue that this new account restriction had something to do with their obligations under the USA PATRIOT Act, a law passed in 2001 that definitely hadn't been updated recently to require some new restrictions on our account.

This is a tactic that many financial institutions rely on. When questioned about their policies, financial companies try to argue that their bad behavior is somehow required by the PATRIOT Act or by some other law. As if to say, "Don't blame us; blame the government."

But as a professional consumer advocate who had interceded with PayPal and other finance companies, I knew this was baloney. I pointed out that nothing in the PATRIOT Act required us to let them have withdrawal access to our bank account. Plus, Courage to Resist had held a PayPal account for years with no issues whatsoever.

At last, Vanessa from the PayPal Office of Executive Escalations acknowledged this. She agreed that it was an internal policy set up by PayPal, and not a legal requirement. And they weren't budging.

During this call, as I paced around my fishbowl of an apartment, I just kept thinking about Chelsea. Even as I was arguing with Vanessa from PayPal, Chelsea was probably freezing cold in that weird burlap smock they'd given her in lieu of a uniform. At that very moment, she was probably sitting upright in her cell, forbidden from even lying down on her cot during the day. She was probably suffering tremendously, and did anyone even care? Was anyone even paying attention?

As soon as we ended the call with PayPal, I was dialing Jeff's number.

"You heard them," I said. "This isn't a legal obligation. They just decided to shut our account down."

"They have to think of public safety and national security," Jeff drawled. Jeff was angry too—though his version of angry was slow talking and sarcastic. Jeff had always been suspicious of PayPal, whereas I had somehow believed this was all a big mistake. But now I realized I might have been wrong. PayPal may have intentionally frozen our account.

And what if the other finance companies followed suit? What if Mastercard, Visa, and our bank shuttered our accounts the way they had shuttered those of WikiLeaks? It would be the end of our organization and our defense efforts.

We weren't a part of WikiLeaks, and nobody from WikiLeaks was even a member of the Support Network. We'd never broken any laws or published any leaked documents on our website. But none of that seemed to matter to PayPal.

"We have to go public about this," I told Jeff, since it was clear we'd exhausted all avenues with PayPal.

"Yep," he agreed. "Press release?"

"Yes. I'll draft one right now."

Even as we were chatting on the phone, I was curling up on my couch with my laptop balanced on my crossed legs, opening up a blank document to start typing. Less than an hour later, I'd sent him a draft, which he edited while I took my dog to the park. I laughed to see his edits on my phone; he'd changed the headline to call PayPal "Evil."

Jeff sent the press release out in the morning while I headed to work. It was raining; that winter it rained almost every day in San Francisco, and I rode a scooter through congested San Francisco streets and arrived at EFF's office in the Mission District. Once the press release was out, I tweeted it, and then I wrote about it from the Support Network's Twitter account throughout the day.

I could see people sharing the story on Twitter, and articles were coming out in *Wired* and on Yahoo News. The best part? Reporters were calling PayPal and asking them to explain themselves.

Independent reporters have always acted as a check on corporate abuses of power. This was precisely the type of story that showed how powerful journalists can be in pushing companies to explain and defend their actions. I read the articles whenever I had a break between meetings and saw a new petition in support of us pop up on the website Fire-DogLake. Within hours, the petition had ten thousand signatures. Other people were calling PayPal directly.

And then, unexpectedly, we won. Jeff texted me. PayPal had lifted the ban on our account mere hours after we'd published our press release.

I got through the rest of the day in a bit of a blur, and helped write a short statement for the Support Network website announcing PayPal had unfrozen our account. Other staff members at EFF swung by my office to congratulate me on the victory.

But something didn't sit right with me.

PayPal had frozen our account for weeks. They'd been utterly resistant to any direct communication from us. And, then, the minute people on Twitter had gotten wind of the account closure and reporters had started calling PayPal, they had caved. It should have felt like a victory, but I felt uncomfortable about it.

I realized that, on some level, I had still believed PayPal must have some good reason for shuttering our account—perhaps something that they just couldn't or wouldn't tell us. Maybe there had been something weird about our account. Maybe a fraudster had tried to use a stolen credit card to donate to our defense fund. Maybe there was even something administrative, like an address on file didn't match. Something.

But when PayPal reversed their decision so quickly in response to the publicity surrounding our press release, it was clear to me in a way I hadn't truly understood before: We really had done nothing wrong. Because if we had done anything wrong at all, PayPal would have been able to defend its decision. If there had been any legal requirement for PayPal to suspend our account, they wouldn't have changed their mind just because people were tweeting at them.

In that moment, I had a fundamental change in my perspective. I knew, with a certainty born from personal experience, what it was like to be singled out by a payment provider without cause. I knew how disempowering it felt to lose access to a financial service. I experienced—personally, viscerally—how an account shutdown made me doubt myself and literally question whether there was something, anything, that we might have done wrong. I also suspected we were not the only ones this happened to.

I wanted to find other people and organizations that had lost access to financial services. I was curious to meet other people who hadn't violated the law but had nonetheless drawn the ire of financial companies. I especially wanted to find those people and organizations who couldn't harness press attention and have their accounts reinstated.

I decided to start tracking down people and organizations excluded from financial services.

This book is the product of an investigation that spanned more than ten years. In the coming chapters, I'll weave together personal stories of people impacted by financial censorship with a discussion of the laws, court cases, and corporate policies that have allowed this form of privatized censorship to continue.

"Financial censorship" isn't a household concept yet, but it should be. It happens when financial service providers limit or shutter accounts of controversial or marginalized speakers who haven't violated any laws. It is a form of privatized censorship where banks and payment intermediaries act as censors in ways the government couldn't do directly without violating the First Amendment. It's a concept that has been discussed in articles and public comments by the civil liberties community, some financial policy experts and researchers, and some elected officials, but many Americans still aren't aware of it. Indeed, many people assume that financial laws protect people and organizations from having their accounts summarily shuttered for exercising their First Amendment rights. But that's not true at all. Existing financial laws do nothing to address the issue of financial censorship.

The impact of this type of financial exclusion is punishment. Activists, journalists, content creators, and others suffer the punishment of losing their financial services. This creates a dangerous chilling effect on these speakers, who may censor themselves or leave their industries. As I will show in the chapters to come, financial exclusion has become a tool to pressure dissenting and marginalized voices into silence.

For individuals, this can mean waking up one day and not being able to pay bills like rent, daycare, or credit card payments. People I interviewed tell me about the hours they've spent on the phone with banking representatives trying to figure out what happened and set up new accounts. One woman I interviewed told me how she's faced repeated account closures to the point that banks didn't want to do business with her—and so she was unable to even have her name listed on her mortgage.

For businesses and organizations, financial exclusion often means losing access to customers and donors. Small business owners I interviewed tell me about the weeks they have lost attempting to appeal a decision and set up new accounts—time not spent building their businesses. Switching to a new payment service can be a slow and painful process, and customer information and subscriptions are often lost in the transition. I interviewed people at nonprofit organizations that spent months unable to receive any donations, so that every day was a moment closer to running out of money and closing their doors.

There is also widespread data sharing among financial services providers. This data sharing means that, for both people and organizations, losing one financial service can put them at high risk for being rejected from future financial services.

Before I go any further, let me outline a few of the constraints on my research, including the boundaries around what I cover in this book and a few things that are outside of its scope.

First, my study is examining a discrete subset of all financial services: bank accounts, credit card transactions, and payment services. These are the tools you would need to, say, order toilet paper online from Amazon or accept subscriptions to your website. There are many other financial services I'm not considering, including investment services, loans, crowdfunding platforms, and online advertisement services. There are certainly censorship issues that can intersect with these topics that are worthy of discussion and analysis, but for the most part they don't threaten one's ability to interact in modern society and support oneself. I would support the right of financial portfolios to divest from fossil fuels and the right of a crowdfunding platform to refuse accounts to sex workers, much though I personally disagree with the latter. But basic financial services like opening a bank account and buying something online operate at a more intrinsic level; losing these services can create an immediate crisis for a person or organization.

When I use the words "financial institution," "financial intermediary," or "financial service provider," I generally mean them to refer to companies that provide these services directly or are part of a larger ecosystem that facilitates these services. I don't mean it to refer to the legal definition created by the Financial Crimes Enforcement Network (FinCEN), which includes things like casinos and telegraph companies.[1] Instead, I'm looking at banks both large and small, payment intermediaries like PayPal and Stripe, and credit card networks.

Additionally, my research is looking at the United States, with a specific focus on US financial companies and a primary focus on US customers. The United States has long presented itself as a bulwark of democratic debate and openness. I think we should hold the US to the highest standards when it comes to corporate citizenship and defense of human rights. Plus, financial laws and human rights law can vary dramatically from country to country. While I've brought in a few international examples here and there, I'll leave deeper discussions of non-US financial censorship topics to researchers who focus on other jurisdictions. I also won't attempt to catalog the obligations of international banks under international law.

This book is mostly focused on people who were engaged in speech that would be legal in the United States. In a few instances when it's especially instructive to do so, I'll bring in examples that fall beyond that scope—activities that exceed our understanding of the word "speech," for example, and a few examples of illegal expression. I'll try to flag this whenever I do so, and I'll do my best to explain why I include that example.

Finally, I'm using the word "financial censorship" to refer to instances in which financial institutions restrict or close accounts of those engaged in speech or actions that would be protected by the First Amendment. Some folks like to police the use of the word "censorship." They argue that "censorship" as a term should only refer to direct censorship through explicit government actions, and they would dislike my use of the term to describe corporate actions. I think that's a pedantic and unhelpful distinction. I'm using the term here to describe how corporate actions are used to shutter debate and silence voices, often with direct or indirect government pressure involved. I'm primarily interested in the impact of these actions—and that impact is punishing speech. Also, I'll sometimes use words like "financial exclusion" or "debanking" to refer to financial censorship, and that's a stylistic choice to prevent the book from getting repetitive.

When I started writing this book, I thought it would be a compilation of stories. But in uncovering these stories, I realized that it's far more than that. This book is about a *pattern*. Through a decade of research, I've found that certain communities and companies are most likely to be targets of financial censorship—those who are already marginalized, disempowered, or unpopular. I've organized the chapters around those groups most directly, frequently impacted by this form of exclusion: activists, journalists, Muslim community members, adult content creators, and the cannabis community. Through their stories, I'll show an ongoing pattern within the United States to silence dissenting and unorthodox voices by limiting their financial resources extralegally. It would be impossible for me to include every example of financial censorship that I encountered in my research. Instead, I'm going to dig deeper into the stories of people and organizations that are emblematic of the larger problem.

Financial companies are the main actors in this book: They are the entities changing their terms of service, shuttering accounts, and refusing to answer questions. But it would be a mistake to think that this form of censorship is purely the whim of the financial companies.

In the coming chapters, I will analyze several known examples of US government officials pressuring financial institutions to shutter otherwise lawful accounts. This censorship by proxy is a way to push financial institutions to do what the government could not do itself directly without violating the First Amendment: punish those engaged in controversial or heterodox speech.

There's a word for the action of government officials abusing their authority to inappropriately compel private action: *jawboning*. I'll explore several known examples of jawboning toward financial institutions. In chapter 1 on political advocacy, I'll describe a case in which government pressure on financial institutions was so heavy-handed that it rose to the level of coercion and was found unconstitutional by the Supreme Court. But not every example of jawboning has a court case around it. In chapter 5's exploration of cannabis and industry censorship, I'll discuss a little-known program called Operation Choke Point, a Department of Justice effort to pressure financial institutions to smother certain legal industries by depriving them of access to banking services.

Each known example of government pressure to shutter financial services is disturbing. But even more disturbing is the fact that we do not know how often this happens. As we explore examples of financial censorship, we should keep in mind that there may be intense, secret pressure from the government to close certain accounts. This government pressure fundamentally changes how we conceptualize financial censorship. These are not just the actions of financial corporations acting independently. These are businesses that seem to be making rational choices in the face of government pressure, industry guidance, and business realities.

The fact that it is possible to ascribe rational reasoning to these choices does not make the impact of financial censorship any less devastating for those struggling with it. While financial censorship is a serious problem, it isn't directly impacting a huge percentage of the population. But it indirectly impacts all of us.

Financial censorship runs counter to American ideals. Where our society has tolerated political differences, freedom of expression, religious freedom, and open discourse, financial censorship is an extralegal tool for shuttering unpopular and dissenting views. It is a mechanism of silencing people who are outside the mainstream. It circumvents the protections established by the First Amendment because it is private companies engaged in shuttering accounts, not the government.

An open society doesn't punish someone for being an investigative journalist, opening a legal business, or posting boudoir photos on social media. Even the idea of punishing people for these activities is appalling to American sensibilities in a way that it wouldn't be in societies that have more authoritarian governments and more censorship-oriented experiences of technology. Yet financial companies are doing exactly that: punishing people who are exercising their First Amendment rights.

People today cannot survive on wads of cash stuffed under a mattress; they need access to payment and banking services to exist in society. When groups and communities can be cut off from financial services due to their beliefs and speech, it's a form of censorship more in line with authoritarian regimes than modern democracy. Whether we allow this type of financial exclusion to continue unchecked speaks to our character as a society.

Of course, there's another far more personal reason that financial censorship hits home for all of us: the corporations described in this book probably have some of your money. It's companies like Chase, Bank of America, PayPal, Visa, and Mastercard—names you undoubtedly recognize—that are shuttering accounts and blocking transactions.

If you are in the United States and engaging in our economy, you're interacting with these companies. They may even be gatekeepers to the majority of your money, your company's money, and the payment systems you use to buy groceries every week.

Given the deep power these corporations have over our own daily lives, it behooves us to understand and question the policies they have set up to deny certain people access to financial services. As informed consumers, we should be shining a light on the policies of the companies we entrust with our finances. It is worth asking: Even if you have never had a problem with these companies in the past, what's to stop them from instituting a new policy that leaves you or your organization suddenly cut off from the financial world?

Not that much, as it turns out. Financial companies have an astonishing amount of discretion when it comes to shuttering accounts. Laws against discrimination don't guarantee a right to financial services, and a lack of transparency makes it extremely difficult for lawmakers or the public to hold these companies accountable.

This isn't just a book about policy. By grounding this book in interviews, I hope to bring this issue out of the realm of policy analysis and show the real-world impact on people. The individuals I interview come from wildly diverse backgrounds, but their experiences share commonalities: they are attempting to find a way through bureaucratic systems that seem designed to stonewall them.

Which brings us to the question: What can be done if financial companies are resistant to addressing the concerns raised by their own customers? In the coming pages, I'll explore some potential solutions. I'll offer my own experiences starting a nonprofit to thwart one particularly dire instance of financial censorship. I and others created a novel nonprofit organization, the Freedom of the Press Foundation, just as I was beginning to research this book. One of our first acts was to establish a donation pathway to WikiLeaks, helping the whistleblower organization survive in the face of a global banking blockade. I'll talk about how we built an organization capable of bypassing the blockade and discuss whether that model is replicable for future activists.

I'll also examine two payment tools that purport to be outside of the centralized, censorship-prone financial system: cryptocurrency and cash. I'll dig into whether cryptocurrency lives up to early hopes that it would be a censorship-proof tool of finance, and I'll discuss recent proposals to eliminate cash and how this could harm many marginalized communities.

Finally, I'll include some simple, practical ways to improve transparency and oversight of a financial system that has too long kept its censorship practices from the public. I'll talk specifically about what financial companies can do today, without any changes in the law, to address this problem. Then I'll talk about how we could design government interventions to get at the root of this problem. I'll explore the work of activists, elected officials, and banking regulators to try to move the financial industry toward more accountability and neutrality—including instances where legislative text already exists.*

In her dystopian novel *The Handmaid's Tale*, Margaret Atwood describes how a fictional authoritarian government denied women access to bank accounts.[2] Women woke up one day to find their credit cards canceled and their bank cards nonfunctional. Whatever money they had was transferred to their male next of kin, whether that was a husband, brother, father, or more distant relative. It was part of a series of actions the government took to hem women in, prevent them from traveling, and shutter their voices. It's a horrifying idea, and one that has stuck with me ever since.

I no longer find Margaret Atwood's description shocking. Today I understand how easy it would be for the banking system to exclude whole swaths of people who haven't violated any laws, and I've already seen how certain communities and groups are targeted. What I find most disturbing now is how little public conversation there is about this practice. With this book, I hope to change that trend, so that we can decide as a society whether to continue down this dangerous path.

* Additional materials, notes, court documents, updates, and suggested solutions for financial censorship can be found at https://financialcensorship.org.

ONE

SILENCING POLITICAL SPEECH AND ACTIVISTS

Debra Cleaver had perfect credit when her personal credit cards were canceled.

It was the summer of 2021. She was buying something online, but her Chase credit card kept getting declined. She tried her other Chase credit card and found it was also declined. That was it. There was no email notification. No phone call.

She documented her experience on Twitter, writing on June 8:

Today I went to buy something mundane on Amazon. Card rejected. Tried another card. Also rejected. Logged into @ChaseSupport. Saw that all 4 of my accounts are closed. No explanation why.[1]

Cleaver is a voting rights activist based in San Francisco. She called me from a cozy office filled with books and framed posters about voting. She sported red round glasses, a pixie cut, and a gray VoteAmerica sweatshirt. She has a quick, contagious smile and a frank approach to talking about her life and work that feels like she's holding nothing back.

Cleaver happens to be one of the most effective voting rights activists in the country. She's personally responsible for innovative projects like Long Distance Voter (which helped people apply for absentee ballots before that was possible online), Vote.org, and her newest nonprofit, VoteAmerica. As the executive director of a new nonprofit, Cleaver is unspeakably busy.

Cleaver was inspired to get into voting rights issues shortly after graduating college. She was in Northampton, Massachusetts, during the contentious 2000 presidential election between Al Gore and George W. Bush. Cleaver and her friends watched the news as Florida was declared in favor of the Democratic nominee. Her friends had all fallen asleep, but she stayed up, glued to news about the election. She was still awake at 3:00 a.m. when the news stations recanted and declared Florida in favor of the Republican Party. Cleaver was stunned. A few weeks later, the Supreme Court decided the presidential election in favor of George W. Bush by stopping the recount of the Florida ballots. To Cleaver, it seemed to be "election rigging in real time."

From that moment on, Cleaver was committed. She knew she wanted to focus on voting rights. She's been passionately geeking out about how to do elections better ever since.

She told me the biggest issue for her isn't voting—it's democracy. "I want to live in a functioning democracy. That's what you have to know about me. And I just still think that electing good people is a path to that," Cleaver said. "It's not that I care about voter registration. It's not that I care about voting. I mean, I do. But I just see all of that as a means to an end."

And what is that end? Cleaver explained that her goal is for people to "have decent, fulfilling lives where they are not actively harmed every day." She believes democracy is the way to get there. "As flawed as democracy is, it's the single best system we have ever invented. And right now, it's being systematically dismantled."

So what happened to her credit cards? When her payments were declined, Cleaver called Chase Bank. She expected to hear that there was some suspected fraud that had temporarily suspended her credit cards. Instead, she learned that Chase Bank had decided to end their relationship with her and had closed her accounts. Chase didn't offer any explanation. Cleaver points out that she had a twenty-four-year relationship with Chase before her credit card accounts were closed and a credit score over 800—which took a dip when Chase decided to shut down her cards.

Cleaver, acknowledging with a laugh that she is "physically incapable of letting things go," made it her mission to find out what had happened. She tweeted throughout the experience, documenting her attempts to get an explanation from bank representatives by calling and going to bank branches in person. She wrote:

have i mentioned yet that they told me over the phone that they closed my accounts because a "wholly owned chase subsidiary" terminated its relationship with me, so chase followed suit? they won't tell me the name of the affiliate, due to "consumer privacy laws."[2]

And her follow-up tweet:

I pointed out that I am the consumer in question, and that I am waiving my own privacy, but the woman was unmoved. So apparently "consumer privacy laws" now exist to protect me from my own financial information. Fascinating.[3]

She persisted in contacting Chase to try to get to the bottom of it, to no avail. She even used her network to get a message to Jamie Dimon, the CEO of JPMorgan Chase. She shared with me the email she got back:

Reference Number: ECW210615-01874

Dear Debra Cleaver:

Thank you for contacting Jamie Dimon, Chairman of the Board and Chief Executive Officer of JPMorgan Chase & Co. This is to acknowledge your email was forwarded to the Executive Office. We appreciate the opportunity to assist you regarding the closure of your accounts. *We confirmed your accounts were closed because we are ending our banking relationship with you. We are not required to provide an explanation for our decision and decline your request to do so.* [Emphasis added] The decision is final and your accounts are not eligible for reinstatement.

If you have other questions, please call us at the number below.

Cleaver has her own theories about why she might have had her credit cards suddenly canceled. She postulates that it might be because a former acquaintance of hers was convicted of fraud, and she helped provide information to the FBI about the case. It's a theory that is a little flimsy:

Cleaver was never charged with any wrongdoing and was listed as a victim in that case.

Another possibility is that Cleaver was singled out specifically for her advocacy. Her nonprofit, VoteAmerica, had its primary bank account with Chase, but VoteAmerica's related 501(c)(4) organization and wholly owned subsidiary LLC were with other banks. Managing multiple banks seemed like a huge hassle, so Cleaver decided to consolidate all the organizational bank accounts under Chase. Cleaver assumed that whatever had prompted Chase to shutter her personal credit cards, it was about her and not the organization.

But it turned out that Chase had a big problem with VoteAmerica. The bank set up the new checking accounts for the related VoteAmerica organizations and allowed Cleaver to deposit $144,000. Then Chase closed the accounts, again offering no explanation.

The difference this time was that Chase was holding $144,000 of VoteAmerica's money. Cleaver began the process of appealing to have the money returned and was met with multiple dead ends. Twice, banking representatives told her that the checks for VoteAmerica's funds were in the mail—but no money arrived. In the end, Cleaver made a formal complaint to the Consumer Financial Protection Bureau, an agency that as of this writing protects consumers from abusive financial practices. Only then were the funds returned.

It took eighty-one days for Cleaver to get VoteAmerica's funds returned by Chase. It was such a battle that today she marks the victory by keeping copies of the two checks on the refrigerator.

Chase was not the only bank that refused to do business with VoteAmerica. Cleaver also applied for accounts for VoteAmerica at First Republic Bank. Soon after she submitted the applications, she was declined. Cleaver showed me the correspondence with the bank representative, who said that the bank was declining the account due to their "strict policy on onboarding politically [*sic*] action accounts."

Cleaver responded to point out that VoteAmerica is a nonpartisan organization. "We don't endorse or oppose candidates for office, and we help all voters regardless of political affiliation. If we were going to do political work, we would have a PAC or an Independent Expenditure committee, and we have neither," she wrote to the bank representative. "The IRS does not grant tax-exempt status to partisan or political organizations, and I would assume that First Republic would trust the IRS to make this determination."

But the First Republic representative responded that nothing could be done. "I did explain in an internal meeting that your organizations are nonpartisan but the bank has decided that they would not like to proceed," she wrote back to Cleaver.

This brief, vague explanation—a claim that the bank had limitations around serving "political" organizations—is the only explanation Cleaver has ever gotten from any bank about why she was denied banking services.

Cleaver is far from the only activist who has lost access to banking services in this way, and examples span the political spectrum. Former senator and ambassador Sam Brownback faced similar discrimination from Chase Bank.

Brownback is particularly focused on the issue of religion. While he and Cleaver are wildly different in their philosophies, they both see their efforts as contributing to more just governments. Brownback sees religious freedom as a check on government power abuses. As he told me, "Authoritarians hate religion because it's an authority higher than them."

Brownback, now in his late sixties, was straight-backed in his chair for our interview, with a blue button-up shirt and black jacket, his gray hair cut close to the scalp. His brow furrowed and his head tilted slightly as he spoke about the dire situation in Nicaragua, where anyone who tries to speak out against the government faces potential imprisonment. Brownback noted, "[President Daniel] Ortega is in his fifth term and is at war with the Catholic Church. Because it's the only institution that's still in Nicaragua that is civil society, that has any organizational structure and a capacity to stand up to the Ortega regime. They're the only ones."

Brownback grew up in Kansas and got his law degree from the University of Kansas in 1982. He represented Kansas first as a US representative, then as a senator, and finally as governor. During his years as an elected official, Brownback opposed same-sex marriage, defended prayer, and voted against abortion—positions that reflected the popular views of his home state of Kansas. In January 2018, he took the role of US ambassador at large for international religious freedom, advising the secretary of state and, indirectly, the president.

Brownback remembered the exact moment he became a committed advocate for religious freedom. It was during his time as a senator, and he answered a call from his staff member Sharon Pate. She told him that a Christian missionary had just been released from jail in Uzbekistan in response to a letter from Brownback. Pate had been urging Brownback to engage in this kind of advocacy, pointing out that something like a letter or even just attention from a US senator could help free imprisoned missionaries or keep them alive around the world.

Talking about it with me, there was awe and pride in Brownback's voice. "I'm at one of my kid's softball games back in Kansas, and I get a call from Sharon. She says, 'He's out. He's out of jail.' And I said, 'What, really?' She said, 'Yeah, that letter? They released him.'"

Just like that, Brownback was all in. He committed to using his influence to bring attention to imprisoned and persecuted religious figures around the world, and he used his time in the Senate and later as ambassador to fight for freedom for not only Christians but also Muslims, Jews, and others.

In 2022, no longer a government official, Brownback founded the National Committee for Religious Freedom (NCRF). After years of championing religious freedom globally, Brownback wanted to protect religious freedom in the United States. He felt that any loss of ground around religious freedom here could set the stage for a reduction in religious rights in other countries. NCRF was designed to be a grassroots organization that helped communities defend religious freedom.

NCRF set up a bank account with Chase a few months after it was started. In May, Sam Brownback went in person to make a deposit at a Chase branch near Kansas City. He was told that the account didn't exist anymore. His reaction was shock.

"I was stunned. What had we done? Because the organization had just been formed, we were just getting our advisory board stood up, we were just getting things started, and the thing is canceled. And I'm just... really, I'm dumbfounded by it." He shook his head to remember it. "We hadn't done anything."

Brownback and his colleagues at NCRF tried to get to the bottom of what happened but immediately hit dead ends. The Chase employees they spoke with said that the decision to close the account had come from the corporate office, and that there was a note in the file that instructed Chase employees not to provide any further information to the customer.

Brownback and NCRF kept meticulous notes of their interactions with Chase and were able to provide me with copies of all the communications from Chase, a time line of events, and a recording from a call with Chase. After weeks of fruitless requests for information, a member of the executive office at Chase in New York told NCRF that the bank would reconsider providing accounts to NCRF if the organization could provide the bank with a list of all donors, a list of intended fund recipients for the next election cycle, and details about how NCRF would select pro-religious freedom candidates to support. As a 501(c)(4), NCRF is allowed to engage in lobbying and support political candidates. NCRF declined to provide those details to Chase.

On October 21, Chase sent another letter to NCRF. This time the bank asserted that something was said during the account opening process that triggered an investigation into money laundering and domestic terrorism. Brownback had brought NCRF executive director Justin Murff with him to open the account.

I asked Brownback what it felt like to hear that something he or Murff had said had caused such an investigation. "Well, it all sounded like somebody searching for an excuse," he replied. He described going to the branch in DC in person to sign the paperwork on the account with Murff, who himself had once worked for Chase, and that everything seemed entirely routine to him.

In November, seven months after closing the account, Chase offered a new reason for the account closure in an email. The bank now claimed it closed NCRF's account because Brownback was a "politically exposed person."

There were many weird things about Chase's decision to deny banking services to NCRF, but the argument that Brownback is a politically exposed person was probably the strangest. A politically exposed person (PEP) is someone who has a high-profile political role, for example, a head of state, or is one of such a person's immediate family members and close associates. The banks consider these people to be at a higher risk of bribery and corruption, so there's extra scrutiny on their accounts—but it generally doesn't mean they can't have accounts at all.

Notably, Brownback was no longer a senator or an ambassador when he founded NCRF. Was it possible that Chase considered every former US elected official to be a PEP? That would be an extraordinary number of people. And could it be the case that Chase's policy was to deny all of them bank accounts? As I reviewed the letter from Chase, I kept thinking, *Surely, if every former US senator was unable to get banking services from one of the largest banks in the country, we'd have heard about that before now.*

Plus, US banking regulators don't consider US public officials to be PEPs. In August 2020, FinCEN issued a joint statement with the Board of Governors of the Federal Reserve System, the Federal Deposit Insurance Corporation, the National Credit Union Administration, and the Office of the Comptroller of the Currency offering guidance to banks about PEPs. While noting that the term isn't defined in the regulations, the joint regulators made their position abundantly clear, writing, "The Agencies do not interpret the term 'politically exposed persons' to include U.S. public officials."[4]

But when it comes to banking regulation, it turns out that those five regulatory bodies aren't the only game in town. There's another entity known as the Wolfsberg Group that offers its own guidance on these and other issues. Originally convened in 2000 at a chateau in Switzerland, the Wolfsberg Group is an association of twelve of the largest global banks, including Bank of America, Citi, Deutsche Bank, Goldman Sachs, and, of course, JPMorgan Chase. Though not a regulatory body, the Wolfsberg Group develops and publishes its own guidelines for combating financial crime, and it works closely with Transparency International, a nonprofit that fights corruption.[5]

The Wolfsberg Group created its own guidance on politically exposed persons in which it argues, among other things, that US domestic persons should have the same high scrutiny as foreigners: "While Financial Action Task Force (FATF) guidance recommends that all foreign PEPs should automatically be classified as high risk, the Wolfsberg Group advocates for the application of an RBA [Risk Based Approach] for all PEPs, *whether foreign or domestic*" (emphasis added). Later in the same document, the guidance states: "FIs should assess the risk posed by PEPs *regardless of whether they are domestic or foreign* [emphasis added] and apply commensurate due diligence standards."[6]

The efforts of the Wolfsberg Group and Transparency International to combat financial crime are laudable, and we can all agree that corruption hurts our democracy and our world. But what's missing from the Wolfsberg guidance is a sense of the harms caused by unnecessary scrutiny and wrongly shuttered accounts. The single-minded focus on combating financial crimes fails to consider other values—like ensuring fair access to financial services for everyone, including those engaged in political advocacy. It's frankly disturbing that the largest banks are developing this type of guidance without input from the civil liberties community.

Brownback felt like Chase never offered a real explanation for why the account was closed. "We eventually ended up getting four different answers as to why they closed the account, none of which, in my mind, seemed to have any resemblance to what was actually going on. But we never got any answer. We never had a meeting with anybody in a decision-making position. It was just…closed."

Brownback and NCRF have tried to use their position to draw attention to the decision by Chase and to raise questions about whether this type of discrimination is happening to other religious freedom groups. They've gone public about the account closure, and they've been doing interviews with the press.

NCRF also began a campaign they called #ChasedAway. It's an effort to gather stories from other religious groups that also had accounts shuttered by Chase. As a former elected official, Brownback felt he could publicly take a stand against a financial giant like Chase. But perhaps there were other, smaller organizations hesitant to speak out.

I spoke with Matt Goddard, one of the staff members of NCRF, about the #ChasedAway campaign. He said that many organizations who face this kind of discrimination end up just taking their money to another financial institution, and "they don't make a stink. They don't want the adverse publicity." He told me that NCRF felt it was important that they take a stand.

"If they can shut us down—and we are chaired by a former United States senator—they can shut anybody down. So we decided we were not going to go quietly."

For VoteAmerica and NCRF, there are unanswered questions about why the accounts were flagged. Were the accounts singled out because all political advocacy accounts with Chase are subject to extra review, or were these accounts specifically identified because of their mandates?

But trying to understand why the banks do something can be an unending rabbit hole: banks often won't say why they do something, or they might change their story multiple times, just as they did with NCRF. So *intent* is always a little hard to pin down in cases of financial censorship.

But *impact* is not. Regardless of what Chase intended, the impact was a massive headache for two advocacy nonprofits that found themselves hamstrung without access to banking services. The impact was hours spent trying to get answers from Chase's obtuse customer service representatives, in the absence of a fair appeals process or any useful transparency mechanisms. The impact was punishing political activists, when other types of organizations are able to set up and maintain accounts at Chase without problems.

Advocacy groups, especially smaller grassroots nonprofits, often operate on a shoestring budget where a brief disruption in funds could have severe consequences for an organization's ability to cover costs and pay salaries. The ability of banks to shutter accounts without notice or explanation gives these financial companies incredible power to disrupt political movements at key moments.

Currently, we do not have mechanisms to ensure banks don't abuse that power.

STOP COP CITY ACTIVIST SHUTTERED DUE TO "NEGATIVE NEWS"

Another political activist who lost her Chase bank account got an explanation about what caused her account to be closed.

Teresa Shen, a therapist living in Brooklyn, has been actively engaged in political advocacy for many years. She and others have been participating in public protests against a sprawling new police complex planned in Atlanta, Georgia.

Critics of the police training facility call it "Cop City." They say that Cop City would destroy hundreds of acres of forest.[7] They also raise concerns about racialized police violence and how the training facility will promote the same practices that led to the deaths of many people of color at police hands. Those closest to the planned Cop City are largely working-class communities of color, who, critics argue, would suffer from having this massive training facility so close by.[8]

Defenders of the police training facility disagree. They argue that the training center could teach law enforcement "to learn de-escalation and harm reduction techniques that reduce the use of force when viable alternatives are available."[9] They say the area to be developed isn't a forest but land that has been cleared multiple times in the past, and that the new facility will have green areas open to the public.[10]

The Stop Cop City protests have been passionate and combative. Carrying signs like "Trees give life, police take it," protesters have held rallies and established an encampment at the proposed training site, including protesters who sit in trees to prevent them from being cut down.[11]

Attempts by Atlanta police to evict the protesters have already resulted in the death of one protester, a twenty-six-year-old activist who died after being shot fifty-seven times by the Georgia police.[12] Police claim the protesters have "destroyed multiple pieces of construction equipment by fire and vandalism."[13]

Though Teresa Shen lives in New York, she traveled to Atlanta to protest Cop City. She got arrested. Shen is facing charges from her participation in the protests, including under Georgia's "domestic terrorism" law.

In 2017, Georgia broadened its statute around domestic terrorism. As the ACLU explained, "The new law broadened the state's definition of 'domestic terrorism' to include certain property crimes committed with the intent to 'alter, change, or coerce the policy of the government' by 'intimidation or coercion.'"[14] Many Stop Cop City demonstrators are facing charges under this expanded law, including Shen.

But unlike other protesters, Shen found herself singled out by a disparaging news article by the right-leaning UK publication the *Daily Mail.* The paper called her "an Antifa terror suspect who is part of the Atlanta cell" and then published details about her family, including scholarships her mother received to attend university in the United States, photos of her family home, and details of her parents' careers, with references to the Chinese government and George Soros inserted to make the article sound especially scandalous.[15]

"It was just a racist piece of garbage that was trying to paint me as some sort of Chinese foreign agent or something. My father is not a tycoon," Shen told *Hell Gate NYC*, a New York City blog.[16] But apparently, that disparaging article was enough to get Shen's account at Chase shuttered.

As Shen described it to *Hell Gate NYC*, she had been a customer of Chase Bank for more than a decade. But, in March 2023, Chase sent

Shen letters informing her that it was closing her savings account, checking account, and credit card. It also closed the account of the therapy group where she worked and was a signer on the account. The letters said that the bank was taking these steps "due to a publicly reported financial investigation."

She called the number provided in the letters. A Chase representative confirmed that her accounts were being closed but wouldn't provide more information. She tried again the next day. As she told *Hell Gate NYC*, the Chase representative offered slightly more information: "He told me, 'I don't really see anything on here other than two words.' The two words were 'negative media.'" At that point, Shen reached out to the National Lawyers Guild, which connected her with Marty Stolar.

When I met Stolar, he was eighty years old and started the conversation by lighting a cigarette. He told me he was intrigued by Shen's case, and that he found her issue "fascinating." Stolar was one of the foremost legal experts on the right to protest. He spent decades defending demonstrators, starting with Vietnam War protesters who were arrested en masse. Stolar himself was no fan of the Vietnam War; he enrolled in law school to avoid the draft and then signed up as a lawyer with VISTA (now called AmeriCorps) to continue avoiding being called up.

His work with VISTA was providing legal services to indigent communities, and they sent him to Chicago to take courses in poverty law and housing law. One evening in 1968 he wandered out from the YMCA in downtown Chicago after classes were over and found himself overtaken by police. He was chased and gassed by the police, who wrongly believed he was taking part in nearby public protests organized around the Democratic National Convention.

He credited that moment with radicalizing him. After that harrowing experience, he actively sought cases where he could represent protesters and made that the cornerstone of his legal work. It would be difficult to find an attorney with more experience representing protesters than Stolar. He has been in the courtroom for some of the US's most important cases around protest and demonstration, from a class action lawsuit against the New York Police Department for surveillance of political movements to representing the Black Panthers.

Stolar thought the domestic terrorism charges facing Shen were ridiculous. "There's nothing different about her case and what the [other] protesters are doing in Cop City. They're doing all the straight political stuff that people try to do. They petition, they tried to put it on the ballot, they demonstrate, they sit in, they block bulldozers."

He said the attempt to call this type of activity domestic terrorism was a "convenient political ploy" to make the activities of the demonstrators sound far worse than it is: "It's merely a naming of conduct which in every other jurisdiction in the country is disorderly conduct or trespassing. To call it domestic terrorism is a farce." He took Shen's case to try to get answers about what happened with her bank account, but he quickly hit dead ends.

Stolar told me: "I wrote to them. I wrote to their president. I wrote to their general counsel. I wrote to the New York State banking regulators. And I got turned back to something called their executive office." He never got the account reinstated, but he did manage to get Chase on the record about why her account was closed: "The final report that I've gotten is for negative publicity. They finally copped to that."

He shared with me the letter from Chase Bank. The letter states: "We confirmed your clients' accounts were exited for negative media." This was a new area for Stolar, and one he found concerning. "I mean, the best I can pull out of that is that the bank, as well as the other banks and financial institutions, have hired some outside company—a set of companies—to advise them about risky people."

Stolar was right. Banks often flag accounts for anything they consider to be "adverse news" or "negative media." In fact, there are commercial services offering this sort of risk management for financial institutions.

In a few days of searching, I found over a dozen companies offering software that would screen for adverse media. "Our global Adverse Media data covers news on money laundering, terrorist funding, bribery, and drug trafficking," explains one that calls itself Sanction Scanner.[17] Companies like Persona offer to save banks time by bringing more automation to the process of reviewing adverse media and argue that "regularly completing thorough adverse media checks is an effective way to reduce your company's reputational risk."[18]

Reputational risk is a step beyond mere compliance risk. It is a way for the bank to consider whether its *reputation* might be damaged by having an association with a banking client. When a bank chooses to screen current and potential clients against any negative news, it can also choose to end a relationship if it believes that the client could have a negative impact on the bank's public image.

While it may sound intangible, this concept of reputational risk ended up in the guidance used by government regulators. For example, the US Office of the Comptroller of the Currency (OCC) refers to reputational risk in its 2019 *Comptroller's Handbook*, stating:

> Reputation risk is the risk to current or projected financial condition and resilience arising from negative public opinion.... The assessment of reputation risk should take into account the bank's culture, the effectiveness of its problem-escalation processes and rapid-response plans, and its engagement with news media.[19]

Financial regulators like the OCC, the Federal Deposit Insurance Corporation (FDIC), and the National Credit Union Administration (NCUA) assess regulated banks and credit unions through a variety of mechanisms. One system they use is called the CAMELS rating system, which is an acronym that stands for Capital adequacy, Asset quality, Management, Earnings, Liquidity, and Sensitivity to market risk. A bad CAMELS rating indicates that the bank has some serious risk management issues and may need more regulatory scrutiny. While there is no "R" for reputation in CAMELS, reputational risk has been used to inform "Asset quality" and "Management." This means that banks that are looking to get the best CAMELS rating possible (and thus reduce unnecessary scrutiny from regulators) have been incentivized to adopt reputation management systems.[20]

The Wolfsberg Group has issued guidance about adverse media. In May 2022, they stated that financial firms should screen for negative news as part of due diligence: "While there remain some limitations and challenges pertaining to broad media searches, negative news screening can be a valuable mechanism which enables financial institutions to have a better understanding of who they are doing business with and the risks to which a financial institution is exposed."[21]

There isn't a single, canonical list of the financial crimes that should be included in the search. The Wolfsberg Group says, "An FI [financial institution] should ensure that the Financial Crime related Negative News is distinguished from other Negative News which is not considered relevant. For example, civil proceedings *may* be excluded from NNS, e.g., speeding fines and public disorder offenses which are not related to Financial Crime. *This is at the discretion and in line with the risk appetite of each FI*" (emphasis added).[22]

The Wolfsberg Group recommended that when a financial institution uses third-party vendors to screen for negative news, it "understands the evaluation of reliability performed by the vendor and the controls they have in place to mitigate the risk of unreliable sources influencing the screening process." It also notes that financial institutions should think about where in the judicial cycle to consider a crime noteworthy. "An FI will need to determine at which stage it wishes to be alerted to the potential Negative News, recognising that alert volumes at the allegation stage will be higher than receiving an alert at conviction stage once the alleged crime has been investigated and may have less AML/CTF [Anti-Money Laundering/Countering the Financing of Terrorism] value."[23]

While the Wolfsberg Group notes some of the problems with negative news screenings, it could have urged banks not to screen for adverse media at all. Or at the least, it could have used stronger language. It could have said: "Banks, please don't include speeding fines and public disorder offenses in your news screenings and stick to only heinous crimes." It could have said: "The Wolfsberg Group recommends that financial institutions not shutter the accounts of people who are merely accused of a crime but instead wait until they are convicted." It could have said: "Only ever consider the highest-rated, most politically neutral, reputable journalistic organizations for assessing whether to shutter someone's bank account."

Wolfsberg's guidance doesn't erase Chase's responsibility for closing Teresa Shen's bank account. After all, it was Chase, not the Wolfsberg Group, that closed her account because her name had been featured in the *Daily Mail*. I offer the influence of the Wolfsberg Group only to show that this problem isn't solely with Chase. Negative news screenings are part of industry-wide guidance that fails to account for the detrimental impact on both individuals and society when certain communities are cut off from financial services.

It's notable that Chase is heavily featured throughout this chapter. I don't think that's because Chase is more discriminatory toward political activists than other banking institutions, though that is certainly possible.

Chase is also an enormous bank with branches across the country—a bank that many people turn to for both personal and organizational accounts. The frequency of examples may just be a result of the bank's size and reach. To know for sure whether Chase's policies regarding political activists are worse than that of other financial institutions, we would need more transparency from across the industry as a whole.

REPUTATIONAL RISK AND GOVERNMENT COERCION

In some instances of financial censorship, we can clearly see the heavy hand of government coercion.

In April 2018, the Department of Financial Services of New York, under direction from New York governor Andrew Cuomo, issued new guidance toward banks and insurance companies. The banking guidance was addressed to "The Chief Executive Officers or Equivalents of New York State Chartered or Licensed Financial Institutions." In the letter, Superintendent of Financial Services Maria Vullo discussed the tragic deaths resulting from recent mass shootings and the growing social backlash against the National Rifle Association and similar organizations that promote guns. She specifically referred to the "reputational risk" that banks might face from "dealings with the NRA or similar gun promotion organizations." The letter ended with some strong encouragement for financial institutions to "review any relationships" they have with the NRA and "take prompt action" to manage those risks.[24]

The official guidance letters weren't the only pressure from officials in New York. The Department of Financial Services also allegedly leaned on insurance companies to stop providing services to the NRA. Vullo "made clear that her real interest lay in causing companies to stop providing insurance to the NRA," and she planned to use her regulatory authority strategically in support of that interest.[25] That same month, Governor Cuomo tweeted, "The NRA is an extremist organization. I urge companies in New York State to revisit any ties they have to the NRA and consider their reputations, and responsibility to the public."[26]

The NRA sued Governor Cuomo and Superintendent Vullo. The organization argued that it had been singled out due to its position on gun rights, and that its advocacy on the issue was protected by the First Amendment. While Cuomo and Vullo didn't directly censor the NRA's advocacy, they pressured intermediaries that the NRA relied on (insurance companies and banking services) to end their relationship with the NRA because Cuomo and Vullo disagreed with the NRA's advocacy positions.

In *National Rifle Association of America v. Vullo*, the NRA argued that this type of pressure was coercion of private companies to indirectly suppress or punish the NRA's speech. The district court agreed with the NRA, but the Second Circuit Court of Appeals disagreed. The Supreme Court heard the case in March 2024 and issued an opinion on May 30, 2024.[27]

This case attracted some strange bedfellows. Perhaps most surprising: the solicitor general for the United States, who represents the interests of the federal government in front of the Supreme Court, sided with the NRA over New York officials. And the American Civil Liberties Union joined, representing the NRA as co-counsel and arguing the case in front of the Supreme Court. The ACLU often doesn't agree with the positions of the NRA. In fact, as ACLU executive director Anthony Romero explained in a blog post, "We abhor many of the group's goals, strategies, and tactics."[28] Nonetheless, Romero explained, the ACLU joined the case because "the NRA has a right, like all other advocacy organizations, to pursue their mission free from reprisals by government officials who disagree with its political viewpoint. The government should not be able to evade the Constitution by doing indirectly what it plainly cannot do directly."

The Supreme Court agreed. In a unanimous decision penned by Justice Sonia Sotomayor, the justices found that there were important First Amendment interests at play and denied the government's motion to dismiss the case. While a government official is free to offer an opinion and engage in public advocacy, she must not use her position to lean on intermediaries like banks as a way to censor or punish speech she doesn't like: "She can rely on the merits and force of her ideas, the strength of her convictions, and her ability to inspire others. What she cannot do, however, is use the power of the State to punish or suppress disfavored expression."

The Supreme Court pointed to *Bantam Books v. Sullivan*, a case from 1963 in which a state commission sent official notices to a distributor of publications it found objectionable.[29] In the *Bantam Book*s case, the

Supreme Court found that government officials couldn't use the threat of legal sanctions as a tool to pressure intermediaries to suppress speech they didn't like. If the government wasn't allowed to censor the speech directly or indirectly because of the First Amendment, then it also wasn't allowed to indirectly pressure others (like distributors) to censor that speech.

In *NRA v. Vullo*, the Supreme Court noted that assessing whether government coercion took place required looking at a number of factors together. It approved of the way the Second Circuit Court of Appeals had weighed the issues (even if it disagreed with that court's ultimate conclusion), which considered four factors in a government official's messaging:

1. The word choice and tone
2. The existence of regulatory authority
3. Whether the speech was perceived as a threat
4. Whether the speech refers to adverse consequences

Importantly, the Supreme Court acknowledged that intermediaries would be particularly vulnerable to pressure from government regulators. Citing an amicus brief from First Amendment scholars, the Supreme Court noted that "intermediaries will often be less invested in the speaker's message and thus less likely to risk the regulator's ire."[30]

This is a landmark case for many reasons, and it's key to understanding the issue of financial censorship. The Supreme Court understood that depriving an organization of its basic financial services is a way of suppressing or punishing speech. This case also reaffirms that censorship doesn't just happen directly; government officials may lean on intermediaries, including banks, to suppress speech they don't like. And, of course, the Supreme Court saw how vulnerable intermediaries like banks are to pressure.

It's also worth noting that a lot of stars had to align for this case to result in a unanimous Supreme Court decision. First, there had to be some First Amendment protected speech in the mix. This case would have been entirely different if, for example, regulators in New York had decided to go after companies that make and distribute guns; unlike political advocacy, manufacturing guns is not First Amendment–protected speech, so there wouldn't have been the same constitutional issues.

Second, government agents had to engage in some ham-fisted pressure tactics against the banking industry to reach the legal standard of coercion. *NRA v. Vullo* shows that there's a level of government coercion on banks that is unconstitutional. But in many instances, government officials may be able to strongly influence banking intermediaries without such direct threats. As John Vecchione, senior litigation counsel for the New Civil Liberties Alliance, explained, "Bankers are not known for their great moral strength in the face of regulators. If you ever talk about long-tailed cats in a rocking chair store, that's the bankers."[31]

While *NRA v. Vullo* shows a clear example of overt government coercion, there may be many other instances that are less public and more indirect. Whenever we see a financial company shutter the account of someone exercising their First Amendment rights, it is worth pausing to consider whether the company is reacting to some sort of private government pressure, including subtle or indirect pressure. As outsiders, we often don't know.

FUTURE-PROOFING BANKING SYSTEMS

It's one thing to stand up for the rights of advocacy groups you agree with. Deciding to stand up for the rights of groups you disagree with is a much dicier proposition. I've explored the stories of advocates from across the political spectrum to tease out this exact issue. Should banks be closing the accounts of political activists? Importantly, should the answer to that question rest on whether or not one agrees with the positions those activists are promoting?

I spoke about this question with Lia Holland, campaigns and communications director at Fight for the Future, a nonprofit that advocates for civil liberties online. She said that for her, it's about "future-proofing technology" so that advocates are not denied basic financial services: "Just because it might make you happy today to see a person that you don't agree with losing access to their money and suffering, that doesn't mean that that same mechanism might not be turned against you down the road." Instead, she urged people to take the long view so that our financial systems are "more resilient to potential misuse regardless of who's in power."

This perspective mirrors some of the arguments the ACLU offered when deciding to get involved in *NRA v. Vullo*. In a media advisory, the organization wrote:

> Across the country, organizations in the fight for racial justice, criminal legal reform, reproductive and LGBTQ rights too often face attacks by state and local government officials who disagree with their point of view. If the court had allowed New York to blacklist a powerful organization like the NRA, government officials would have had even greater power to target less powerful organizations—especially those who speak for our most vulnerable communities.[32]

Dedicating one's life to changing the world can come with a lot of sacrifices, but access to financial services should not be one of them. Shuttering the banking services of activists and advocacy groups does not just directly stifle the dissent of those impacted. It also sends a dangerous message to anyone else who is thinking about engaging in public advocacy.

It also gives financial institutions an undue amount of power over our political discourse. In these and the examples in the coming chapters, financial institutions show time and again that they are ill suited to wielding this power. Whenever we look into whether advocacy or certain types of speech are legitimate and worthy of protection, we have to consider not only the content of the speech itself but the appropriateness of who is judging that speech.

Banks are wholly inappropriate for that task.

TWO

JOURNALISM IN THE CROSSHAIRS

"We were punished."

That's how Joe Lauria, the editor in chief of *Consortium News*, described PayPal's decision to cut off their account.[1]

Lauria has spent decades writing about international affairs, with the bulk of his career working as a United Nations correspondent, first for the *Boston Globe* and then for seven years at the *Wall Street Journal*. Those years taught him a skepticism of governments. He doesn't parrot government propaganda—and he's quick to call out other publications that do.

Consortium News was created in 1995 to be an internet-first news outlet—something that's quotidian today but was groundbreaking at the time. The founder, Robert Parry, was a journalist best known for helping break the Iran-Contra scandal in the 1980s. In the wake of the Iraq War—when countless media outlets across the United States drummed up fears of weapons of mass destruction in Iraq—Parry wanted to create a more independent news outlet. Parry said he was concerned about a healthy democracy: "We looked at the underlying problems of modern democracy, particularly the insidious manipulation of citizens by government propaganda and the accomplice role played by mainstream media. Rather than encouraging diversity in analyses especially on topics of war and peace, today's mainstream media takes a perverse pride in excluding responsible, alternative views."[2]

Even after Parry passed away in 2018 and the baton was passed to Lauria, *Consortium News* has served as an independent voice. It offers a critical view of US engagements overseas and has provided ongoing, scathing coverage of US encroachments on press freedom.

When PayPal closed *Consortium News*' account in May 2022, it held $9,000 of *Consortium News*' funds.[3] PayPal didn't offer an explanation for why it shut down the account. But Lauria believes it was directly connected to their coverage of the war in Ukraine.

I spent hours reading through articles both on the *Consortium News* website and criticizing *Consortium News* to try to understand its role in the larger media landscape. In the weeks before PayPal's decision to shutter their account, *Consortium News* published multiple articles about the Russian invasion of Ukraine, and they didn't merely paint Russia as an aggressor that must be stopped at all costs. Many of the articles on *Consortium News* were critical of the Ukrainian government's current approach to the war and US involvement. One article published on *Consortium News* before the PayPal shutdown featured an interview with a Ukrainian academic whose book about President Volodymyr Zelenskyy painted his "neoliberal" economic policies as unpopular.[4] Another article discussed a curfew in the Ukrainian city of Odessa on the anniversary of a violent clash between pro-Ukraine and pro-Russia protesters.[5] There was also an opinion piece from writer Caitlin Johnstone titled "Being Anti-War Isn't Easy," which argued that modern wars include a public messaging campaign that makes them palatable even to people who dislike the idea of war. "In theory people are just opposed to the idea of blowing other people up for no good reason," wrote Johnstone. "In practice they're always hit with a very intense barrage of media messaging giving them what looks like very good reasons why those people need to be blown up."[6]

PayPal never confirmed whether the account was closed for coverage of the war against Ukraine, and in fact provided hardly any explanation of why it had shuttered this pushy news outlet. As Lauria explained in an interview with podcast *Scheer Intelligence* on KCRW:

> I only could surmise from their user agreement that they think we've published false information. What is that false information? What's being left out purposely, deceptively, by the major media about these important facts to create a context for this Russian invasion of Ukraine.
>
> And historians can talk about the Versailles treaty causing resentment in Germany, which led to the rise of Nazism in World War II, and that's fine; that's not excusing. But we can't talk about the context and the causes of this war. That's all we report; we don't support either side. That might be a problem, because we're not standing with Ukraine, but we are just trying to give a factual analysis of what caused this incredibly dangerous conflict.[7]

Lauria also feared that PayPal wouldn't be the only financial service to cut them off: "We're worried about our bank account. We're worried about another government-linked agency trying to sully our reputation. And we are not permitted to—well, we are so far, but the walls are closing in. PayPal may be the first step."

Journalists started reporting on the account closure, including Matt Taibbi, *Democracy Now!*, and *The Hill*'s Kim Iversen. On social media, people were furious at PayPal.[8]

On May 4, 2022, Lauria published an update on *Consortium News* noting that PayPal had "backed off" and would be unfreezing the organization's funds, and he speculated that it was a response to the public outcry. The update from PayPal seemed to include the possibility that *Consortium News* could again begin receiving funds through PayPal: "Access to your account will remain limited until you perform the steps required to lift the limitation."[9]

However, two days later Lauria published another blog post. He said that a representative from PayPal's Escalation Department told him that the notice about reinstating the PayPal account was in error and that *Consortium News* was permanently banned. Lauria wrote:

> An agent from PayPal's "escalation department" then said she could not provide any information about why the account was blocked because Robert Parry, the *CN* founder whose name is on the account, is deceased. She said they could only speak with him. PayPal is refusing to change the name to the current editor-in-chief because the account was permanently banned (even though days ago he submitted the documents necessary for a name change). The "escalation" agent also said she could not discuss details because she was worried about her "employment."[10]

Consortium News isn't the only news outlet to have its account shuttered by PayPal in this way. *Mint Press News* is a small, independent outlet in Minnesota that started in 2012 as the passion project of journalist Mnar Adley. It offers alternative perspectives on many international news issues. It is particularly critical of Israeli violence against Palestinians. In April 2022, *Mint Press News*' PayPal account and the personal PayPal account of their senior writer Alan MacLeod were closed without notice.[11]

MacLeod spoke out about it, saying, "This is a warning shot fired at anyone even remotely antiestablishment. Alternative media operations run on shoestring budgets and rely on enormous corporations like PayPal to operate correctly. If they can do this to us, they can do it to you."[12]

Mint Press News was founded by Mnar Adley when she was twenty-four years old. When we met, Adley was poised and confident, wearing a stylish hijab of silver and white. While she founded *Mint Press News* in her twenties, she told me the idea was planted years earlier. An American citizen who spent the first nine years of her life in the United States, Adley then moved with her family to Jerusalem for four years. Returning to the United States was jarring. She told me about how strange it felt to be living in a place with a secure home, groceries, manicured lawns—no checkpoints, no restrictions, no military personnel on the streets pointing guns. She was stricken with survivor's guilt for the easier life she enjoyed in the United States, and she struggled with PTSD from her early years in a land torn apart.

When she saw news coverage of what was happening in Israel in the early 2000s, it felt wrong to her. "I witnessed firsthand what it was like to live under an apartheid system and witness grave human rights abuses," she told me, "only to come back to the United States to see how the media worked in the interests of the permanent war state."

As a teenager just coming back from Jerusalem in the early 2000s, she felt the mainstream media wrongly painted the violence unfolding in Israel as a religious fight and that it missed a huge piece of what was going on. Adley felt it should be viewed "through the lens of colonialism, ethnic cleansing, and apartheid and military occupation."

Talking to Adley, I initially got the impression that she was an idealist—someone who felt she could change the world through journalism. But as our interview progressed, that seemed to be the wrong word. She was collected, fierce, and frankly jaded in her discussion of efforts to document wars around the world. "Relentless" is probably a more fitting word.

Like *Consortium News*, *Mint Press News* never got answers from PayPal about why it lost its account. And just as those with *Consortium News* believe, Adley thinks the site was targeted in a crackdown on so-called fake news.

"Fake news" is a label that has been cast at *Mint Press News* before. But the website isn't full of articles about how the earth is flat or how aliens are controlling our government. It is filled with articles criticizing America's involvement in overseas wars.

As with *Consortium News*, I tried to understand what was going on with *Mint Press News* by spending hours reading articles published on the site as well as articles from outsiders criticizing the outlet. The most controversial and debated article on *Mint Press News* is about the use of chemical agents in the Syrian civil war.[13] While the United States had initially decided to stay out of the Syrian conflict, President Barack Obama had warned that the use of chemical agents would be a "red line."[14] Then there were a series of deadly chemical attacks in Syria, including a particularly horrifying attack in Ghouta that left hundreds of people—including children—dead. This prompted the United States to authorize air strikes against the Syrian government. *Mint Press News* raised questions about what happened in Ghouta. It published an article with interviews from people in Syria, including fighters and family members of fighters, who questioned whether the al-Assad government was behind the attacks. The article was subsequently criticized as promoting fake news.[15] *Mint Press News* didn't remove the article but did update it to note: "Some information in this article could not be independently verified."[16]

During our interview, I asked Adley about the allegations that *Mint Press News* has published fake news. She didn't flinch from the question. Instead, she said that we are living in an information war, and that those in power have a specific agenda to ensure that the United States stays at war—and information is disseminated to the media to advance that agenda. She pointed to media stories that were later debunked—like the famed weapons of mass destruction that fueled US engagement in Iraq—and said these ideas "were pushed and perpetuated by the mainstream corporate media outlets from the *Washington Post* to the *New York Times*, CNN, Fox News." She saw *Mint Press News* playing an integral role in countering mainstream media narratives.

I also asked Adley how it felt to learn that the *Mint Press News* PayPal account had been suspended. "I was kind of shocked at first, but then I was like: *Why do I feel shocked about this? This is not the first time we've been targeted*," she recalled. "But it was the first time we had been targeted in a financial way."

The message Adley received explained that the account had violated PayPal's terms of service. She was certain it was due to *Mint Press News'* articles. She tried calling PayPal but got no definitive answers: "I kept getting transferred everywhere, but never to somebody at a high-level decision-making position."

PayPal never confirmed that it closed *Mint Press News* and *Consortium News* accounts over concerns about fake news. It never offered an explanation at all. But we do know PayPal was increasingly interested in the issue of fake news at that time.

In October 2022, a few months after the account closures of *Mint Press News* and *Consortium News*, a new version of PayPal's Acceptable Use Policy was publicized that included a prohibition against "sending, posting or publication of any content or materials that, in PayPal's sole discretion," are harmful or "promote misinformation." PayPal's terms promised a $2,500 fine for each violation, to be removed directly from one's PayPal account.[17] David Marcus, former president of PayPal, was dismayed by the change, writing on Twitter, "It's hard for me to openly criticize a company I used to love and gave so much to. But @PayPal's new AUP goes against everything I believe in. A private company now gets to decide to take your money if you say something they disagree with. Insanity."[18]

Reporting on this new policy prompted public condemnation as well as a letter of inquiry from senior House Republicans.[19] It also prompted concerns from the civil liberties community. As Aaron Terr, a senior program officer at the Foundation for Individual Rights and Expression, explained, "Whatever motivation PayPal has for establishing these vague new categories of prohibited expression, they will almost certainly have a severe chilling effect on users' speech. As is often the case with ill-defined and viewpoint-discriminatory speech codes, those with unpopular or minority viewpoints will likely bear the brunt of these restrictions."[20]

In the face of this huge public backlash, PayPal walked back its position. A PayPal spokesperson told Axios that the policy went out in error and included incorrect information. "PayPal is not fining people for misinformation and this language was never intended to be inserted in our policy. Our teams are working to correct our policy pages. We're sorry for the confusion this has caused."[21] Removing this controversial section of its terms of service did not result in *Mint Press News* or *Consortium News* getting their accounts reinstated.

WHO DEFINES JOURNALISM?

Having spent a lot of time on the websites of *Consortium News* and *Mint Press News*, it's clear that both news outlets are reporting on foreign policy from an antiauthoritarian perspective. They are critical of US foreign policy interventions and unabashed in that position. There are also questions about the sources of their articles. In taking positions that run counter to mainstream outlets, are these news outlets promoting false information? *Mint Press News*, in particular, has faced repeated criticisms of spreading misinformation.

Wartime news coverage is notoriously tricky. Nation-states are highly invested in projecting certain narratives about a war that align with their interests while downplaying contradictory narratives. That's not a conspiracy theory; that's just common sense. The widespread reach of social media has brought videos of war zones and the voices of people living through wars to global audiences, but often provocative images and videos that lack context can spread and be reshared in ways that further strip away context and nuance. It can be dangerous and difficult for journalists to report in war zones, and armies are understandably reticent to share details of their location, actions, and future plans.

As a result of these and other factors, the true story of a war may not be known until long after the conflict has ended. That story may even evolve over time based on witness reports, analysis by independent NGOs, and government reports—whether released on purpose or through whistleblowers.

I've come to think the phrase "fake news" as it's commonly used is unhelpfully vague. It can be used to discredit antiestablishment independent media that counters government narratives, call out digitally altered and enhanced media that is used to prop up authoritarian government narratives, or describe whimsical, weird conspiracy theories, like how condensation left in the wake of high-flying aircrafts is a nefarious chemical agent.

The question isn't whether some websites spread false information. We already know that happens. The real question is this: Who should decide what is false information and what should be done about it?

Press freedom is a hollow term if it's only used to defend journalists who are popular and uncontroversial. Journalistic outlets that challenge government power, corporate interests, and popular opinion are far more likely to face censorship than their mainstream counterparts. That's because these outlets are more likely to attract the ire of the powerful while having fewer allies to defend them. Sometimes the dissenting voices that face the most censorship eventually prove to be particularly valuable to society for their efforts to report on abuses of power and spur reform.

As we continue to examine the role of payment intermediaries shuttering the accounts of news outlets and journalists, we need to hold space for two different values at the same time: first, that truth in journalism is important and necessary for a functional democratic society, and second, that payment intermediaries are ill equipped and inappropriate to decide which journalism is truthful or socially beneficial.

Payment services don't have any incentive to consider the value of controversial and unpopular speech or how it may benefit our society. These services don't have systems to ensure transparency, fair decision-making, and useful appeal processes for closed accounts. Especially when we consider the complexity and challenges of providing accurate, real-time reporting on war, financial services providers can't act as competent judges of journalism.

Most importantly, financial companies are not positioned to help determine the impact of censorship on our democracy.

Fake news and misinformation are serious problems that require real solutions. Social media platforms and other information sharing services have been looking for ways to limit the spread of misinformation, offer additional context on articles with questionable information, and make fake news harder to find. Academics are studying the problem, and lawmakers are examining whether and how new legislation can help address the issue. Schools are even experimenting with teaching media literacy so that students can identify false information online. There are many tools for tackling this thorny issue, which is good because it's probably going to take a range of tactics to address these issues.

Censorship by payment processors should not be one of the tools we turn to. It's too blunt of an instrument, wielded by companies that have no incentive to value speech. But this tool has been used to punish controversial news sites, and for a long time.

To really understand the impact of financial shutdowns on journalism, it's important to go back and look at the most famous example of financial censorship: the banking blockade by Visa, Mastercard, PayPal, and Bank of America against the whistleblower website WikiLeaks. It serves as the canonical example of how financial institutions can shutter the accounts of organizations in response to controversial speech, serving as a devastating punishment without governmental niceties like a trial or appeals process.

THE WIKILEAKS BANKING BLOCKADE

Like a lot of people in Iceland, Kristinn Hrafnsson is skeptical of bankers.

"We got used to calling them 'banksters' here," he told me, tying together the words "banker" and "gangster."

Hrafnsson is the current editor in chief of the whistleblower website WikiLeaks, and our conversation occurred while the prior editor in chief, Julian Assange, was held in Belmarsh Prison in London, England. Hrafnsson called from a stark, poorly lit room in Iceland and wore thick-rimmed glasses. These, combined with his well-trimmed white hair, gave him the impression of a serious and scholarly type. Like other professional newscasters, he spoke slowly and with gravitas. The Icelandic accent added a cottony burr to his voice.

As a reporter, Hrafnsson investigated shoddy banking practices and fraud that contributed to the financial crisis of 2008. That crisis was a major blow to economies around the world, but it was particularly devastating in Iceland, where the country's three largest private banks defaulted and the economic blowback prompted mass protests. Much of the Icelandic government resigned from the shame of it.[22]

Investigating the financial crisis is what led Hrafnsson to WikiLeaks. In 2009, he was working on a major story about how Iceland's Kaupthing Bank had loaned billions to a private financier.[23] Recognizing just how important this story would be, Hrafnsson alerted the news station so they could adjust the trailer for the upcoming episode.

"About two hours later, me and my colleagues were called into the general manager of the TV station's office. We were told that we were sacked and had to leave the building," he told me. He stopped short of accusing the television station of firing him under pressure from the bank to kill the story but pointed out that the timing of getting fired was a "remarkable coincidence." The station declined his offer to run the story before he left.

Hrafnsson didn't drop his investigation. Instead, he took it to a different news station, and the coverage caused an uproar both in and beyond Iceland. He told me that no sooner was the story out than Hrafnsson found himself charged under Iceland's Bank Secrecy Act, a law designed to protect the privacy of financial information that has also been weaponized against journalists.[24] He remembered his shock at this. He laughed to describe it, shaking his head and saying, "I'm not a banker, I'm a journalist." He explained that it took months to get the charges dropped.

This was the first time Hrafnsson really understood how powerful the financial companies could be in silencing journalists who challenge or embarrass them.

That same year, a colleague suggested Hrafnsson check out WikiLeaks.org. He visited the website and was shocked by what he found. "I couldn't believe my eyes," he recalled. "They had published the entire loan book of that big bank."

The loan book was a list compiled by Kaupthing Bank's board of directors that provided details on all the bank's large loans as well as the bank's own estimation of the quality of those loans. It proved beyond a doubt that Kaupthing Bank knew it had insufficient collateral from its most substantial borrowers.

Reporting on Kaupthing Bank's loan book would prove to be one of the pinnacles of Hrafnsson's career. "It was not just a vindication, a confirmation, but an awakening for me," Hrafnsson said. He realized how revolutionary the transparency tools of WikiLeaks could be in helping hold major institutions accountable.

Hrafnsson joined WikiLeaks shortly after. He couldn't know it at the time, but his battles with the financial industry were far from over.

PayPal, Visa, Mastercard, and Bank of America blocked payments to WikiLeaks within a few days of one another in December 2010. The financial companies didn't say they colluded in making that decision, but it's unquestionable that they were aware of what the other companies were doing—after all, they were all quite public about it.

But it wasn't only peer pressure that motivated the payment companies. They also got pressure from US elected officials, the most vociferous of whom was a US senator. Senator Joe Lieberman, formerly a Democrat but identifying as an independent since 2006, was the chair of the Homeland Security and Governmental Affairs Committee. He'd been on the warpath against WikiLeaks in the wake of their publication of a series of State Department cables that offered in-depth insight into US foreign policy. It was the beginning of what would be known as Cablegate, a massive leak from whistleblower Chelsea Manning that would amount to over 250,000 cables published by WikiLeaks and its partners. It was one of the most significant leaks of government documents in US history.

Shortly after the first set of cables was published, Lieberman's staff called Amazon, which provided hosting services for WikiLeaks, and asked, "Are there plans to take the site down?"[25] Amazon promptly cut off WikiLeaks, and Lieberman rushed to publicly applaud the company, publishing a press release that called on other companies to follow suit:

> The company's decision to cut off WikiLeaks now is the right decision and should set the standard for other companies WikiLeaks is using to distribute its illegally seized material. I call on any other company or organization that is hosting WikiLeaks to immediately terminate its relationship with them. WikiLeaks' illegal, outrageous, and reckless acts have compromised our national security and put lives at risk around the world. No responsible company—whether American or foreign—should assist WikiLeaks in its efforts to disseminate these stolen materials.[26]

It's important to pause here and correct a massive misstatement from Senator Lieberman. WikiLeaks had not violated any laws by publishing classified information. Indeed, there's a tradition in the United States of the press publishing classified information—sometimes from whistleblowers who risk their freedom to shine the light on corruption, and often from government sources who leak it intentionally and with no consequence. While leakers may face criminal charges for sharing classified documents, publishers generally do not. In those instances where the government has attempted to charge news organizations for publishing government secrets, the courts have overwhelmingly sided with the publishers.

President Richard Nixon's Justice Department attempted to prevent the *New York Times* from publishing the Pentagon Papers, documents provided by whistleblower Daniel Ellsberg that showcased the scope of America's failed war in Vietnam. In a seminal case, the Supreme Court dismissed claims that national security gave the government a trump card for preventing classified information from being published and upheld the First Amendment rights of publishers.[27] Decades later, the Supreme Court considered whether a radio journalist who played a recording provided to him by a source could be held liable when the tape was illegally recorded. The Supreme Court again upheld the rights of the press, stating that it was not illegal for a journalist to publish newsworthy materials provided to her, *even if someone else broke the law to obtain or distribute those materials*.[28]

Today, news organizations across the United States publish classified information all the time. If we were going to throw every organization that published secrets in prison, every major news publisher in the United States would be behind bars.

When the banking blockade was instituted against WikiLeaks, no charges had been brought against the publisher. Julian Assange, then editor in chief of WikiLeaks, was already a divisive figure in the United States, and he became more so in the subsequent years. That controversy has contributed to a lot of mistaken impressions about his role in publishing these documents. He didn't hack into government databases and steal information. Rather, as forty law professors wrote in an open letter to the Department of Justice about the case, Assange's activities were like those of any tech-savvy investigative journalist working with a source to report a story involving leaked national security data.[29] He communicated with Manning, and then the WikiLeaks team securely received the documents, took steps to remove data inappropriate for publication, and developed a publication plan.[30]

Notably, WikiLeaks was not alone in publishing the materials from Manning. The documents were published simultaneously by news organizations around the globe, including the *New York Times* (US), *The Guardian* (UK), *Der Spiegel* (Germany), *Le Monde* (France), and *El País* (Spain). None of these news organizations nor any of their reporting staff was ever accused of a crime. Additionally, despite howls from the US State Department and others, no person has even been identified as harmed by the leak or the published reports.[31]

Human rights groups and press freedom advocates warned that attempting to hold Julian Assange liable for publishing secrets could have dire consequences for press freedom in the United States and would violate the First Amendment.[32] The *New York Times* and other outlets that collaborated with WikiLeaks in publishing classified information publicly chastised the government for even considering prosecuting Assange, writing that "publishing is not a crime."[33]

For our purposes, none of these details matter. Our focus is the banking blockade, and so the piece of data we need to capture is this: when the banking blockade was instituted against WikiLeaks, there were claims that the site had broken the law but no charges had been brought against them—and wouldn't be for years.

So when we consider the WikiLeaks banking blockade, we must remember that the financial companies were acting without a court's intervention. But not entirely without government intervention—pressure from Senator Lieberman in particular may have played a major role in their decision.

Two days after Lieberman's press release urging companies to follow Amazon's lead and cut off WikiLeaks, PayPal stopped processing donations to Wau Holland Stiftung, the fiscal sponsor of WikiLeaks. On December 4, 2010, PayPal blocked Wau Holland's PayPal account and put a 180-day freeze on the funds held in the account. Those funds were subsequently released following communications from Wau Holland's attorneys.[34] On December 7, Visa and Mastercard stopped processing donations to WikiLeaks. On December 18, Bank of America also blocked WikiLeaks.

None of the financial companies said their decision was a direct result of government pressure. Instead, they mostly claimed it was because of terms of service violations. Mastercard stated that it was shutting off WikiLeaks because "rules prohibit customers from directly or indirectly engaging in or facilitating any action that is illegal."[35] Bank of America issued a statement saying that its decision to cut off WikiLeaks "is based upon our reasonable belief that WikiLeaks may be engaged in activities that are, among other things, inconsistent with our internal policies for processing payments."[36]

PayPal's general counsel, John Muller, published a statement on the PayPal blog noting that the company "was not contacted by any government organization in the U.S. or abroad. We restricted the account based on our Acceptable Use Policy review."[37]

It seems likely that Lieberman's office did contact at least some of the payment providers directly, just as it contacted Amazon. In an antitrust lawsuit launched years later, a complaint from Icelandic hosting provider Datacell noted that Mastercard had acknowledged direct communication in comments to the European Commission. Per the complaint: "On August 25, 2011 MasterCard admitted in a letter from its counsel to the European Commission that Lieberman's and [Representative Pete] King's staffs contacted it regarding Sunshine Press."[38] So it's clear Senator Lieberman and others were publicly calling on companies to cut off WikiLeaks, and there's evidence they were also reaching out privately.

Kristinn Hrafnsson remembered the moment the banking blockade took effect. Hrafnsson said that the global news coverage of Cablegate resulted in an "incredible spike" in the donations from people around the world who valued WikiLeaks' work and wanted to support their efforts. But that outpouring of support was cut off almost immediately as the blockade took effect.

The first reaction to the blockade, Hrafnsson said, was shock:

> We were absolutely astonished. And I couldn't believe it at first. I thought it would be lifted immediately; it must have been some mistake. Knowing from the financial system that these card companies had gone to great lengths to maintain that they were absolutely politically neutral entities, that there was no difference between the essence of a dollar bill or a credit card.... So I just couldn't believe that they would be taking these extraordinary steps.

The impact of the blockade on WikiLeaks was immediate and severe. "This of course cut the blood flow to the organization," Hrafnsson acknowledged. "We had a totally new reality and needed to scale down."

In October 2011—nearly a year after it began publishing Cablegate—WikiLeaks published an overview of the impact of the financial blockade.[39] The report showed its devastating consequences. WikiLeaks offered a graph showing the falloff in donations as soon as the blockade went into effect, noting that "the attack has destroyed 95% of our revenue" and that it "cost the organization tens of millions of pounds in lost donations at a time of unprecedented operational costs." WikiLeaks also warned about the message this blockade would send to other organizations: "Any organization that falls foul of powerful financial companies or their political allies can expect similar extrajudicial action."

WikiLeaks announced that it would discontinue publishing leaked documents, noting, "Our scarce resources now must focus on fighting the unlawful banking blockade."[40]

It wasn't just WikiLeaks that suffered consequences from the banking blockade. The financial freedom of everyone who wanted to make a donation to WikiLeaks was also impacted. They were blocked from spending their money in support of their values.

Senator Lieberman praised the companies blocking WikiLeaks, issuing a joint statement with ranking member Susan Collins (R-ME): "Companies that are cutting off their services to WikiLeaks in the wake of its release of 250,000 stolen and classified State Department cables are doing the right thing as good corporate citizens and deserve the support of the American people."[41]

Pressure from Lieberman and Collins wasn't the only factor that may have influenced the financial companies. Some companies, especially Bank of America, had reasons to target WikiLeaks even before Cablegate was published. In late November 2010, a few weeks before Cablegate, Julian Assange said in an interview with journalist Andy Greenberg that he had a trove of unreleased documents that "could take down a bank or two." He referred to it as a "megaleak" and promised it would be published soon:

GREENBERG: Is it a U.S. bank?

ASSANGE: Yes, it's a U.S. bank.

GREENBERG: One that still exists?

ASSANGE: Yes, a big U.S. bank.

GREENBERG: The biggest U.S. bank?

ASSANGE: No comment.

GREENBERG: When will it happen?

ASSANGE: Early next year. I won't say more.

GREENBERG: What do you want to be the result of this release?

ASSANGE: [Pauses] I'm not sure. It will give a true and representative insight into how banks behave at the executive level in a way that will stimulate investigations and reforms, I presume.[42]

While WikiLeaks didn't name the bank in question, all signs pointed to Bank of America. As Andy Greenberg explained in his book *This Machine Kills Secrets: How WikiLeakers, Cypherpunks, and Hacktivists Aim to Free the World's Information*:

> Right on cue, Bank of America acted—or overreacted—swiftly. It commissioned an internal team of more than a dozen staffers who worked day and night to track down potential moles. It hired a chief information security officer and brought on defense contractor Booz Allen Hamilton to audit its security and to review millions of documents in its archive that might damage the firm if they were leaked. It even began preemptively buying up website names like Brianmoynihanblows.com and Brianmoynihansucks.com, references to its CEO, as a defensive measure to prevent the domains from falling into the hands of critics.[43]

WikiLeaks never did publish that trove of documents about a US bank, but the threat of that publication further complicates the issue of the financial blockade. And it may have made the finance companies more willing to participate in the blockade.

"I think it's highly likely that it played a part in their animosity and their willingness to take such extraordinary steps," Hrafnsson told me. "I'm absolutely certain that it played a part in the decision to be so open to the friendly suggestions from the political elite to do something and take decisive action against the organization."

Hrafnsson also pointed to leaked documents from security contractor HBGary released just a few months after the blockade took effect. Those documents showed a pitch to Bank of America and the US Chamber of Commerce that offered a strategy for discrediting WikiLeaks. As Eric Lipton and Charlie Savage of the *New York Times* reported, "One idea was to submit fake documents covertly to WikiLeaks, and then expose them as forgeries to discredit the group. It also suggested pressuring WikiLeaks' supporters—notably Glenn Greenwald of Salon.com—by threatening their careers." While Bank of America denied hiring HB Gary or seeing the PowerPoint presentation, the details of the anti-WikiLeaks strategy is another data point in the war between WikiLeaks and the financial companies.[44]

THE RIGHT TO NOT ENGAGE IN BUSINESS

To understand the issues swirling around the banking blockade against WikiLeaks or the purposeful closure of anyone's bank account, it's useful to step back and consider the legal framework around banking. Specifically, can financial companies like Visa and Bank of America just cut someone off for any reason?

In the United States, we have largely allowed companies to chart their own course. They can choose to do business—or not—with whomever they please, as long as those decisions do not violate antidiscrimination laws.

There are some other limitations on whether companies can pick and choose customers. For example, regulated utilities like your electric company or water company can't decide they don't want to provide service to certain customers within their service territory.

The law also holds a special place for companies that transmit messages, goods, and people. These are considered *common carriers*: companies that have an affirmative obligation to serve all customers and treat all their customers the same. Companies like cargo trains, taxicabs, package delivery services, and telephone companies are all considered common carriers.[45]

There's no great system for determining who is and isn't a common carrier. John Bergmayer, legal director for the nonprofit advocacy organization Public Knowledge and one of the foremost experts in common carriers, acknowledged with a laugh that it's deeply complicated: "I probably worked on it professionally for years before I really understood it."

When we met to discuss it in 2024, he told me that it's a historical concept that has been refined slowly over generations. "Basically, everything used to be regulated, sort of like a common carrier. If you were a physician and you were a public physician, that was a public calling and it was regulated. Same thing with being a baker, or just any business." Bergmayer explained that these regulatory traditions date back all the way to medieval Europe before modern capitalism even existed. But over many years, most businesses stopped being considered common carriers, and the term began to apply only to entities that transport and store goods (like warehouses), people (like hotels), and communications (like telephone wires), so long as they provided those services to the public for a fee.

Bergmayer points to three factors that weigh heavily on whether something counts as a common carrier:

- Whether a company has a *natural monopoly* on the market, thus making competition unlikely;
- Whether there is a *network effect* such that the more people use a service, the more valuable it becomes; and
- Whether the incumbent company has *gatekeeper power*, making it easy for them to block competitors from entering the market.[46]

The Supreme Court recently weighed in on the issue and found that social media companies like Facebook and YouTube had a First Amendment right to curate the content on their sites and thus weren't common carriers.[47] But the opinion left open whether services like email, which transmits messages, or payment networks, which transmit financial transaction data, could be subject to regulations that made them accept all customers.[48]

For now, what's important to note is that credit card companies like Visa and Mastercard, payment intermediaries like PayPal, and banks are not currently considered common carriers. Even though a number of financial companies are such powerful market players that businesses are basically required to accommodate their contractual terms of service in order to survive, these companies do not have an affirmative obligation to serve everybody.

Even so, there are also some limitations on when and how financial companies can reject accounts, including state and federal antidiscrimination laws as well as some finance-specific laws. But these aren't nearly as strong as one might assume. For example, the Equal Credit Opportunity Act (ECOA) bars creditors from engaging in discrimination. However, it only applies in certain situations—such as when someone is applying for a home loan or a credit card. It also only protects against discrimination based on certain protected classes—race, religion, national origin, sex, marital status, and age—and whether a percentage of one's income is from public assistance, or because they exercised any right under the consumer financial protection laws.[49] Receiving an online payment isn't a financial service covered by ECOA. Even if it were, investigative journalism is not a protected class.

So what about cases where businesses are not considered common carriers and antidiscrimination laws aren't triggered, as is apparently the case for most of the examples of financial censorship we are considering? In those instances, it really comes down to the contract the company has with the customer—and that's all.

Vinhcent Le, senior legal counsel of tech equity for Greenlining Institute, explained that companies have a lot of leeway about what they put in their contracts with customers. The government can step in when contract agreements are extremely unfair, but that rarely happens. As he summarized: "You're relying on the government to come in and say that certain contract provisions just aren't allowed, but that's very rare and very piecemeal. We're a very pro-business country. Our jurisprudence has just developed that way."

AS WIKILEAKS GOES, SO GOES JOURNALISM

Hrafnsson told me he has a hard time imagining exactly what WikiLeaks would be like if it hadn't suffered a financial blockade for years. He pointed out that it wasn't just the lost donations that were costly to the organization. Fighting the blockade also took untold amounts of time and effort from the staff and resulted in multiple protracted court battles. Without the blockade, things would have been fundamentally different: "We would have been able to grow the organization. In the world we live in today, money is power. It would have been power to resist the challenges that have been thrown at us left, right, and center. So it would have been a totally different environment."

He said that the legal defense of Assange has become an incredibly expensive and time-consuming battle for the organization, and everything might have been different if there had been resources to proactively fight those legal challenges earlier. "I'm a journalist. I'm not a lawyer," Hrafnsson noted, a tired smile in his voice. "But I talk more to lawyers now on a daily basis than to my children and my entire family."

Regardless of how one feels about WikiLeaks, the financial blockade was a dangerous instrument used against journalism. Under pressure from a US senator, a group of financial companies collectively refused to provide services to WikiLeaks—effectively shutting off their financial support at a critical moment. If any journalistic organization that embarrasses the US government can find their financial accounts shuttered, whether at the behest of angry senators or not, then what news outlets will continue to serve their role as a check against government power?

Just as WikiLeaks was taking on government secrecy, WikiLeaks was confronting the financial behemoths directly by threatening to leak documents that would embarrass a major US bank. This raises the question: If those who challenge the power of financial institutions can find their own financial resources cut off, then who will dare challenge these companies?

This isn't just about WikiLeaks. This is about whether the tactic of financial exclusion is a tool that companies like PayPal and Visa should be using against controversial speakers. Regardless of one's personal opinions about WikiLeaks, we should all be concerned about handing financial companies such incredible power to punish controversial journalists.

THREE

BANKING WHILE MUSLIM

Muhammad Ali Mojaradi told me that studying Persian poetry is a way to learn about humanity. "You could find every dimension of human life expressed," he said, his face lighting up as he talks about it. "Someone who's into fashion can read hundreds of pages of versified explanations of fashion styles. There are poetry books about food. You could read hundreds of pages of versified recipes and descriptions of how food should be served."

But much of this enormous treasure trove of Persian poetry is hard to access, especially for English speakers. "There's a tiny percentage of the whole canon that exists in translation. A very, very small percent. The rest of it is just out there and either untranslated and, honestly, unread as well."

Mojaradi aims to fix that. Graduating from the University of Michigan during the COVID-19 pandemic, Mojaradi faced a lackluster job market and no obvious ways to put his degree in economics and finance to good use. So he doubled down on what he'd already begun doing during college: translating Persian poetry from Farsi to English and bringing that literature to global audiences. Through his popular Instagram account and Persianpoetics.com website, he started to bring this literary world to life for countless readers.

Mojaradi, wearing a traditional Persian skullcap called an *araqchin*, has a casual approach when he talks to me. His affect seems to span two different ages: the restless energy of a recent college graduate and the musty academic vibe of a seasoned poetry professor. He's also spanning two cultures: the Detroit-raised Gen Z social media influencer and also a member of the Iranian diaspora trying to understand his own cultural heritage.

In addition to his work as a teacher, Mojaradi is also a bit of a sleuth. He specializes in debunking online myths about Persian poetry. In one YouTube video, he investigated a quote circulating online attributed to the Sufi mystic and poet Rumi. Documenting each step on YouTube, Mojaradi hunted down different websites where this quote appears until he found one with the Persian text, and he immediately noted an error in the meter of the phrase—a signal this might be a fake quote, as Rumi isn't known for his sloppy metering. Mojaradi continued his research, bringing viewers along until he discovered that the quote derived from a work of historical fiction by John Moyne, a deceased scholar of Rumi's work.[1] In other words, like many of the reader-submitted quotes Mojaradi investigates for accuracy: *not Rumi.*

Mojaradi offers online courses for students interested in learning Farsi or those who want to dive deep into specific texts or Persian poets. He also offers one-on-one instruction for students who pay a little more. As an online teacher, Mojaradi receives lots of small payments from different people taking his classes. That makes him incredibly reliant on payment intermediaries. But he's faced problem after problem with his banking services, starting with having his account flagged and frozen by PayPal and then Venmo (which is a subsidiary of PayPal).

In one letter to Mojaradi, PayPal asked for "an explanation of the reference to 'Persian'" as well as other details. Persian (also called Farsi) is a language spoken by tens of millions of people worldwide and also refers to the predominant ethnic group in Iran. The United States has instituted sanctions against Iran to deter weapons development and terrorism, but these sanctions are aimed at the country—not at specific ethnic groups or language.[2]

Mojaradi told me he was taken aback by having his PayPal account frozen and getting questioned about his business. "It was such an unsettling and nerve-racking feeling because you just think: 'Okay, I have all this money stopped up here and, if they cut me off, how am I going to get paid by people? What's going to happen?'"

Mojaradi was also keenly aware of the massive power imbalance between him and PayPal. "Because it's a private company, there's no higher body of authority I can appeal to," he said. "In theory, I could sue them, but there's no easy way to do that. It's their discretion."

PayPal eventually relented and reinstated Mojaradi's accounts, but that wasn't the end of his troubles with financial access. He also set up a Chase business banking account on the advice of his accountant, only to find it repeatedly frozen and scrutinized by the bank. After setting up everything online, he was notified that he needed to come to the branch in person. Once there, he was asked details about what Persian meant and what services he offered. The resulting mess was difficult to follow, even when he walked me through it and sent me the convoluted correspondence with Chase: "Another month or so went by and it was closed again. Then I went to the bank and there was some other issue. Then some branch didn't want to help me, so I went to the other branch that I talked to, and they said, 'Oh, we don't know what's going on.'"

Sick of his account getting repeatedly frozen, Mojaradi decided he was finished with Chase and tried to close the account. Here again he faced difficulties: instead of handing him a check for the remaining balance of his account, Chase said they would mail it in several weeks.

Mojaradi is far from the only Muslim American facing these kinds of banking problems. The Institute for Social Policy and Understanding, a nonprofit research organization that examines the experiences of American Muslims, conducted a poll in 2022 and discovered that over a quarter of Muslims faced challenges while banking, such as having accounts closed or suspended. That's in comparison to the roughly 12 percent of the general public who reported banking issues in that study. These problems also extended to organizational accounts, where Muslims were far more likely to face issues with their business and nonprofit accounts than the general public.[3]

There are a lot of potential factors that could have drawn PayPal's attention to Mojaradi's account. Many of his students are Middle Eastern or have Middle Eastern names. Mojaradi himself is Iranian American and has visited family in Iran. He's traveled internationally to study Persian poetry. But the questions he got from PayPal and later Chase indicate that it was the word "Persian" in his business that caused his account to get flagged.

Mojaradi tried to minimize the risk by urging his students to only ever list the date of classes, not the details of what they are paying for. He explained: "I would always tell people: 'Don't write "Persian class." Don't write "Farsi class."'"

But the banking issues have cost Mojaradi paying students. Two told him explicitly that they wouldn't be taking more classes because they weren't comfortable with the questions they were getting from payment intermediaries. He also told me about one British Iranian student who got calls from a bank's compliance department over her payments to him. She became frustrated over the invasive questions and wanted to fight back, somehow. "No, don't fight them," he warned her. "This will cause a huge problem for you. Just give them the information."

In the end, she stopped taking classes with Mojaradi, even though she had bought a class package for a few hundred dollars. "Maybe she just got spooked about it," he offered. "She could still take classes, if she wants. It's still sitting there."

After seemingly endless issues with his banking services, Mojaradi started speaking out about what was happening to him on social media. Journalist Rowaida Abdelaziz of *Huffington Post* discovered his story and profiled him in an article about the challenges facing Muslims in banking.

That decision to go public was a major step for Mojaradi, and it came with some definite costs. He worried that people would think he had done something wrong, or that he was a drug dealer or some other kind of criminal. And some of those fears came true when his profile was published online. "Some people on the internet were on the *Huffington Post* article saying: 'He's lying. Clearly, he's a drug dealer, a terrorist, or something like that. They're not looking into people for no reason.' Things like that."

I looked through the comments on *Huffington Post* a few months after the article was published. Many of them have already been removed for violating community standards, but some of the remaining ones are skeptical. Accusatory. One user going by Mike Smith wrote, "What the article is NOT telling you is that Muslim terrorists have used this type of 'platform' in the past to funnel funding without detection."[4]

Another using the name Daniel Cihomsky wrote, "They have to, Islamic terrorists move money through these kinds of accounts. You just have to deal. Remember Islam's religious war with the West is a racist war too. So what comes around goes around." And a James Huffer said, "Good, there should be no relief for terrorists."[5]

Surviving the suspicions of random internet readers is a cost Mojaradi carries for the decision to speak out publicly. And it's not just a one-time thing. Because he used his real name for the *Huffington Post* interview, the resulting news article will be accessible to future employers, landlords, business partners, romantic prospects, and anyone who might try to dig up dirt on him.

We know about the issues of financial discrimination facing the Muslim community thanks to people like Mojaradi who are willing to bear those costs.

While this chapter is focused on the ways American Muslims struggle with financial access due to misapplied sanctions laws, it's important to remember that they are far from the only group that has faced persistent barriers to financial access. Black Americans, Indigenous people, immigrant communities, and unhoused people, among others, face friction in establishing and maintaining financial services. However, the financial access burdens placed on Muslim Americans uniquely show the dangers of overbroad sanctions enforcement.

In the United States today, economic sanctions are largely based on two foundational laws: the Trading with the Enemy Act (TWEA) and the International Emergency Economic Powers Act, which is known as IEEPA and pronounced like a sort of gleeful cry: *Ah-eeepa!*

TWEA was instituted shortly after the United States entered World War I and gave the US broad authority to prohibit commerce with its wartime foes. In 1977, as the Cold War fueled tensions between the United States and the Soviet Union, Congress passed IEEPA, which granted ongoing authority to issue economic sanctions during national emergencies.[6]

Sometimes, economic sanctions are broad bans that prohibit almost all commerce with a particular nation, as is the case with US sanctions against Cuba and North Korea. These types of sanctions are called embargoes. Other times, economic sanctions prohibit commerce connected to an illegal industry or activity, such as terrorism, narcotics trafficking, computer crime, or election interference.

The United States also maintains a Specially Designated Nationals (SDN) List, which consists of individual people, groups, and companies whose assets are blocked by the US government. Dealing with an entity or person on the SDN List is illegal. These economic sanctions are often referred to as "targeted sanctions" because they specify particular individuals and entities rather than entire countries.

The idea behind economic sanctions is that they can act as a form of pressure against another country or group without the United States having to send in troops or launch missiles. Defenders of economic sanctions argue they can have huge impacts around the globe. For example, Rachel

Lyngaas, chief sanctions economist for the US Department of Treasury, has argued that economic sanctions levied against Russia have damaged Russia's economy and hurt its ability to wage war against Ukraine. "While Russia has the resources to maintain its war in the short-term, its leaders face increasingly painful tradeoffs that will sacrifice long-term prospects—as underinvestment, slow productivity growth, and labor shortages will only deepen."[7]

But there are also many critics of economic sanctions who argue there are brutal humanitarian costs. Additionally, as journalist Jacob Weisberg wrote, "They don't work. Though there are some debatable exceptions, sanctions rarely play a significant role in dislodging or constraining the behavior of despicable regimes."[8]

I won't weigh in on whether economic sanctions are a humane or even useful tool, and whether they should or shouldn't be used to advance the United States' international agenda. Instead, I'll examine the censorship costs of sanctions compliance programs.

In these attempts to comply with and execute economic sanctions, US financial institutions are freezing accounts, closing accounts, and blocking transactions of people who aren't doing anything wrong and who are not the rightful targets of US economic sanctions. These account restrictions and closures especially impact ethnic and religious minorities. The account holders are often engaged in legal forms of speech when their accounts are flagged for review, such as for Muhammad Ali Mojaradi. It is likely that the automated review systems that flag accounts are unable to differentiate between First Amendment–protected speech, like poetry education, and unprotected acts, like terrorist financing.

To understand how sanctions programs are implemented, it's also vital to understand incentives. Banks are extremely incentivized to develop sledgehammer-sized sanctions enforcement programs because even the smallest slipup can bring a barrage of regulatory scrutiny and extreme fines. On the other hand, banks rarely get called to task for racial or religious discrimination because, as I heard from those trying to sue financial actors for discrimination, it's very difficult to prove illegal discrimination in banking practices when the bank can claim it was enforcing sanctions.

Shahroo Yazdani, an attorney who specializes in financial sanctions, told me that many of the people who have financial accounts wrongfully restricted often don't go public because they are fearful of what government scrutiny could mean. "Often you have to think about the cultural aspect of it too, which I think is often overlooked. You're dealing with people who often, and I'm not saying this is always the case, but most often you're dealing with people who come from sanctioned countries and countries where they cannot trust their own government, or they have grown up with a stay-under-the-radar mentality." Yazdani explained that people worry that they'll get audited or jeopardize their immigration status if they try to speak out against wrongful account closures. This means that the public doesn't hear from many of the people losing their financial services over misguided sanctions enforcement. Yazdani noted that certain communities are more impacted by sanctions enforcement than others. She estimated that 80 percent of the calls she receives on this issue are from people of Iranian descent, with people from South and Central America a distant second.

Yazdani told me that, for many financial institutions, these enforcement systems are motivated by a fear of fines: "Violating sanctions for them can cost them upwards of $360,000 per violation. So for them, it makes more sense . . . to cast a wider net when it comes to sanctions and then potentially catch people who shouldn't be in that net, but have really restrictive policies to be sure they are not getting fined."

A bank doesn't have to intentionally set out to violate international sanctions to get in trouble with regulators. "Regardless of intent, if there's a violation, they will be fined," Yazdani noted.

There is so much complexity to how sanctions are supposed to be implemented and the amendments that have been passed to refine sanctions law. But a lot of the people enforcing these programs at financial institutions aren't experts. "Quite frankly, the sanctions knowledge is not there. There's just not enough people who understand sanctions most often in financial institutions," Yazdani explained. She told me that "they're very, very complicated" with "technical carve-outs that are really difficult to implement."

I asked Yazdani if there are a lot of people who are not supposed to be the target of sanctions who are nonetheless having their accounts shuttered or frozen. "Oh, yeah," she confirmed. "I see that maybe ten times a week, something like that."

The discussion with Yazdani made clear to me that sanctions programs are also expensive. Financial institutions need to pay experts to build these convoluted enforcement programs or invest a significant amount in training their existing staff to understand all these nuances and carve-outs. While individual compliance officers may try to reduce these discriminatory harms and some financial institutions invest substantial resources to try to build less discriminatory systems, there is always a question of the bottom line. For many financial institutions, it is easier to just close accounts and block transactions. As Yazdani put it: "It's easier, and again just financially makes more sense, for them to not spend the money on the people they need to hire to actually look at a case-by-case scenario every time."

As is so often the case around financial censorship, the financial incentives matter. Setting aside the human costs of war, when the US government decides to impose economic sanctions instead of engaging in open warfare with another country, the government is saving a lot of money for itself. It's not having to pay for weapons or troops or shipping people around the world. Instead, it just pays employees of the US Office of Foreign Assets Control (OFAC) to enforce the sanctions programs. Indeed, the US government may even come out ahead; the steep fines financial institutions pay for any unwitting sanctions violations go back to government coffers.

So *financial institutions* absorb the costs. They have to pay expert staff to set up and enforce sanctions programs, potentially pay fines if any transactions slip through the cracks, and then hire enough people to review complex cases. The banks can save money by hiring fewer experts and just closing accounts that skirt anywhere near a sanctions issue. That's easier and frankly cheaper than analyzing the details, digging into the law, and risking a fine to consider the speech ramifications.

LUNCH IN THE BRONX

Shahana Hanif has been fighting for her community pretty much her whole life.

A New York City councilwoman, she told me that her district is the largest Bangladeshi working-class community in Brooklyn. And that community was deeply shaken by the aftermath of the terrorist attacks of 9/11, when anti-Muslim and anti-immigrant sentiments spiked. A fifth grader at the time, Hanif decided to organize other kids in her neighborhood to send a letter to the president, George W. Bush. "I grew up going to the mosque, me and my sister. During the school year, it was every weekend. And then, during summer, it was every day. That was one of our safe spaces. And also, it's where I made my first set of friends," she explained. But that mosque and community didn't feel safe when Americans were equating Islam with terrorism in the wake of 9/11. In their letter, Hanif asked the president to intercede to stop the bullying she and her classmates were facing. "I think the message was that we're getting bullied right now, and we think you can stop this."

Audacious. Deeply rooted to her community. Trying to make government work for her and her community. Even in elementary school, Hanif was showing the characteristics that would have her elected to the New York City Council at age thirty. She is the first Muslim woman ever elected to the council (and, as of our conversation in July 2024, still the only Muslim woman elected) and the first woman to ever represent her district. Perhaps it's unsurprising that when her Venmo transaction was blocked, she decided to fight back.

In 2019, Hanif met some girlfriends for lunch at a Bangladeshi restaurant in the Bronx. They split the bill and Hanif used Venmo to pay one of her friends. She referenced the name of the restaurant—Al Aqsa—in the comments on Venmo. The transaction was blocked.

She received an email shortly afterward from Venmo noting:

> On December 21, 2019, you sent a payment for the amount of $14.00 for, "al-aqsa." We're trying to understand:
>
> * Your reference to "al-aqsa,"
>
> * purpose of this payment, including a complete and detailed explanation of what you intended to pay for and the establishment/location if applicable.

Hanif spoke out on Twitter, sharing a screenshot of the message from Venmo and writing:

> #EatingWhileMuslim #VenmoingWhileMuslim means @venmo will block transactions that are Muslim phrases or reference Islam. i was just tryna

pay @RimaBegumji
. reminded me of #PersianShenanigans
anyways, this Bangladeshi meal was in the Bronx at Al-Aqsa Restaurant.
pls eat there [Bangledeshi flag emoji][9]

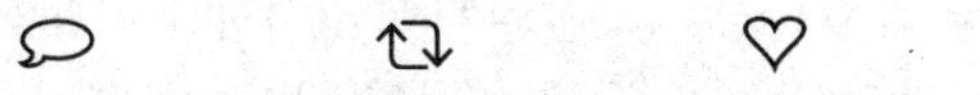

Her story was picked up by Sydney Pereira of *Gothamist*, who wrote, "It was another day being a Muslim woman in America for Shahana Hanif."[10]

Hanif told me that, as a Bangladeshi Muslim living in the post-9/11 era, she and her community have faced an incredible amount of surveillance. Having her Venmo transaction blocked felt like part of that.

> I felt scared. I was like, "Will I not be able to use Venmo?" Because that is literally a tech tool that is meant for this moment. We're in a digital era, and if this is happening to a subset of communities, including those who speak, read, and write very well in English.... It made me think no one is invincible here. Anybody at any moment can experience this kind of surveillance. And this was surveillance while banking.

Al Aqsa is the name of this Bronx Bangladeshi restaurant, and it's also the name of a variety of other restaurants and grocery stores in New York and beyond. "Aqsa" is an Arabic word that means "further" or "furthest." It's also a word of cultural and religious importance: Al-Aqsa is the name of a mosque in Jerusalem considered to be one of the holiest places in Islamic tradition.

Hanif decided to use this experience to push back against discriminatory policies by Venmo. She contacted the Council on American-Islamic Relations of New York (CAIR-NY), who filed a complaint against Venmo with the New York City Commission on Human Rights. The complaint alleged that Venmo's practice of blocking words associated with Muslim and Middle Eastern terminology was discriminatory. As the complaint said:

> Flagging every transaction involving a person of the same ethnicity or religion as a sanctioned country, subjecting it to heightened and

> burdensome administrative scrutiny, may technically be a way to "comply" with OFAC sanctions. However, that does not change the fact that such a practice is overbroad and discriminatory. Suppose the NYPD were to stop and question every individual of a particular race just because a suspect of a crime belonged to an ethnic group, displayed certain characteristics, or ate at particular ethnic restaurants; that would clearly be profiling. That is precisely what is happening here.[11]

CAIR-NY acknowledged that OFAC might require Venmo to screen for sanctions violations, but it didn't require Venmo to create a program that discriminated against Muslims. The organization argued that this type of sanctions compliance program had a *disparate impact*. "Disparate impact" is a phrase that comes from discrimination law. It means there's a policy in place that purports to be neutral on its face but nonetheless has a disproportionately negative impact on a class of people.[12]

While Venmo's sanctions enforcement policies may not be explicitly discriminatory toward people of color and Muslims, it hits them differently. Ethnic and religious minorities are far more likely to have their financial services disrupted under the auspices of sanctions enforcement than white Christian Americans.

"So, generally disparate impact refers to looking at the ultimate effect that a law or action will have, and trying to measure discrimination based on the reality," Carey Shenkman, Of Counsel for CAIR-NY and one of the attorneys who assisted Council Member Shahana Hanif in her complaint, explained to me when we met over coffee in the Bay Area in July 2024. "Disparate impact would look at the end result. Even without a statement of intent or a statement of discrimination, there's still going to be numbers that really make it suspect or close to obvious that there's an inequality there."

Hanif's case encapsulates so many of the problems with existing sanctions enforcement. It was a nondescript, small payment between friends that was flagged because Hanif referenced the name of a Bangladeshi restaurant. The name happened to be a common Arabic word that also has religious importance to the Muslim community. Even though she had clear documentation from Venmo that they blocked her transaction over using that Arabic word, and even though she had a robust legal team working with her on a complaint, and even though New York has strong civil rights protections, she got no relief from the New York City Commission on Human Rights. She also never got answers to her questions about what words Venmo looks for when scanning transaction data and what information they collected on her. She did nothing wrong, but her accounts were scrutinized and her entirely innocuous transaction was blocked.

But this example is particularly illustrative because it's possible to appreciate Venmo's perspective. In 2003, the Treasury Department designated an organization calling itself the "Al-Aqsa International Foundation" as a Specially Designated Global Terrorist entity. That means any dealings with that foundation would be illegal and violate US sanctions. OFAC maintains an online lookup tool for the SDN List. When I search it for the word "al-aqsa," there are nearly two hundred entries that come up in the search results. One is simply an entity called "Al-Aqsa." OFAC includes an address in Brussels, Belgium. Through the lens of Google Maps, I can see a white building on a busy street corner with a sign about solidarity with Palestine.

The online lookup tool is a blunt instrument. Most financial institutions invest in more sophisticated screening services, many of which now promise the use of artificial intelligence to reduce false alerts. Venmo would face an enormous fine if so much as a single sanctions-violating transaction were to slip through, and one of the few tools it has to minimize those fines is to argue it has a strict sanctions enforcement program. So is it reasonable for Venmo to double-check that Americans eating at a Bangladeshi restaurant in the Bronx aren't supporting an international terrorist organization with a similar name?

I've tried to imagine a hypothetical parallel to this type of financial scrutiny for a group that isn't historically marginalized in the United States. What would it be like if, for example, OFAC's sanctions list included commonly used English words that aren't necessarily religious but still have historical, religious overtones within Christian cultures—perhaps words like "communion" or "trinity." Would every parent of a student at Trinity College find themselves having to explain to their banks that they weren't violating US sanctions when they sent in tuition payments? Might every sale of a copy of bell hooks's *Communion* trigger an investigation? English speakers from Christian communities would feel the weight of intense scrutiny over them—a sense that they were being watched, that merely going to church, shopping, and eating with friends could cause financial companies to probe into the details of their relationships and transactions and keep records that were unerasable and inaccessible to them.

"Seriously, Venmo," these beleaguered hypothetical Christians might say, "can't you tell the difference between someone buying thirty dollars in Christmas decorations off of Etsy and someone sending money to a terrorist group in another country that happens to have the word 'Trinity' in its name?"

"We could," hypothetical Venmo might say, "but that would require us to hire at least twice as many people to review transactions."

When first learning about how American Muslims were disproportionately impacted by sanctions compliance programs, I kept wondering why antidiscrimination laws did not help. Weren't our laws designed to ensure that people would not face discrimination due to their religion or ethnicity? The case of Mohammed Farshad Abdollah Nia demonstrates how antidiscrimination protections can fall short at protecting Muslims from unfair account closures.

Nia is an immigrant from Iran and lives in San Diego, California. He opened an account with Bank of America in 2015 and used his Bank of America credit card for many years without any issues.

Then, in 2019, Bank of America requested Nia provide proof of his US residency. Nia submitted his Form I-797C, which Bank of America said was an acceptable form of proof. They closed his account anyway.

Rather than accept the decision, Nia decided to sue. And he didn't just sue on his own behalf; he launched a class action lawsuit on behalf of other Iranians who had faced discrimination by Bank of America.

Nia's case caught the attention of elected officials.

Representative Ilhan Omar (D-MN) and Senator Elizabeth Warren (D-MA) organized a number of their colleagues to send a letter to the heads of US banking regulators.[13] The letter talked about Nia's case against Bank of America, noting, "Rather than engaging in a fact-based inquiry to determine how to serve customers who are located in the U.S. and entitled to access financial services, many banks opt for overcompliance, restricting or closing accounts indiscriminately, often with little or no notice, or pathways for redress."

In March 2024, US district judge Cynthia Bashant issued an order that largely sided with Bank of America. Notably, the judge determined that Bank of America was acting in good faith and was therefore protected by IEEPA. According to the decision, "The IEEPA liability clause sets a standard that, so long as actors are working in good faith to comply with directives under IEEPA, they are shielded from liability under statutes such as ECOA discrimination and Section 1981."[14]

This matters because ECOA (the Equal Credit Opportunity Act) and similar laws are supposed to protect financial account holders from discrimination. But what the Nia lawsuit shows us is that the existing financial discrimination laws aren't up to the task: Muslim Americans are still disproportionately losing accounts, facing account freezes, and having their transactions blocked. As long as the financial companies are "acting in good faith" to execute economic sanctions, it's basically impossible to hold them accountable for discriminatory practices.

As the National Iranian American Council, a nonprofit organization that advocates on behalf of the Iranian American community, wrote, "If allowed to stand, this ruling effectively validates the status quo in which banking access can be denied for tens of thousands of members of impacted communities on the basis of nationality, national origin, or national heritage, while limiting options for challenging those discriminatory policies in the courts by granting banks the benefit of the doubt in their enforcement."

#BANKINGWHILEMUSLIM AND A BANKING BILL OF RIGHTS

When representing Council Member Hanif over her flagged Venmo transaction, attorneys at CAIR-NY also gathered stories from impacted community members. They promoted a social media campaign that was part of a broader coalition effort to raise awareness about banking discrimination faced by Muslims. People shared stories using the hashtag #BankingWhileMuslim on Twitter and other social media channels, in addition to sending stories directly to CAIR-NY.

Burhan Carroll, a staff attorney for CAIR-NY, told me that the first step of the campaign was just to "get a sense of the scale of the problem." CAIR-NY feared that Muslim community members didn't even know to reach out when their financial accounts were blocked and didn't realize it was part of a larger pattern of discriminatory banking policies.

The campaign revealed the problem was widespread. Carroll explained: "It turns out that this is affecting a broad swath of the New York Muslim population. It's affecting everyone from ordinary community members to members of the city council."

Through their legal research, CAIR-NY determined that there were few options for the New York Muslims facing these problems. Carroll told me:

> Under existing New York State banking law, it is basically allowed for banks to terminate your account, terminate your services without any kind of notice, without any kind of reason for that closure. And that struck us as inherently unjust. Regardless of what your religious affiliation is, it should not be the case that New York State residents can have their banking services denied to them outright, unilaterally, by their banks for any reason.

That was the inspiration behind a bill introduced in the New York State legislature that is attempting to create a "Banking Bill of Rights" for financial account holders. The reason for the bill, Carroll told me, is that the existing antidiscrimination laws aren't strong enough. The proposed bill would seek to bring more accountability to financial institutions by making them provide an explanation for why accounts are closed and then giving customers a chance to appeal those decisions.

Eliana Bisgaard-Church, legislative director for Assemblymember Zohran Mamdani, the bill's sponsor, told me that her office began working on this issue after hearing from advocates as well as state regulators about discriminatory banking practices. "It became very apparent that there is a fundamental lack of due process right for individuals with various financial practices, primarily their credit and debit card applications and cards, once actually issued. And these have a very clear bias. We see rates among Muslim and Black clients being far higher for denials and case closures without any rationale."

In addition to providing transparency and a right of appeal, the legislation includes a private right of action, which means that customers could sue financial institutions who didn't follow the rules outlined in the bill of rights. The idea is to protect New Yorkers from discriminatory exclusions by increasing transparency.

Bisgaard-Church said this could serve as a model for other states or future federal legislation. "These protections shouldn't just exist for New Yorkers. We certainly believe that they should be afforded to everyone no matter where you are."

CROWDFUNDING FOR THE MUSLIM COMMUNITY

For Amany Killawi, social entrepreneurship has a spiritual dimension.

"For me, it was religiously inspired in the sense of 'What are you going to accomplish in your time on earth?'" she told me during an interview in 2024. She talked about a future day of judgment. "You're going to account for how you spent your time. How do you set yourself up so that on that day, you feel very proud?"

Killawi will likely have a lot to be proud of. The middle of seven children, she recalled that her first community project was to get a girls' sports club at her mosque in Detroit, Michigan. "Why do the boys have a sports club, but the girls don't?" she asked with a laugh during our call. The club she started gave the young women in the mosque a space to play volleyball, basketball, soccer, and other sports. From there, Killawi moved into student government and then on to youth organizing and mentorship. Inspired to continue in service to others, she studied to be a social worker.

She told me that the traditional American dream is missing a piece about service to those around us. "I think for a lot of people, they figured out how to make the American dream work for them individually, but we haven't figured out how to make it work collectively."

That collective vision for Killawi is rooted in lifting up multiple voices, especially from the Muslim community. She told me that as the daughter of immigrants, she always felt like she was between two worlds. It made her very conscious of the opportunities she had and galvanized her to want to use those opportunities to make a difference. "There's a sense of obligation," she explained. "I have a unique privilege. How am I going to leverage living here and the opportunities I have that my cousins don't have, say overseas, for good?"

Even before she graduated with her degree in social work, Killawi had begun community organizing. "My first crowdfunding campaign was actually to work with inner-city Muslim youth to build an incubator where they could pitch their ideas and get funding and get started. And the idea was to essentially encourage them to become community activists and give them real challenges and give them the money and have them launch or use that as a launchpad."

Killawi raised $10,000 for the incubator, using the crowdfunding platform Indiegogo. Through that project, she connected with Chris Blauvelt and then Omar Hamid, two other Muslim Americans interested in funding projects that could change the world. The three teamed up on an ambitious plan: a donation and crowdfunding platform built by and for the Muslim community. Killawi told me that while there were a massive number of niche crowdfunding platforms at the time, none of the ones they found appeared geared specifically to the Muslim community. That seemed like a lost opportunity.

"Muslims give differently," Killawi explained. "They have different giving patterns. And we knew that we wanted to build a platform that was unique to us." She noted that Muslims are supposed to give 2.5 percent of their wealth to charity every year, a religious duty called zakat. "That's a very important requirement. It's one of the five pillars, and it's supposed to purify your wealth so that wealth is circulating and not just staying in the hands of a few."

In 2013, Killawi and her cofounders created LaunchGood.com. The idea was to help Muslims spend money in line with their values, whether that was funding humanitarian relief to victims of natural disasters or funding a start-up venture specific to the Islamic community. They started with $10,000 from an angel investor and were repeatedly rejected for venture capital funding, but they persevered. Part of that was storytelling: they were able to launch campaigns that told sympathetic stories to potential donors. Killawi herself helped write and frame the early campaigns on the website so that they would be compelling to a broad audience of Muslim donors.

In July 2015, LaunchGood had their first viral campaign. There had been a series of arson attacks on Black churches in the Southern United States, and LaunchGood donors were quick to respond. "The Muslim community came together and said, 'Hey, one-third of the American Muslim community is African American. This is our community, too, and they're hurting,'" Killawi told me. What started as a small online effort to send flowers to a church where multiple members had been killed quickly grew to funding efforts to rebuild. "So the community came together and just crowdfunded a hundred thousand. I remember President Obama talking about the campaign," she recalled with pride.

Killawi said this speaks to how the Muslim community defines itself: "Each campaign would become ideally a chapter in this global storybook of who we are as a community, especially post-9/11. I think a lot of us were just done defending and we were kind of tired of that narrative, and we just wanted to build."

At first payments were not an issue for LaunchGood. That changed in 2019, when they suddenly had problems with their payment processor. Many registered nonprofits use the LaunchGood platform to raise money, and LaunchGood's payment processor took issue with one of them. Killawi said it was extremely frustrating because it was a reputable charity ("I mean, Justin Trudeau attends their galas. They get government funding"). But rather than work with LaunchGood to address the concerns, the payment provider ended their relationship.

"It was very traumatic for us. We had Ramadan coming around the corner," Killawi explained. Ramadan is a holy month for Muslims and it's the time of year when LaunchGood sees most of its donations happen.

LaunchGood quickly switched to another payment service, but that relationship also didn't last long. "[The company] literally told us, you have too many Muslim and Arabic names. It's too much work for us to remediate the false positives," Killawi said.

They switched to a third payment service provider. Killawi reported that at first, everything seemed great. "Their head of compliance loved us. She actually wrote us a letter, a reference letter of recommendation. She was very happy with our team; we were very transparent with them. Their CEO's daughter had a campaign on LaunchGood."

But as with the other payment providers, the third company dropped LaunchGood. Killawi still doesn't know exactly why. "They couldn't point to any one thing. We kept asking, 'What's the issue?' But just the idea of LaunchGood, I think a Muslim platform and our campaigns being global and the humanitarian causes, I think they were uncomfortable. And they off-boarded us."

In each instance, Killawi told me they were facing a tight time line to find and transition to a new payment provider. The word Killawi used again and again in describing the experience was "frustrating." "I mean this whole time we could have been building new products. It's almost like you're starting back from zero because if you can't process payments, in our case, you have no company."

Killawi told me that the experience of losing payment services was awful and made them question whether there was something they had done wrong or if there might be some file about LaunchGood with the FBI or the banks. They tried to run checks on LaunchGood but could find nothing. Then they started hearing from others who were losing their banking services. Killawi told me about different people in her extended network who lost financial services for their organizations—a medical billing company for a practice of mostly Muslim doctors, a Muslim matchmaking service, a nonprofit for Muslim health-care professionals, a travel company owned by Muslims, and many others. Hearing stories from so many other people helped normalize Killawi's experience so she no longer felt like her company had done something wrong.

Killawi and her cofounders began speaking publicly about the financial discrimination LaunchGood and other Muslim-owned organizations faced, sharing stories on Twitter using the hashtag #bankingwhileMuslim. Through this outreach, LaunchGood was able to capture congressional attention. Representative Rashida Tlaib (D-MI) and twenty-one other members of Congress sent a letter to the heads of the banking regulatory agencies saying that LaunchGood had been unfairly targeted by big banks and asking, "If this type of consistent banking discrimination can happen to them, what chance is there for smaller charities and nonprofit organizations, particularly those that are Muslim-affiliated?"[15]

Killawi wants to make sure that this doesn't happen to LaunchGood again. Part of that is about building in redundancy. For every step along the payment stack, LaunchGood now has a backup service provider ready to step in if they lose an account. Killawi is also looking ahead. She's investigating whether LaunchGood could itself serve as a payment provider for others. She said LaunchGood might be better positioned than any other financial service provider to meet the needs of a global Muslim community in this area: "We know how to underwrite this community better than anyone else, and we can do it in a way that manages the risk better than any other bank might be able to."

She noted that today, banks and payment providers are missing out on ways to help Muslims support the causes they care about. "There's a cost to that bigotry. Let's put it this way: economically, if we want to speak the language of banks and just the bottom line, there's a cost to that."

LaunchGood's story highlights how the financial discrimination faced by the Muslim community severely hampers the community's ability to organize and engage in charitable giving. The problems they are facing with accessing financial services are all too common for Muslims in America, and the consequences are predictable: unnecessary friction in transferring to new payment services, massive personnel costs in managing banking issues, and disruptions to their services at a time when they could be building their business. LaunchGood is fighting back and helping draw attention to the challenges Muslims face in accessing the financial system, but how many other Muslim organizations face these problems in silence? And how many small Muslim start-ups quietly fold when faced with repeated barriers to accessing even basic financial services?

DUE PROCESS TURNED ON ITS HEAD

Albert Fox Cahn, executive director of the Surveillance Technology Oversight Project, told me he has heard from many Muslim Americans dealing with these financial account closures and restrictions, and that there are a few commonalities in the cases: "There is a through line in how we treat a lot of these suspected sanctions violations, suspected money laundering: that you preemptively are seizing funds first, closing accounts first, and asking questions later...It feels like due process is being turned on its head."

When I asked what can be done about it, Cahn suggested that one way to address this is to ensure that financial compliance laws don't trump antidiscrimination laws. "I would want to add to all federal legislation and regulation governing AML, KYC [Anti-Money Laundering, Know Your Customer], and other financial sorts of compliance a provision that explicitly does not preempt state and local civil rights laws."

He told me that state and local officials hesitate to enforce civil rights protections when faced with the possibility of preemption by federal legislation. Plus, the federal civil rights laws around banking aren't strong enough. As he explained, "Unless you're talking about explicit redlining and violations of the Fair Housing Act, I feel like there's a real gap there between the rights people have on paper and what can actually be enforced in many cases."

Cahn is right about that gap. After all, it's already illegal for financial institutions to discriminate based on race or ethnicity. But those laws aren't proving useful in holding these companies accountable when they close the accounts of many Muslims and immigrants. So it's not enough to make something illegal. We have to consider how antidiscrimination laws exist within the fabric of other banking regulations and government priorities. As long as banking regulators prioritize sanctions enforcement over civil liberties and financial access, financial institutions will do the same. It's worth questioning the entire system and asking what role—*if any*—financial institutions should play in enforcing economic sanctions.

Writer and anthropologist David Graeber wrote, "The ultimate, hidden truth of the world is that it is something that we make, and could just as easily make differently."[16] When it comes to our financial system, it's easy to believe that the way things have been in the past is the way they must always be. But it's possible to imagine an entirely different approach to financial regulation. For example, what if government lawyers had to prove to a judge that financial institutions knowingly assisted in violating economic sanctions before they could be fined? What if we strengthened antidiscrimination laws so that the penalties rivaled those for violating sanctions? What if financial institutions were considered neutral intermediaries, like the electric company or the water company, and it was the originator of a payment alone, not their financial company, that would be held liable for violating economic sanctions?

What I'm saying is that incentives matter. The system we've built through our existing sanctions laws favors account closures and overcompliance. But it doesn't have to be that way. We can imagine a system that shifts the incentives so that financial institutions have every reason to protect account holders and stand up for their rights to engage in legal speech and advocacy. In the coming chapters on industry best practices and government regulation, I'll discuss specifically how we can change incentives to keep accounts open and our financial system neutral.

FOUR

CONTROLLING BODIES AND SEXUALITY

It seemed like nobody wanted to publish Mark Coker's book. The problem, the young author was told repeatedly, was that other books on his topic hadn't sold well. So even though he was certain that the book that he'd cowritten with his partner, Leslieann, was polished and engaging, and even though he was represented by an established New York literary agency, he just couldn't land a publishing deal. But he wasn't deterred. Instead, he concluded that the publishing industry itself was deeply flawed.

"I thought, This isn't right, that publishers are basically censoring books based on their perception of commercial merit," Coker told me. He believes that books are more important than money, and that there is value in countless books that don't have obvious commercial appeal. He offered an example: "Say you're a grandmother, and you want to write your family recipes and publish it, so your grandchildren can enjoy them. That book is just as important to humanity as a *New York Times* bestseller."

His mantra became: let readers decide.

"I thought, What if I could invest in every single book? What if I could say yes to every author? And the way to do that was an e-book. Do it electronically. There's no paper glue and cardboard boxes to ship around and burn fossil fuels and burn up expenses. It's all digital bits and bytes," he explained. Smashwords, the company he created, is a digital platform where anyone can publish their own books. It offers writers generous percentages of each sale while allowing them to retain the rights to their written works.

This approach was in alignment with how Coker had lived his life. The son of Berkeley student activists, Coker learned to distrust those in power early on. One of his first solo projects was a website that enabled small, individual investors to access stockholder calls with public companies—companies that had historically refused small investors access to their earnings calls. He launched his own public relations firm in his twenties and rode the wave of the dot-com bubble. After that bubble burst, he turned to book writing—and, facing setbacks in publishing his own novel, he realized there was a problem he could solve for authors everywhere.

Smashwords (now merged with Draft2Digital) soon became one of the largest self-publishing platforms in the world. By 2012, Smashwords had over 58,000 authors and small publishers on the platform and over 190,500 published books.[1] By the end of 2022, it had over 160,000 authors and small publishers and over 600,000 published books.[2]

Coker had just finished giving a presentation on self-publishing at the 2012 San Francisco Writers Conference when he looked down at his phone to see an alarming message from PayPal. The payment company was telling Coker that certain erotic fiction on Smashwords violated PayPal's terms of service. If the company didn't remove the offending content within three days, PayPal would shutter their account.

"I was just standing there, just kind of shocked and bewildered," he told me. "I saw the life of the business just flashing before my eyes." PayPal wanted Smashwords to remove any e-books that contained bestiality, rape for titillation, incest, and underage erotica. Through contacts in the writing community, Coker was able to get in touch with a vice president at PayPal who told him that the requirement wasn't something that PayPal wanted to impose; allegedly, PayPal was just trying to comply with demands from unnamed banking partners that were necessary for PayPal to process transactions.

The topics that PayPal was flagging appear frequently in mainstream fiction. PayPal's rules could flag classic works by Vladimir Nabokov, Anaïs Nin, William Shakespeare, Percy Bysshe Shelley, Ovid, and Sophocles, as well as by modern writers, from Jodi Picoult to George R. R. Martin. Widely popular works like Martin's *A Game of Thrones* could be seen as violating these rules.

The Smashwords platform was wired to PayPal both for purchasing books and for paying authors around the world. Even if he could somehow find another payment processor, Coker feared the problem would just repeat itself. As he wrote in a letter to his authors:

> These same requirements will eventually rain down upon every other payment processor. PayPal is trying to maintain their relationships with the credit card companies and banks, just as we want to maintain our relationship with PayPal. People who argue PayPal is the evil villain and we should drop them are missing the bigger picture. Should we give up on accepting credit cards forever? The answer is no.[3]

Plus, Smashwords wasn't alone in facing pressure from PayPal. Other platforms such as All Romance Ebooks and Bookstrand received similar letters.[4]

In the case of Smashwords—as in the case of every example offered in this book—the target of financial censorship had not been found guilty of any criminal activity. But did PayPal or their financial partners have a reason to believe that Smashwords was committing a crime? To answer the question, we need to understand the United States' approach to sexual speech.

Sexual speech can be written text, images, videos, immersive 3D experiences, interactive chats, or combinations of these and other mediums. Sexual speech can include depictions of nude body parts, but it doesn't always. Sexual speech can be entirely fictional, or it can have various degrees of reality. All of which is to say that the concept of sexual speech is unbelievably broad, covering everything from ancient Greek plays to erotic comic books to sexy podcasts.

There are many cases involving the government trying to censor different forms of sexual speech and the First Amendment offering some—but not complete—protection for that speech. In 1957, the Supreme Court decided in *Roth v. United States* that sexual speech must have some form of social value in order to be protected under the First Amendment. As Justice William Brennan wrote, "All ideas having even the slightest redeeming social importance—unorthodox ideas, controversial ideas, even ideas hateful to the prevailing climate of opinion—have the full protection of the guaranties, unless excludable because they encroach upon the limited area of more important interests. But implicit in the history of the First Amendment is the rejection of obscenity as utterly without redeeming social importance."[5] Brennan made a distinction between sexual speech (which is protected by the First Amendment) and obscenity (which is not protected), noting that obscenity "deals with sex in a manner appealing to the prurient interest."[6]

In 1973, the Supreme Court revisited its earlier opinions and threw out the old obscenity standard. In *Miller v. California*, the Supreme Court created a three-part test for whether sexual speech would be protected under the First Amendment: first, whether the average person applying contemporary community standards would find that the work, taken as a whole, appeals to the prurient interest; second, whether the work depicts or describes, in a patently offensive way, sexual conduct specifically defined by the applicable state law; third, whether the work, taken as a whole, lacks serious literary, artistic, political, or scientific value.[7]

This narrowed the protections set forth in *Roth*, which only required that speech have some sort of redeeming social value. It also brought up the idea of localization—first, that there be "community standards" and also by specifically naming "applicable state laws." The concept of obscenity would thus be a state or community definition, not a national one. This raises some wild questions when it comes to sexual speech online. On the one hand, the internet is a global community. Then again, we could also see each social platform or website as its own distinct community with its own "contemporary community standards."

In the context of online speech, the most important Supreme Court case has been *Reno v. the American Civil Liberties Union*, decided in 1997. In this landmark case, the court struck down as unconstitutional two provisions of the Communications Decency Act that would have made it a crime punishable by up to two years in jail and/or a $250,000 fine for anyone to engage in online speech that was "indecent" or "patently offensive" if the speech could be viewed by a minor. The ACLU organized other civil liberties organizations in challenging this law. The District Court for the Eastern District of Pennsylvania agreed with the ACLU, stating, "The Internet may fairly be regarded as a never-ending worldwide conversation. The Government may not, through the CDA, interrupt that conversation. As the most participatory form of mass speech yet developed, the Internet deserves the highest protection from governmental intrusion."[8]

The Supreme Court upheld the district court ruling, noting that "notwithstanding the legitimacy and importance of the congressional goal of protecting children from harmful materials, we agree with the three-judge District Court that the statute abridges the 'freedom of speech' protected by the First Amendment."[9]

One piece of the Communications Decency Act that survived the Supreme Court's evisceration was Section 230. This section provides some legal immunity to online platforms who act as hosts for the speech of others. So, for example, Meta is generally not liable for the posts of its users and Google is generally not liable for the comments posted by users on YouTube videos. This provision has been cited as one of the reasons the internet has thrived in the United States. After all, if every website had to review and approve every comment or post from every user or else face legal liability, our internet experience would be far less participatory than it is today.

Congress responded to the Supreme Court's ruling on the Communications Decency Act by passing the Child Online Protection Act of 1998 (COPA), which attempted to punish commercial website operators with civil and criminal penalties if they published sexually explicit material without also verifying a user's age and blocking access to minors by using credit card authentication or other tools. COPA was declared unconstitutional by the courts and made two trips to the Supreme Court before their refusal to hear a third appeal effectively killed it.[10]

In 2018, years after PayPal censored Smashwords, the US Congress passed the FOSTA-SESTA package, which combined two bills that both tried to tackle the online promotion of sex trafficking. The law creates civil and criminal penalties for those who assist in sex trafficking, but it also includes broad language that includes websites and apps that "knowingly facilitate" sex trafficking.[11] Many civil liberties organizations raised concerns that, regardless of its noble intentions, the bill would censor online sexual speech. Elliot Harmon of the Electronic Frontier Foundation (EFF) called it a "bill that silences online speech by forcing Internet platforms to censor their users," and EFF filed a lawsuit against it.[12] While EFF's lawsuit succeeded in getting the Court of Appeals for the DC Circuit to helpfully narrow some of the definitions of the law, FOSTA-SESTA remains on the books, and the Supreme Court never weighed in on its constitutionality.[13]

For the purposes of this book, the main takeaway is that sexual speech is protected from censorship by the government by the First Amendment, but the law carefully polices a line between speech and nonspeech "obscenity." Courts consider a three-part test to determine if something is worthy of First Amendment protection or is nonprotected obscenity, including whether the average person applying community standards would find the work appealing to prurient interests, whether the work is patently offensive per relevant state laws, and whether the work lacks serious literary, artistic, political, or scientific value. Finally, a recent law about sex trafficking creates new liabilities for website owners hosting sexual speech.

The fictional, erotic novels and short stories published by Smashwords would certainly pass the Miller test, as they have literary and artistic value, and they couldn't be interpreted as facilitating sex trafficking by even the most imaginative interpretation. They are written fiction stories.[14]

When we consider the case of Smashwords and other booksellers fighting the PayPal block, it's useful to remember that the activity of these publishers is clearly protected by the First Amendment. Smashwords did not break any law. The actions of PayPal are then *extralegal*; it is a form of censorship that has nothing to do with what is legal speech. If PayPal wasn't censoring Smashwords due to any legal obligation, why were they doing it?

Smashwords was in ongoing conversations with representatives of PayPal as they tried to deal with the ultimatum to remove a subset of erotica from the platform. Mark Coker blogged openly about those conversations: "PayPal tells us that their crackdown is necessary so that they can remain in compliance with the requirements of the banks and credit card associations (likely Visa, MasterCard, Discover, American Express, though they didn't mention them by name)."[15]

The reports from Mark Coker and the prohibition against rape, incest, and bestiality could point to the rules of certain credit card networks. Credit card networks set out rules about who can interact with their services and in what ways, and those rules apply to the financial institutions that issue those branded credit cards and, depending on the rule, may also apply to payment intermediaries who facilitate credit card payments. But the rules trickle down: Financial institutions pass the rules on to the other financial companies they do business with, to merchants accepting credit cards for services, to customers using credit cards for purchases. Each corporate cog in the machine might add its own gloss to the legal terms, inspired by, building from, or reinforcing ideas originally found in the rules of the credit card networks.

Visa and Mastercard both have sections of rules that prohibit the use of their brand or mark in ways associated with certain sexually explicit content. For example, the Visa rules currently state:

> 1.3.3.4 Integrity Risk and Use of the Visa-Owned Marks
>
> A Member must not use the Visa-Owned Marks:
>
> *In any manner that may bring the Visa-Owned Marks or Visa Inc. or its affiliates into disrepute* [emphasis added]
>
> In relation to, or for the purchase or trade of, photographs, video imagery, computer-generated images, cartoons, simulation, or any other media or activities including, but not limited to, any of the following:
>
> – Child sexual abuse materials
> – Incest
> – Bestiality
> – Rape (or any other non-consensual sexual behavior)
> – Non-consensual mutilation of a person or body part
>
> A Member that does not comply with these requirements will be subject to non-compliance assessments prescribed under the Visa Integrity Risk Program.[16]

Mastercard has similar language in its rules, which currently state:

> 5.12.7 Illegal or Brand-damaging Transactions
>
> A Merchant must not submit to its Acquirer, and a Customer must not submit to the Interchange System, any Transaction that is illegal, *or in the sole discretion of the Corporation, may damage the goodwill of the Corporation or reflect negatively on the Marks.* [emphasis added] The Corporation considers any of the following activities to be in violation of this Rule:
>
> 1. The sale or offer of sale of a product or service other than in full compliance with law then applicable to the Acquirer, Issuer, Merchant, Cardholder, Cards, or the Corporation.
>
> 2. The sale of a product or service, including an image, which is patently offensive and lacks serious artistic value (such as, by way of

> example and not limitation, images of nonconsensual sexual behavior, sexual exploitation of a minor, nonconsensual mutilation of a person or body part, and bestiality), or *any other material that the Corporation deems unacceptable to sell in connection with a Mark* [emphasis added].[17]

Both rules list explicit sexual activity that might be illegal, but then the companies have a lot of leeway to ban sexual speech as they see fit. At the same time, these same companies may purport to be committed to neutrality and human rights. Mastercard, for example, insists in its Human Rights Statement: "When it comes to transactions permissible by law, we respect individuals' right to transact privately with others."[18] But this messaging, which seems to jar with the sweeping language of the official rules, may well leave financial intermediaries that connect to the Mastercard network with uncertainty about how to handle lawful but potentially "brand-damaging" speech. It's easy to see how payment intermediaries and banks could take the most conservative interpretation and always err on the side of censorship.

One thing is clear: the language PayPal used to tell independent booksellers that they must stop selling erotic fiction bears a striking similarity to these rules set out by the credit card networks.

THE FIGHT FOR TRANSGRESSIVE FICTION

After Mark Coker sent out his first email to the Smashwords community about the new rules from PayPal, word started to spread. News outlets covered the story, and digital rights and free expression advocacy groups began speaking up.

The National Coalition Against Censorship and the American Booksellers Foundation for Free Expression sent a joint letter to PayPal warning that its broad brush could easily censor erotica that may have artistic and literary value.[19] In my role at EFF, I organized a joint letter from thirty-three civil liberties organizations and publishers including the Authors Guild, the Comic Book Legal Defense Fund, the ACLU of California, and Reporters Without Borders. We called on PayPal to stop censoring speech.[20] Smashwords kept up the pressure, both in direct conversation with PayPal and through public blog posts. And erotica writers themselves fought against the censorship. Remittance Girl, who blogs and writes literary erotica, spoke about how this censorship impacted women writers in particular: "The vast majority of us are women. And we are especially socially vulnerable to having our sexuality used against us, to being shamed for our desires, to having our sexual identities decided upon by men."[21]

At first, PayPal seemed to defend its policy. In a post from their director of communications, Anuj Nayar, which has subsequently been removed from its blog, PayPal asserted that using its service was not a right: "PayPal is a payments company. The right to use PayPal's service is not the same as the right to speak."[22] The blog post ended by inviting comments but saying the company wouldn't budge: "We always welcome your feedback—but please know that we'll continue to keep this policy in place as long as it protects our interests as a business."

Visa did not issue an independent statement, but Remittance Girl contacted Visa directly and published their response. Visa stated that it had not contacted PayPal about this issue: "We want to clarify that Visa had no involvement with PayPal's conclusion on this issue." Visa asserted it would not try to censor legal fiction: "Visa would take no action regarding lawful material that seeks to explore erotica in a fictional or educational manner."[23]

Mastercard also responded to an inquiry from Remittance Girl and stated that "MasterCard had no involvement in the decision made by PayPal to refuse to process payments for certain books." It further clarified: "In this particular scenario, MasterCard would not take action regarding the use of its cards and systems for the sale of lawful materials that seek to explore erotica content of this nature."

It's worth pausing here to note how these denials from Visa and Mastercard change our perception of this situation. Of course, we are trying to piece together exactly what happened while the financial companies involved have little incentive to be transparent. Smashwords is pointing to pressure from PayPal, PayPal is pointing to pressure from other financial companies, and now a blogger is reporting that she received confirmation from the credit card companies that they had no direct involvement.

In this circular blame game, readers, writers, and society are ultimately the ones who suffer. This also points to a larger issue we see throughout the stories of financial censorship: unless you happen to work inside one of the financial companies making these decisions, it is nearly impossible to know with certainty the origin of a censorship request.

PayPal's general counsel at the time, John Muller, reached out to me after we published our online petition. He wanted to talk about our concerns—in person.

I drove down from San Francisco to San Jose with my colleague Lee Tien, a First Amendment attorney who had been with EFF for twenty years and who was unfailingly generous in teaching me about the law when I joined the organization. As we drove, I recalled advice my first mentor in the consumer advocacy space, Beth Givens, had given me, which I thought about often even if I didn't always heed it. She told me to never meet directly with companies, as it would merely give them a chance to try to convince you that they were on your side and soften your approach toward them. It was better to judge corporations based on their publicly available materials than accept their friendly overtures in person.

I haven't honored that advice; over the years I've met many times with corporate employees, including those with influence over internal policies, those lobbying for legal changes, and line engineers building the technology itself. But every time I meet with them, no matter how cordial the meeting, Beth's advice rings in the back of my head. As I stepped into a meeting with PayPal's legal officer, I remembered that this man, however polite and even if he acquiesced to our coalition's efforts, was not my friend.

By the time we arrived for the meeting, Muller had already decided he wanted to change PayPal's policy. What he wanted was to know whether we agreed with his change in tack. Going forward, PayPal would adjust its stance on written fictional erotica. It would try to embrace something like the Miller test set forth by the Supreme Court. As they wrote on their blog post in a few days:

> First and foremost, we are going to focus this policy only on e-books that contain potentially illegal images, not e-books that are limited to just text. The policy will prohibit use of PayPal for the sale of e-books that contain child pornography, or e-books with text and obscene images of rape, bestiality or incest (as defined by the U.S. legal standard for obscenity: material that appeals to the prurient interest, depicts sexual

> conduct in a patently offensive way, and lacks serious literary, artistic, political or scientific value).

PayPal also promised that this policy wouldn't be used to ban whole genres of books:

> In addition, the policy will be focused on individual books, not on entire "classes" of books. Instead of demanding that e-book publishers remove all books in a category, we will provide notice to the seller of the specific e-books, if any, that we believe violate our policy. We are working with e-book publishers on a process that will provide any affected site operator or author the opportunity to respond to and challenge a notice that an e-book violates the policy.[24]

I was pleasantly surprised by the exchange with Muller. We had come armed with ample examples of meritorious literature that dealt with the topics PayPal was trying to ban. But he didn't need to hear any of that; he wanted to cut straight to the chase and get our feedback on their updated policy. From that conversation, it seemed that PayPal was going to let the courts decide what counted as obscenity and try to follow their lead as much as possible. That was exactly what we had hoped for.

We drove back to San Francisco happy with the result. I quickly emailed our coalition with an update about what happened, and Rebecca Jeschke, EFF's press director, sent out a press release.

Mark Coker of Smashwords rejoiced. "This is a victory for all writers and readers. It removes credit card companies, banks and payment processors from the business of censoring legal fiction. It creates a new precedent that should allow other payment processors who have previously discriminated against legal fiction to relax their policies," he wrote on the Smashwords blog.[25]

Some in our coalition were more tempered in their response. "It is too early to conclude that PayPal has completely abandoned the idea of policing the content of books purchased online," said Joan Bertin, then executive director of the National Coalition Against Censorship (NCAC). "We hope so but won't know until the company releases a formal policy. We have to see how it is enforced."[26] NCAC also raised questions about the feasibility of censoring individual books, as "it would be impossible to individually screen all e-books bought and sold online." Bertin's concerns have stuck with me, and I've become increasingly aware of how easy it is for a company to change a speech-friendly policy with a change in leadership.

The fight over erotic fiction was far from over. Just a few months after the battle between Smashwords and PayPal, the Nifty Archive Alliance had their Stripe account suspended. Stripe is a payment intermediary similar to PayPal, and the Nifty Archive Alliance is a registered 501(c)(3) that has a mission to encourage and nurture LGBTQ writers.

The Nifty Archive Alliance supports the operations of the Nifty Archive, which is a website where writers can self-publish romantic stories and erotica. The Nifty Archive has been a resource for the gay community for decades. Started in 1992, stories were originally shared on Usenet, a precursor to the modern World Wide Web. The Nifty Archive survived a move to Gopher, another protocol for sharing documents before the modern web, and then finally arrived at the World Wide Web. While today many of the original domains established at the dawn of the internet have been taken over by new owners, Nifty is still a hub for the LGBTQ community to share their romantic and erotic fiction by submitting it over email. Stories are shared pseudonymously, and they explore wildly diverse sexual fantasies across a range of imaginary scenarios and worlds, from battle fronts to laboratories.

The Nifty Archive has been around for so long, it now serves as a time capsule from an early time in gay history. Community members started sharing sexy stories twenty years before federal recognition of gay marriage, and so it can be seen as the erotic stories of an oppressed people. Created by and for the LGBTQ community, the stories explored romance and sexuality before there were mainstream models of queer and transgender sexuality widely featured in books, movies, magazines, and more.

Similar to Smashwords, Nifty Archives ran into trouble because it provides an online space for controversial erotic fiction. Stripe suspended Nifty's account because it feared that certain stories exploring taboo topics such as bestiality would run afoul of the Visa and Mastercard rules. Stripe didn't just shut down support for the section of the site that had those stories; it froze payments to the entire 501(c)(3).

Whereas the fight over Smashwords happened entirely in the open, with erotica writers, tech journalists, and First Amendment lawyers weighing in, the debate between Nifty Archive and Stripe was brokered behind closed doors. After Nifty's account was restricted, Nifty contacted EFF for help. On hearing EFF's concerns, Stripe reversed course and reinstated Nifty's account, and the nonprofit was once again able to receive funds.[27] What's perhaps most interesting about the Nifty case is the timing. It happened mere months after the massive coalition triumphed in getting PayPal to change its stance on erotic fiction. It seems that PayPal doing the right thing paved the way for Stripe to stand up for free speech as well. This is likely an important lesson in creating change in the world of financial censorship in general, though it applies more broadly to advancing civil liberties in the tech policy space: one company willing to stand up for digital rights can embolden others in the same industry to follow suit.

One view of the Smashwords and the Nifty Archive cases is that free speech triumphed over the censorship of financial companies, and in some ways that's true. But it's also an overly simplistic interpretation. Even if activism was triumphant in these two situations, it's unrealistic for advocacy organizations and others to police the enforcement decisions of financial companies. That's not scalable to the global reach of companies like PayPal and Stripe, much less to a company the size of Visa.

Plus, the censorship by financial companies of written, fictional erotica is an ongoing problem. I spoke with Sinclair Sexsmith, an author, editor, and educator who has written extensively about issues related to consensual kink and queer sexuality. They teach courses on writing erotica and have published erotic fiction on their website, Sugarbutch. Sexsmith has been denied a PayPal account for much of their adult career. This is particularly problematic as Sexsmith relies on online payments for much of their education and speaking work.

For years, Sexsmith used a partner's PayPal account to receive payments, but they were left without a PayPal option once that relationship ended.

After the breakup in 2022, Sexsmith spent hours working their way through the customer service tree to talk to someone at PayPal on the phone, explain the situation, and get a ticket opened for their account. Two days later, their new account was again shut down. Sexsmith shared screenshots with me of the notification from PayPal, which said in bold type, "You can't use PayPal anymore," and then explained in smaller font, "At PayPal, we value a safe community for our customers to do business. We noticed activity in your account that's inconsistent with our User Agreement and we no longer offer you PayPal services." There was no additional information provided. Sexsmith told me, "It's become one of the major ways to move money, and have money and hold money, especially online. And it does feel like I'm cut off." Apparently saving erotic fiction on sites like Smashwords and the Nifty Archive did not translate to protection for solo erotica writers like Sexsmith publishing on their own blogs.

Cindy Gallop, a feminist and entrepreneur in the adult space who herself has been repeatedly blocked from parts of the traditional financial system, has argued there is a massive missed opportunity for financial companies.[28] By providing services to these businesses that create content around human sexuality, the finance companies would be unlocking a huge market. After all, while Sexsmith, Nifty Archive, and Smashwords are just three accounts, they are representative of a vast swath of content creators who are underserved by the existing financial system.

These examples illustrate how payment processors go far beyond the legal definitions of obscenity when enforcing policies about sexual speech. In each instance, the enforcement decisions stepped into the realm of moralizing. Payment processors aren't just trying to enforce the law but are interpreting nebulous agreements with other payment intermediaries with whom they have relationships. When in doubt, the payment companies err on the side of shuttering speech.

Erotica is complex and personal, and there are stories exploring the darkest sides of human sexuality that have value, whether for their intrinsic literary qualities or because they proved helpful for someone's personal growth. These cases make us ask: Are payment processors like Square and PayPal and credit card companies like Visa and Mastercard capable of assessing the merit of transgressive erotica? As a society, do we want these companies to have veto power on sexual fantasy?

BANKERS POLICING THE HUMAN BODY

Gabriel Bienczycki doesn't think of himself as having anything to do with the sex industry. "As a completely non-sexual series, we didn't expect it to be a source of any controversy," he told me in an email interview.

He founded True Naked Yoga in 2018 with his friend Tom Severini. The website offers guided instructional videos for yoga practiced in the nude. The unclothed instructors demonstrate often advanced yoga movements, either in well-lit studios or in bright, serene natural landscapes. The videos have a calming, almost hypnotic quality, and the instructors move smoothly between poses in ways that allow the viewer to see the subtle flex and stretching of muscles.

Severini hears frequently from members, and it's clear to him that people aren't relating to True Naked Yoga as sexual content. Instead, members reach out frequently talking about the health benefits and asking for new classes that will help them rehabilitate from an injury, lose weight, or gain strength. He listed some of the success stories from the program: "We've heard from ex-professional athletes who now use our programs. In response we created programs for runners, cyclists, swimmers. Cancer survivors who would rather exercise with the idea that they have nothing to hide. Members who lost over a hundred pounds doing yoga."

Yoga has skyrocketed in popularity in the past fifty years in the United States, but naked yoga actually has deep historical and cultural roots. It's mentioned as far back as the Bhagavata Purana, a revered Hindu text that dates back to at least the sixth century CE. Different versions of naked yoga and meditation have existed across multiple cultures. The historical practice is rooted in ascetic philosophies renouncing physical comforts and emphasizing simplicity and frugality as a tool to deepen spiritual awakening. Naked yoga has also been around Western cultures for decades. Paul Corsden's 1974 documentary *Naked Yoga* aired on television in the UK and was nominated for an Oscar in 1975, and men's-only naked yoga classes were popularized in New York City studios in the early 2000s.[29]

Bienczycki, whose background in dance led to a love of yoga, says that financial companies don't know how to categorize a business that allows nudity but isn't sexual. True Naked Yoga got lumped into a category with sexual content even though the website took pains to be nonsexual, which Bienczycki felt was a fundamental misunderstanding of the content. "Our videos are shot from modest angles, don't linger on genitalia, and absolutely don't feature any sex or suggestive acts," he pointed out.

Their credit card processor was Stripe. Stripe reviewed their account in December 2021 and didn't find any problems with their business. But, in August 2022, Stripe told True Naked Yoga that they had to find another payment processor—and only gave them four days before shutting their account.

Bienczycki and Severini didn't know what to do. "My stomach dropped. I was upset, angry, and felt helpless," Severini recalled. "It felt so unfair that they could just shut our account like this after being a good customer for almost three years. Nothing had changed with our content on our site."

Bienczycki was especially upset by how little time Stripe gave them to fix the situation. As he explained:

> Due to the extremely short notice given by Stripe, we were in a state of panic for those entire 4 days. We worked so hard over the prior 3 years to establish ourselves, gain the trust of the community, and amass the subscriber base that allowed us to have a functioning business and continue spreading the benefits of naked yoga. That progress seemed absolutely doomed in those few days as we scrambled to find another provider.

Unfortunately, finding another credit card processor wasn't simple; it took True Naked Yoga a month to find a replacement.

Attempts to appeal Stripe's decision met with dead ends. Severini said that it was impossible to talk to anyone at Stripe about what happened:

> There is no phone number to reach them or even a direct email for a rep. There was a website chat, but during the month that this was happening it was disabled. They don't even have a conventional support ticketing system. You have to fill out a form online and wait. The emails we received back were not informative and every time I would reach out I would get an email from a different employee with a similar response, but no one ever gave us an answer. They always made it seem like they would get back, but they never did. Just kept us hanging until the account was shut down without any further emails.

He shared one of the emails he received from Stripe. The tone is caring, engaged, and completely disconnected from the specific situation True Naked Yoga was facing:

> I hope this email finds you well and many thanks for contacting us back about your query on if a migration process can be carried out if your account is closed as well as the deadline extension you requested. I really appreciate your time and patience towards this event and therefore, I'll be more than glad to assist you properly.
>
> In this case, after a thorough research on my end, I along with my team will keep reviewing your account. Once we finish our examination, we will let you know the outcomes from it. Again, many thanks for your patience and big understanding towards this plight.
>
> In the meantime, if you have any other doubt or concern about another topic, you may let us know about it and we will be happy to help.

True Naked Yoga is a subscription service. Its business model relies on monthly subscriptions from members to cover costs and make a profit. When Stripe banned them, they were unable to process monthly membership fees or sign up new customers, effectively halting the company's growth. Even after they found a new credit card processor a month later, True Naked Yoga couldn't just import their prior membership list—members had to affirmatively opt back into the service. Bienczycki said that this resulted in a huge loss of customers and it took months to recover.

Much of True Naked Yoga's ability to survive during and after their financial censorship was due to an already established and committed membership base. That community was able to rally so that the company could rebuild once it had a new credit card processor. This might not have been the case had Stripe's shutdown happened earlier in True Naked Yoga's existence, when its community and brand were still finding their footing. Less established companies that face similar shutdowns might not be able to rebound as quickly—or at all.

CUSTOMER SURVEILLANCE PROGRAMS

It's important to pause to describe one of the most impactful facets of financial censorship: the customer surveillance programs that make it possible. One of the primary justifications for freezing and even closing financial accounts is perceived legal obligations, especially legal obligations on the part of financial institutions to "know your customers." So what does that actually mean?

Financial institutions are required by law to set up customer due diligence programs, but financial institutions have some flexibility in how they design and implement those programs. These customer identification programs (CIPs) help the bank know who their customers are and ensure those customers are not violating any laws. Know Your Customer (KYC) obligations are the legal requirements financial institutions have to verify the identities of their customers. These identification programs are part of Anti-Money Laundering (AML) and Countering the Financing of Terrorism (CFT) or Terrorist Financing (TF) obligations, which are just like their names indicate: requirements that are designed to help combat money laundering and terrorist financing. Often, these requirements are referred to by different combinations of acronyms, like KYC/AML or AML/TF.

All of these programs are designed and implemented at financial institutions to surveil customers. At a minimum, this includes collecting a customer's name, date of birth, physical address, and government-issued identification number. Banks may ask customers to provide proof of their identity and address such as a driver's license, passport, or utility bill. These programs also involve monitoring the financial transactions of customers for behavior that the financial institution deems suspicious.

Financial institutions will both share customer information with the US government through required reports and other permitted channels, and make that data available to government agencies upon request, without requiring a judge to issue a warrant.[30]

KYC obligations are threaded into different parts of US banking law, particularly the inaccurately named Bank Secrecy Act, and were expanded under the USA PATRIOT Act.[31] Covered financial institutions are required to ascertain the identity of customers, but the financial institutions have some discretion in how they go about establishing that identity. They are also required to report to the government about any currency transactions over a certain threshold ($10,000 as of this writing), or a group of related smaller currency transactions that add up to that amount or more.[32]

Civil liberties organizations fought against KYC regulations. In testimony to a House subcommittee in 1999, legislative counsel Greg Nojeim of the ACLU called on Congress to reject proposed amendments to KYC obligations and strengthen financial privacy rights for Americans, saying, "Customers of financial institutions who are not engaged in illegal activities should have a statutory right to know when personal information about them has moved into the law enforcement world."[33]

Financial institutions are also required to file a Suspicious Activity Report (SAR) whenever a covered financial institution notices customer activity that seems "suspicious." These reports can be filed on transactions as low as $2,000. The Financial Crimes Enforcement Network's guidance on when to file an SAR is rooted in preventing money laundering. It urges banks to look for potential "red flags" that might indicate inappropriate activity and then ask questions such as these:

- Is the amount of the transaction unusually large for the typical customer or for the MSB [Money Services Business]?
- Does the customer make the same or similar transactions more frequently than normal?
- Does the type of transaction seem unusual for the customer or the MSB?[34]

One of the biggest problems with monitoring for suspicious activity is that there are different understandings of what counts as suspicious. As Peter Van Valkenburg, director of research at the cryptocurrency research and advocacy organization Coin Center, told me on a call in 2024, "That term is generally undefined in the examiner handbooks, and definitely undefined in the actual law itself. So it's really just whatever you think is suspicious."

While these programs are supposed to be about stopping illegal activity like money laundering and terrorist financing, they are inextricably intertwined with restrictions placed on entirely legal accounts for customers who haven't done anything wrong. That's because in an effort to comply with these laws, banks set up customer monitoring programs with an eye toward catching problematic behavior. And those programs inadvertently flag any number of legitimate accounts.

Once an account is flagged, even if the flag was inappropriate, the account can be restricted, transactions can be blocked, and sometimes the account can be closed entirely. Financial institutions are required by law to set up customer identification and monitoring programs, but they are not incentivized to ensure that customers who have not violated the law can access the financial system.

As Van Valkenburg explained, the problem is that it is expensive to bank clients who trigger these review systems, even if in the end they didn't do anything wrong: "The banks don't find it profitable to bank them anymore, given the incredible compliance costs that they have to undergo in order to provide services to those people. So that's a huge problem. And the only way around this is to unwind the ratcheted-up financial surveillance that we now expect financial institutions to do."

This is a major theme seen throughout stories of financial censorship: it's not economical for financial institutions to slow down and carefully consider the ramifications their account decisions have on speech and society. Changing this system will involve fundamentally changing the incentives of financial institutions and, as Van Valkenburg said, unwinding financial surveillance.

BANKERS POLICING ADULT CONTENT

Often the censorship decisions of financial companies are hidden and secretive. But that's not really the case when it comes to explicit adult content such as pornography. On adult sites, the heavy hand of financial censorship is often overt and even directly negotiated between the website and the financial providers.

I met with Mike Stabile, director of public affairs for the Free Speech Coalition. The Free Speech Coalition is a trade association for the adult industry. Founded in 1991, the small staff engages in advocacy and lobbying to help fight social stigma, misinformation, and discriminatory policies that affect the adult industry. They also have a variety of resources for performers, including online guides to help performers report consent violations or know their rights if they face racial discrimination. Stabile confirmed that adult content sites will frequently give passwords to their banks so that bankers can review all the content on the website.

Surprised at the idea that there are a bunch of bankers trolling around porn sites for free, I asked if this was just something that a site would do when setting up with a new bank. Stabile replied, "Oh absolutely. It's not even a new bank. It is your old bank, even. But certainly, with a new bank. They will go in and look at all the content and say, 'This scene—no. This word—no.'"

Whatever the banker flags, the adult content site will need to take down to get their account approved or keep it in good standing. Stabile told me the censorship often seems arbitrary. A banker might censor a certain word on one website but not have a problem with that word used on a different website owned by the same company. The positions of the banks might change over time and might be subject to interpretation by the individual banker reviewing the site.*

When Stabile explained this, I felt like I'd stumbled onto something big. How long have financial service providers been logging onto pornography sites and offering editorial feedback on specific words, images, and videos? I wondered if this was the root of all the other problems we see around financial censorship. Perhaps these companies got so used to making granular content decisions about pornography sites that they began to think this was part of their role. Almost no one would stand up and fight for the editorial choices of pornography sites, so the financial companies could settle into the role of online editors without anyone pushing back. Over time, perhaps these companies started to think of censorship as their prerogative.

Stabile told me how the threats to the adult industry have changed over time. With the move to digital, the credit card companies have stepped forward as the vanguards of American modesty. He compared

*I was so surprised by this that I asked Cathy Beardsley, CEO of adult payment facilitator Segpay, about this practice. She confirmed in an interview with me: "They [banks and credit card companies] use spiders, and they'll go through the websites monthly looking for terms and words that will get flagged, that we have to then have our merchants clean up. So we try to do that ahead of time so that our merchants aren't getting flagged by anyone."

the relationship between Visa and Mastercard to the rest of the payment industry as being akin to a mafia lord. "The head guy, Visa and Mastercard, doesn't give specific instructions. They give sort of vague pronouncements." Everyone below them in the chain will interpret their edicts, and there's a lot of room for different interpretations.

When it comes to payments, there are a few layers of middlemen to navigate. They conclude:

1. A payment processor that manages the transaction between the merchant, banks, and card networks. Sometimes there's also a separate payment gateway that sends payment information from the merchant website to the payment processor.
2. The acquiring bank (the merchant's bank).
3. The credit card networks.
4. The issuing bank (the customer's bank, which will issue the credit card to the customer).[35]

This means that for any online payment involving a credit card, there are typically a minimum of four financial entities involved, and any one of them could flag a transaction and prevent it from going through.

Stabile explained that the acquiring banks tend to be conservative in their interpretation of Visa's and Mastercard's rules because they don't want to risk their relationship with the credit cards. Then the payment processor may be even more conservative in their interpretation of the rules.

The end result? Bankers hopping into porn websites to point out all the content that needs to be changed or deleted, and porn sites feeling they have no choice but to comply. Every entity in the chain of payment confirmation is incentivized to take conservative approaches to online speech because they are far more afraid of risking their relationships with banking partners than they care about any individual transaction.

Stabile told me that the Free Speech Coalition (FSC) has had its own banking issues. Even though it is a trade industry association engaged in advocacy and has no explicit content on its website, FSC was rejected from getting a bank account for a new project they wanted to start. This surprised them because they already had a business account at that bank. But the banker told them they couldn't approve another adult-oriented account, even one that was just geared toward advocacy and education. They were also warned against trying to appeal the decision, as more attention drawn to their account might jeopardize their existing banking services.

Stabile didn't want to share the name of the bank out of fear of retribution.

SHERIFF DART'S INTIMIDATION TACTICS

Sheriff Tom Dart of Cook County, Illinois—the county that encompasses Chicago and surrounding areas—sent a letter in 2015 to credit card companies Visa and Mastercard asking that they stop providing services for the online classified website Backpage.com. "As the Sheriff of Cook County, a father, and a caring citizen, I write to request that your institution immediately cease and desist from allowing your credit cards to be used to place ads on websites like Backpage.com," he wrote.[36]

Backpage was created by media companies who had lost much of their advertising revenue as more of their readers moved online instead of buying newspapers and magazines in the physical world. Backpage offered online advertisements for a whole host of things—community events, used cars, apartments, jobs. While Backpage's terms explicitly prohibited the use of the site for prostitution or trafficking, it had a section for advertising for "adult" services, including subcategories such as "escorts," "body rubs," and "adult jobs." In effect, this meant Backpage was an efficient means for sex workers of various types to advertise to potential clients, and for clients to get in touch with sex workers.

Dart argued that his campaign against Backpage was motivated by a concern that people were abusing Backpage.com for nefarious purposes such as human trafficking, even though that's not what the site is designed for.

Mastercard and Visa responded to Dart's letter by shutting down services to Backpage. This kickstarted a court case specifically around the legality of a government official using his office to intimidate financial services into ending relationships with one of their clients.

Backpage sued Sheriff Dart, alleging the sheriff had violated the First Amendment. While this case happened years before *NRA v. Vullo*, it grappled with many of the same issues about whether it's legal for the government to pressure a financial company to shutter someone's account over their legal but controversial speech. The Center for Democracy and Technology, the Association for Alternative Newsmedia, and EFF submitted a joint amicus brief in the case, arguing that this was a dangerous form of government censorship, even if it was indirect.[37]

The US Court of Appeals for the Seventh Circuit sided with Backpage and the civil liberties organizations, ruling that Dart's actions violated the First Amendment through government intimidation. The court acknowledged that Sheriff Dart—just like anyone, government official or otherwise—has a First Amendment right to express his opinion. But when he sent an official letter on government stationery and began with "As the Sheriff of Cook County," that stepped beyond the bounds of expressing a private opinion and into the realm of acting as a government official. The court likened what Sheriff Dart was doing to Backpage to "killing a person by cutting off his oxygen supply rather than by shooting him."[38]

Why does this case matter?

Often in cases of financial censorship, there's a whiff of government involvement but it's hard to prove. Credit card companies or payment processors might not say they were directly contacted by the government, but perhaps they think they are acting in a way the government would prefer.

With the *Dart v. Backpage* case, like *NRA v. Vullo*, the government pressure is not secret. Each case offers a clear view into how government officials pressured financial companies to punish speakers. In both cases, the government used intimidation tactics to try to bully financial companies into shutting off services for people and websites engaged in forms of protected speech. The courts thankfully understood how this would be an effective form of censorship. Notably, these cases only address examples of overt government censorship and leave unexamined situations in which government pressure is more subtle or the censorship is rooted solely in the policies of the financial companies.

SPEECH BATTLEGROUNDS AROUND ADULT CONTENT

Like many before her, financial circumstances prompted Allie Eve Knox (not her real name) to explore sex work as a career—specifically, a whole bunch of debt.

"When I graduated from grad school, I was in super debt," she told me in an interview. "I was in like $100,000 of debt. I was working at the university at the time, and I had like $10 left at the end of the month. I never saw a light at the end of the tunnel."

With two bachelor of fine arts degrees and a master's degree under her belt, Knox found herself in the same place as a lot of recent graduates: qualified to work but not finding the career opportunities that would make it possible for her to make a dent in her debt while still carving out a reasonable life for herself.

In her twenties, she'd done some nude modeling for *Playboy*, so she'd had some experience with the adult industry. Now thirty, she turned back to it as a way to make money in the evenings. She adopted the name Allie Eve Knox and got to work camming—where she got sexy in front of a camera from the privacy of her own home. She immediately started making money. She thought she'd found a way out of her crushing debt, a way to fix her larger financial problems. Knox uses a variety of subscription services to connect with fans, sells video chats with clients, and sells tokens like her panties online.

Her connections are virtual. They are also legal.

One of the common misconceptions about sex work is that it's categorically illegal. But when we examine the issue a little more, we discover that there are countless ways in which human desire and sexuality have been monetized that don't violate the law and are squarely protected by the First Amendment—including erotic calls, selling worn underwear, and posting naked photos online. There are also clip sites, which are online repositories of videos that customers pay to access at any time, as well as cam sites, where performers will live stream content and customers can pay to watch in real time. "I never meet anyone, ever," Knox said.

By not meeting people in person, Knox helps protect her privacy and herself. "It's so safe," she explained. "If I have a problem, I just shut this computer."

In fact, one of the riskiest parts of her line of work is having to deal with the online intermediaries who try to collect information on her. This includes clip sites that collect detailed information about her as well as any financial institutions.

Like many people in the adult industry, Knox has faced a seemingly endless set of challenges in dealing with financial companies. Knox points out that many traditional cam sites will take a substantial cut from viewer payments—40 to 50 percent of what a performer might otherwise make. She and other performers have sought to find a way to receive money directly from their fans.

Knox's first experience with financial censorship was with PayPal. Her account was shut down within a couple weeks of setting it up. She said that PayPal shuttered her account on the accusation that she was "soliciting sexual services." But at the time, she'd only done two things with PayPal: sold a pair of socks and gotten a tribute for her birthday. This was shortly after she'd started camming professionally, and she said her PayPal account wasn't linked in any way from her camming page. While she never got an explanation, her suspicion is that her account got flagged because the person who had sent her a tip had sent other performers tips as well.

PayPal may have been the first, but it was far from the last payment service that booted Knox. She listed some of the financial services that approved and then shuttered her account: Cash App, Google Wallet, Venmo, Square Cash (which was connected to Snap Cash), and Circle.

Knox also experimented with cryptocurrency. One of her fans showed her how to download the Coinbase app and use it to accept tips from people. She was excited that Coinbase wasn't taking huge fees, that the payments couldn't be reversed, and that she could see the payments within a few minutes. She became a public advocate for cryptocurrency, to the point that she was on a documentary that aired on Showtime in 2017, holding a QR code up to the camera with her Coinbase wallet. The day after the episode aired, Knox found her Coinbase account closed as well. Knox also became deeply involved in SpankPay, a cryptocurrency payment service aimed at providing services to the adult industry that was shut down when one of their banking partners ended its relationship with them.

Today, Knox faces massive barriers to using the financial system. "The mortgage company did not feel comfortable putting me on the loan, because I'm too 'high risk.' So they couldn't put my info on the loan. So everything had to be in my husband's name." She ended up putting all of her loans—her car payment, her home mortgage—under her husband's name.

"That's a real fucking problem when he becomes your ex-husband," she pointed out. Disentangling herself from her now former partner has become a mess. "I have been making his credit perfect for the seven years our things have been linked. I still don't have credit. I have no credit for any of the things I've bought and paid for."

Knox is not alone in facing these kinds of problems. Many people engaged in sex work or even sex work–adjacent fields face financial discrimination. The policing of sexual and nude imagery is an area of financial censorship that especially impacts minority communities. Journalist and author Violet Blue has written about the dangers of weblining—discrimination or redlining that happens in the digital world, including when payment intermediaries shutter accounts of certain communities unfairly: "What's happening to female entrepreneurs in the sex business can no longer be written off as isolated incidents. Weblining's targeted populations are porn performers, sex workers, independent retailers, erotic writers and the internet's new generation of online pornographers: business sectors comprised of a disproportionately large number of women and LGBT people."[39]

In a *CUNY Law Review* article titled "High Risk Hustling: Payment Processors, Sexual Proxies, and Discrimination by Design," researchers argued that the financial policies that debank sex workers are a convergence of laws and policies steeped in bias against communities already marginalized by society, the privatization of financial infrastructure, and the adoption of automated risk assessment tools. As the authors note, "Platforms have created policies that conflate sex with harm, illegality and risk, and deputize private actors, platforms, and individual users to do the work of police and the state."[40]

The researchers also point out that the financial platforms use vague definitions around what kind of content is prohibited, giving the payment companies leeway to decide what they will and won't allow:

> Platforms' prohibited activities are often vaguely defined, affording broad discretion to payment processors to decide what uses are permissible and even to change their assessments on a day-to-day basis. This leaves users with little information on how to comply. PayPal, for example, prohibits use of the service for activities that relate to "*certain* sexually oriented materials or services" (our emphasis), although it does not define or clarify which sexually oriented materials or services are prohibited.

Losing access to financial services can have devastating consequences. As Dr. Natasha Tusikov, a criminology professor at York University, wrote, "Losing trusted, commercially popular payment services can destroy businesses, particularly small outfits that do not have the resources or technical capability to shift to alternative forms of payment like cryptocurrency."[41]

While there are a range of payment options for adult content creators, Tusikov showed that some financial companies set policies that the rest of the industry is forced to accept because it cannot risk its relationship with those key players. "Certain payment actors, particularly the major US credit card companies, exert structural power over the online payment system. They determine the rules and processes for what constitutes acceptable and prohibited transactions and govern who can be granted merchant accounts to accept payments via credit cards."[42]

This brings us to another important court case, though this case remains unresolved as of this writing. In December 2020, *New York Times* columnist Nicholas Kristof wrote a lengthy opinion piece about the website Pornhub. Noting that the website has a cheery image and is among the most visited sites online, Kristof told the heart-wrenching story of a young woman whose life was destroyed after naked videos she'd taken of herself at thirteen were uploaded to Pornhub repeatedly.* At the end of the article, Kristof called on financial companies to cut off Pornhub, writing, "If PayPal can suspend cooperation with Pornhub, so can American Express, Mastercard and Visa."[43]

*Kristof indicated the videos were of a fourteen-year-old, though the subsequent lawsuit asserted she was thirteen.

The article received a lot of attention—including from Bill Ackman, the billionaire hedge fund manager and CEO of Pershing Square Capital Management. Outraged by the article, Ackman texted Mastercard's then CEO, Ajay Banga, whom he had met through a mutual friend. Ackman shared Kristof's article with his tweet: "Amex, VISA, and MasterCard should immediately withhold payments or withdraw until this is fixed. PayPal has already done so."

Banga replied, "We're on it."[44]

PayPal had cut off Pornhub in November 2019, leaving the website scrambling to pay their performers.[45] Within a week of Kristof's article and shortly after Ackman's text to Mastercard's CEO, Visa and Mastercard both suspended services to Pornhub.[46]

I want to pause here and acknowledge that while I disagree with Kristof's recommendation that payment processors bear responsibility for policing online speech, his research into illegal material spread online helps us understand this issue. I hope these stories spur public policies and societal changes that will help us better protect victims. Our criminal system should do a better job at tracking down and holding accountable rapists and human traffickers, and we are failing in our duties as a society when we don't protect those among us who are most vulnerable. I hope we can all agree on that, even if we disagree about whether credit card companies should be leading the fight against sex trafficking.

As of this writing, there is an active lawsuit filed by Serena Fleites, the woman profiled in the Kristof article who had her videos nonconsensually uploaded to the website. She is suing MindGeek (the corporation that owns Pornhub) and Visa, and she's alleging that the defendants violated federal and state law.

It's beyond the scope of this book to weigh in on whether Pornhub failed to act appropriately and swiftly to remove illegal material from its site. That's a question the courts are considering. For our purposes, this case is important not because of whether Pornhub acted inappropriately but because the credit card company Visa is listed as a party in the lawsuit as well.

Visa sought to have the charges against it dismissed. In its memorandum to the court, Visa argued that "routine payment processing does not constitute 'participation' in a sex trafficking venture" and pointed out that the alleged actions were committed by third parties who uploaded content onto Pornhub, and no one is saying that Visa even processed any payments specifically related to videos of Fleites. Visa characterized the lawsuit against it as an attempt to hold a payment network liable for conduct by people downstream in the payment chain who were unrelated to Visa. "If allowed," the memorandum warned, this lawsuit "would upend the electronic payments industry."[47]

The International Center for Law and Economics (ICLE), a nonprofit policy organization that analyzes legal and economic policies, weighed in through an amicus brief, pointing out that any large firm with a role in commerce could be deemed liable under the theory of this case: "FedEx, for example, would be liable for continuing to deliver packages to MindGeek's address. The local waste management company would be liable for continuing to service the building in which MindGeek's offices are located. And every online search provider and Internet service provider would be liable for continuing to provide service to anyone searching for or viewing legal content on MindGeek's sites."[48]

ICLE also pointed out that the majority of the content on Pornhub's website was legal pornography. ICLE urged the court to consider the larger ramifications, noting that if Visa is held liable for a situation like this, it could result in a massive increase in the cost of providing a credit card network—and those costs will ultimately be passed down to consumers who will pay bigger fees for credit or be denied access to payment cards.

But the judge considering the motion to dismiss was not swayed.

In August 2022, Judge Cormac J. Carney, of the US District Court for the Central District of California, ruled that Visa could not yet be dismissed from the lawsuit, writing, "If Visa was aware that there was a substantial amount of child porn on MindGeek's sites, which the court must accept as true at this stage of the proceedings, then it was aware that it was processing the monetization of child porn, moving money from advertisers to MindGeek for advertisements playing alongside child porn like plaintiff's videos."[49]

One of the issues Judge Carney focused on was that Visa ended services to Pornhub after the Kristof article. In response, Pornhub removed a massive swath of content from their website—some ten million videos, or around 80 percent of its content, according to documents in the lawsuit. Judge Carney notes:

> But Visa quite literally did force MindGeek to operate differently, and markedly so, at least for a time. And the astonishingly strong response from MindGeek—who is otherwise alleged to stonewall and even harass victims—is consistent with Plaintiff's allegations that unnamed former MindGeek employees have explained that MindGeek constantly worries that Visa could cut it off and makes decisions based on what content the "major credit card companies are willing to work with." [...] When MindGeek crosses the line, or at least when MindGeek is very publicly admonished for crossing the line, Visa cracks the whip and MindGeek responds vigorously. Yet, here is Visa, standing at and controlling the valve, insisting that it cannot be blamed for the water spill because someone else is wielding the hose.[50]

This line of reasoning is chilling, and anyone paying attention to this case should be deeply worried.

It's obvious that the two largest credit card companies—Visa and Mastercard—have powerful market dominance that gives them leverage to demand almost anything at all from those further down the chain. Staying in the good graces of the credit card companies isn't just a preference for online businesses—it's a matter of survival. So the court should not be surprised that Pornhub would do nearly anything, including self-censoring 80 percent of its content, in an attempt to appease the credit card companies. If anything, this should be a lesson in how dangerous it can be for credit card companies to weigh in on speech issues.

If credit card companies are held liable for the potential illegal content hosted by websites that have any kind of payment or advertising service, it creates an untenable burden on credit card companies to review and police every piece of content on any aspect of the web that has any form of payment. Even for a company as large as Visa, that's an impossibly huge and unrealistic task. And remember: while the target of this lawsuit happens to be a porn site, any site that allows user-generated content can have illegal material on it. In fact, social networking sites the world over deal with users uploading sexual content daily, even when the sites are marketed as being nonsexual in nature. Any site that allows users to interact and upload content will inevitably face the fact that some users will use the site for sexual expression, and there's a good chance that some will use the site to upload illegal sexual content.

If a credit card company thinks it can be dragged into a lawsuit for merely providing payment services to adult sites, it will prompt them to shutter services to all adult sites (and possibly all sites hosting any form of user-generated content) or take the most conservative approach possible in reviewing explicit material. This means that any content that is sexual or related to the human body can be demonetized, denying income to many law-abiding people and especially adult content creators—the majority of whom are women.[51]

It also creates uncertainty through the chain of online payments. Remember, Visa isn't the only player involved in approving an online transaction. There's the payment processor, the acquiring bank, and the issuing bank. Visa is likely being singled out in this case because it's the largest credit card network, but the line of argument could apply to all other financial institutions involved in online payments.

Tasking financial intermediaries with assessing the legality of online speech would be ushering in a new era of internet censorship. It is hard to overstate how far-reaching and dangerous it would be for the courts to hold Visa liable because users decided to upload illegal content onto Pornhub.

In August 2022, right after Visa's motion to dismiss was denied, Visa and Mastercard suspended payments for advertisements on Pornhub.[52] Visa issued a statement condemning sex trafficking, highlighting that they disagreed with the court's decision, and noting, "We do not make moral judgments on legal purchases made by consumers, and we respect the rightful role of lawmakers to make decisions about what is legal and what is not."[53]

This lawsuit hasn't been decided yet. There's still time to get this right. The courts have an opportunity to step back and consider the larger ramifications of deputizing financial institutions to police all forms of sexual speech online.

Pornography online remains extremely popular. In 2019, Pornhub alone received some 115 million daily visits.[54] (Yes, daily.) That's more visits than the 81 million people who voted for President Joe Biden in 2020. But while many people may be viewing online porn, there are also many people fighting to see it wiped from the internet. Groups like the National Center on Sexual Exploitation (NCSE) are supporters of legislation that ostensibly aims to go after sexual exploitation, but they have an ultimate goal of stopping the "public health crisis of pornography."[55] In May 2020, NCSE and its UK subsidiary organized a coalition letter to the credit card companies stating that "pornography itself is a form of sexual exploitation, causing physical and mental trauma." The letter called on the card companies to "stop processing payments for the pornography industry."[56]

To put a finer point on it: This isn't just about sexual exploitation. This isn't about stopping human trafficking. This is about censoring all forms of pornography. The advocacy campaigns pressuring credit card companies to cut off services to sites that include nude or sexual content are backed by groups that aren't merely trying to censor illegal content. These groups are working to censor legal sexual speech that involves consenting adults.

This is no secret; they are publicly publishing coalition letters describing their goals.

When activists pressure financial companies to cut off websites hosting naked or sexual content, it circumvents the public policy and legal system. As a point of comparison, when someone is charged with a crime in the United States, they have an array of rights that were put in place to ensure that the system is fair. Defendants have a right to see the evidence against them, offer a defense, be heard by a neutral third party, read any judgment against them, and make an appeal. When someone loses access to financial services, there are no such rights. Targets of financial censorship have no right to an explanation for why they are being cut off, no opportunity to make a defense, and no chance to appeal the decision.

Some of the most important battles around online speech today are happening in the contracts between finance companies and websites. That means that the general public, elected officials, and even the judicial system aren't in the driver's seat when it comes to deciding where we draw the line around sexual speech. Instead, bankers are making sweeping decisions about what types of sexual speech should exist online today.

FIVE

CANNABIS AND INDUSTRY CENSORSHIP

When we finally got documents from the government, I was very briefly delighted.

I had worked with David Greene, a friend of mine on the EFF legal team, to submit a Freedom of Information Act request about a Department of Justice program creepily called Operation Choke Point. Months later—or possibly a year, enough time that I had literally forgotten we submitted the request—the DOJ responded. I printed the eighty-plus pages we'd received and started reading.

I first started hearing about industries losing their banking services in 2014. Frank Keating, then the head of the American Banking Association, wrote an op-ed in the *Wall Street Journal* accusing the Department of Justice of running a secret campaign to pressure banks to shutter the accounts of legal businesses.[1] "Why is the Justice Department telling bankers to behave like policemen and judges?" Keating wrote. "Justice's new probe, known as 'Operation Choke Point,' is asking banks to identify customers who may be breaking the law or simply doing something government officials don't like. Banks must then 'choke off' those customers' access to financial services, shutting down their accounts."

I was intrigued by this so-called Operation Choke Point. I was already tracking the impact of financial exclusion on movements and individuals, but I hadn't considered how certain industries were shuttered from access to financial services. I kept tabs on the issue and looked for more evidence, but I just could never get a clear picture of what was really going on. So I brought it up with David, who agreed to file a FOIA request.

An hour after I started my review, I was surrounded by papers and my frustration was peaking. The Justice Department had sent us dozens and dozens of pages without confirming a single detail about the program. This was supposed to be a fully operational DOJ program that involved interagency cooperation. Operation Choke Point would impact the policies of financial companies in ways that would trickle down to everyone who used the banking system. There were sweeping legal and ethical ramifications. But the DOJ offered no insight whatsoever into this program. We had received no training guidelines, no operating procedures, no internal memos, no reports on the efficacy of the program—nothing that could indicate whether this program that supposedly pressured banks to shutter the accounts of certain legal businesses actually *worked.*

It's always been clear to me how dangerous it could be for financial institutions to block services to political activists, journalists, content creators, nonprofits, and others. But I had to learn more about the impact of financial exclusion on businesses to really understand its dangers. That's because in the US, businesses often have a lot of privilege. Our society values businesses and offers them a range of legal protections and tax benefits. Businesses have wielded their significant resources effectively to influence our political system, ensuring they continue to benefit from favorable laws.

All of that is true, but it's also not the whole story.

I've come to understand that there are a number of industries that wield an outsized influence on our political and legal system. They are adept at defending themselves while creating barriers to new industries that challenge them. Younger, smaller industries are often more vulnerable to attack, even if they offer alternatives that appeal to consumers. Many of the industries that are most vulnerable to financial censorship are newer fields that challenge older, established industries. Additionally, whenever examining how corporate financial accounts are closed, it's useful to look for evidence of government influence. The impact of government pressure is notable in the case of Operation Choke Point, in which government regulators leaned on financial companies to deny services to certain industries.

Rather than explore all the different ways financial exclusion impacts different industries, I am going to go deep on one field of business that has been especially burdened by financial censorship: cannabis. Cannabis is a young industry that has been fiercely fought by police unions and corporate prisons, the beer and beverage industry, and the pharmaceutical industry—which stands to lose billions of dollars with marijuana legalization.[2]

Though still illegal at the federal level, cannabis is used by millions of people in the United States. The laws against it prop up police surveillance, shatter families and communities, incarcerate tens of thousands of people, and oppress people who don't have the finances to afford lawyers. Most of all, laws against marijuana have been used to persecute Black people and other communities of color. Outdated marijuana laws, like other drug laws, are deeply connected with these larger societal issues.

The Marijuana Policy Project (MPP) is a nonprofit founded in 1995 to try to fix all of that. MPP advocates for marijuana reform, and it focuses on ballot initiatives. While partisan division in Congress has stymied federal marijuana reform, marijuana ballot initiatives are sailing through with voter approval. As of this writing, the overwhelming majority of US states have legalized cannabis for medical purposes, and twenty-four states have approved recreational use. MPP has been driving these changes in legislatures and ballot proposals.

In October 2023, the San Francisco Fire Credit Union refused to process a donation to MPP, claiming that they did not want to support dispensaries. I heard all the details because the individual trying to send the donation was EFF cofounder John Gilmore.

I've known John for years as a soft-spoken, long-bearded hippie who was the only EFF board member I'd routinely bump into in the common rooms of EFF. A computer programmer turned start-up investor turned philanthropist, John has spent more than two decades fighting the drug war by donating to nonprofits working for reform.

We met up in Sacramento in late 2023. I'd moved there temporarily after the COVID-19 pandemic forced EFF to go remote, and John was passing through on his way home from an event in Tahoe. I picked him up from the train station and we drove to a downtown bar, John lugging a plastic shopping bag and a beat-up roller bag with a stuffed animal strapped to the front. With his purple tie-dye T-shirt clashing with his worn plaid button-up, John hardly gave the appearance of being a millionaire philanthropist.

John told me he has been a customer of the SF Fire Credit Union for more than a decade. I'm not surprised he supports credit unions; many people are drawn to credit unions as an alternative to big banks like Chase and Bank of America. Credit unions have a reputation for being more humane, more personal.

John told me he went in person to the credit union in the fall of 2023 to send a wire transfer to MPP as his annual donation. The customer service representative at SF Fire Credit Union didn't have any issues, and John received his confirmation number and headed home. The next day, the credit union contacted him. They were blocking his donation to the Marijuana Policy Project because the organization had the word "marijuana" in its name. The credit union, John was told, had a policy against supporting dispensaries, and their compliance department had blocked the transaction.

John, who sits on the board of directors for the Marijuana Policy Project, was quick to explain that MPP was not a dispensary. A 501(c)(4) nonprofit recognized by the IRS, MPP is one of the top two nonprofit organizations lobbying to reform cannabis laws in the United States. They don't sell or distribute marijuana. Nothing they are doing is illegal.

The credit union did not care about John's explanation. It still refused to process the donation.

Of all the people I interviewed for this book, John was perhaps the most prepared for the possibility of financial censorship, having seen so many organizations in the drug policy space suffering due to the selective and inscrutable enforcement of banking policies. "My experience with banks is that they're not entirely reliable," John told me. "I tend to have a variety of bank accounts."

Thanks to that decentralization, he was able to turn to another financial service and use that to get funds to MPP. SF Fire Credit Union never allowed the donation through and never apologized to John or the Marijuana Policy Project for denying the transaction.

I spoke with Matthew Schweich, MPP's executive director, about how it felt to have a major donation to his organization blocked by a financial institution. "It's very frustrating but unsurprising. I've been here working on cannabis reform since 2015, and have encountered these issues over and over again," he said.

He doesn't let the unending issues with banking services stop him from doing the work; eventually, he said, his organization is always able to find a way through. But that doesn't mean he likes it: "It does offend me as someone who believes in free speech that a bank or financial institution would refuse to transfer money when it's been made absolutely clear that the recipient is a nonprofit."

Schweich pointed out that while some banks may hesitate to provide services to cannabis companies that are legal at the state level but not recognized at the federal level, none of that would apply to MPP, which is a fully legal nonprofit at the federal level. "We are not in violation of federal law. In fact, we go to great lengths to follow all the laws, state and federal level. We operate just like any other nonprofit, and we advocate for certain policy positions. It is clearly unjust that we, as a nonprofit, would have any banking service made unavailable to us," Schweich explained. "I believe it's a form of prejudice by these individuals who make these decisions." He noted that it's extremely easy to verify that the Marijuana Policy Project is a legal nonprofit.

I reached out to the SF Fire Credit Union. Their chief marketing officer, Josephine Chew, wrote back to me, first telling me, "I've checked in with our compliance and call center teams and we are unable to locate any instance of such [a] complaint." I followed up with the details about what happened including the dates and John's info. I expected the credit union wouldn't want to tell me about specific customer accounts, so instead I asked for their overall policies. I asked whether the credit union allowed donations to nonprofits for marijuana reform, what systems it used to flag problematic transactions, and what policies the credit union had about marijuana-related organizations.

A week later, Ms. Chew wrote back with a terse response. She didn't answer any of my questions and said, "While we cannot comment on the specifics of this situation given customer privacy laws, SF Fire Credit Union complies with all federal law including its position on marijuana. Additionally, you may want to consult our industry association—America's Credit Unions—for perspective."

Then she sent me a few links about how their industry association (formerly known as Credit Union National Association or CUNA, now just America's Credit Unions) had lobbied Congress to ensure banks could provide services to cannabis companies. Perhaps she was trying to show that the credit unions were on the right side of this issue. Instead, it just showed how dysfunctional SF Fire Credit Union's own compliance systems are: it had blocked an organization lobbying for reform to marijuana laws even as their own industry association was also lobbying for reform around marijuana laws.

I texted John to tell him about what happened and share the message from Ms. Chew. I laughed at the text he fired back, which was scathing: "These idiots blocked a fully legal donation to one of the political allies of CUNA who is working on the issue they say is a legislative priority for credit unions! They not only shot me and MPP in the foot, but also their own industry's advocacy! Cluelessness squared."

I personally think SF Fire Credit Union's initial decision to block the donation to MPP could be forgiven—every financial institution wrongly flags accounts for additional review from time to time. What I cannot wrap my head around, having looked at it from every direction, is why the credit union didn't reverse their decision after John explained MPP was a registered nonprofit that hadn't breached any laws. It seemed like something was fundamentally broken within the compliance review systems of SF Fire Credit Union. Anyone who did even the most cursory examination of MPP would immediately realize it was a legal nonprofit, not a dispensary.

The story of a nonprofit advocacy group like MPP highlights how difficult it is for anyone with any connection to cannabis to obtain and maintain financial services. Even fully legal organizations like MPP that merely have "marijuana" anywhere in their name face barriers to accessing financial services, and even credit unions are not immune from taking a heavy hand in policing marijuana rules. How much more difficult is it for companies that have a direct connection to cannabis, such as dispensaries that are legally authorized to sell cannabis in states like California, Washington, and Oregon?

In 2014, FinCEN offered guidance about how financial institutions could provide services to marijuana-related businesses. This included guidance on how a bank could perform due diligence on customers, report suspicious activity, and consider its own risk tolerance when offering services to marijuana companies. It also noted that "the decision to open, close, or refuse any particular account or relationship should be made by each financial institution based on a number of factors specific to that institution."[3]

At first blush, this type of guidance seems promising. It does not seem like FinCEN is entirely banning all forms of marijuana banking, after all. It offered guidance for how financial institutions could make banking work. And shouldn't that be enough? I can imagine a free-market argument based on this guidance. FinCEN is offering something that seems like a path forward. So a few enterprising banks should be stepping up to fulfill this demand.

Author and small business owner Gene Marks, writing for *The Guardian*, explained that while independent and community banks may choose to provide services to the cannabis companies, that's not adequate to meet the industry's needs:

> I don't mean to throw shade on these organizations, because many of them are excellent. But they oftentimes don't offer online banking, international access, wire transfer, investment options, financial stability and other capabilities of a larger institution. When it comes to the cannabis industry, federally chartered banks like Wells Fargo, PNC Bank, JPMorgan Chase, TD Bank and Key Bank are not playing ball.[4]

As a result of this banking exclusion, the cannabis industry relies heavily on cash. And with that reliance comes a slew of risks: physical cash, though resistant to censorship and surveillance, can be a target for criminals, can suffer physical damage or loss, and doesn't lend itself to online sales. Nate Lipton, the CEO of a company that sells horticulture equipment, wrote in the *Arizona Republic*, "This cash-only situation has made dispensaries a major target for violent crime."[5] He described how a man was robbed at gunpoint at a dispensary minutes from where Lipton lives in Tucson, Arizona.

A less understood drawback of this cash-heavy environment is that, as soon as we start dealing with revenues equivalent to even a medium-sized business, the money is actually quite bulky. Just moving it around becomes a challenge. US senator Jeff Merkley (D-OR), who is among several members of Congress working to pass legislation to ensure cannabis companies have access to financial services, described to the Senate Banking Committee how he had trailed one cannabis entrepreneur on a trip to pay quarterly taxes:

> Forcing legal businesses to operate in all cash is dangerous for our communities. I saw this with my own eyes when I joined an Oregon businessman, Tyson Haworth, on a trip to our State capital in Salem to pay

> his tax bill. He had his quarterly payment of $70,000 in a backpack. He turned it over on a table, and it just kind of spread out across the whole table, and some of it fell onto the floor, and it was, like, wow, that is a lot of money to be carrying around in a backpack.[6]

That image has stuck with me: a man walking into a government building with $70,000 in cash stuffed into a backpack, dumping it all on a table until some of it cascaded down onto the floor. It's just one of the many realities of an industry that's still facing major barriers to the financial system.

Cannabis exists in a strange gray zone of the law—businesses are legal in many states, paying taxes and registering for business licenses. While marijuana has not been legalized at the federal level, it's not like the DEA is busting down the door of all these state-recognized marijuana dispensaries. FinCEN has offered some guidance to banks on offering services to cannabis companies, but that hasn't been compelling to nationally chartered banks. At the same time, financial institutions do not go out on a limb to help any individual account. Losing a few does not hurt their bottom line, whereas any extra regulatory scrutiny can be very expensive.

Importantly, banks have lots of good reasons to err on the side of caution. After the 2008 financial crisis, banks were lambasted in the press, financial executives were dragged in front of congressional committees to testify, and the Dodd-Frank Act attempted to crack down on predatory lending practices. And then in 2013, the Justice Department launched Operation Choke Point and overzealous FDIC examiners started pressuring financial institutions to shutter accounts for legal businesses. So why would a bank ever embrace risk?

Instead of "risk tolerant," a better framing of the approach we need from banks on this issue is "inclusive and neutral." Just as any utility service or public resource, inclusive and neutral banking services are about meeting the needs of everyday people to exist in society. Inclusive and neutral banking can ensure that basic banking and payment services are available as a right for anyone who wants and needs them, including tax-paying businesses.

If we had an inclusive and neutral banking system, then a company that could get a business license and pay taxes would also be able to get a checking account to use for purchasing a business license and paying those taxes.

THE CHALLENGES OF INCONSISTENT BANKING

Justin Bunton is used to being the adult in the room. A human resources (HR) professional, Bunton helps companies stay compliant with employment law, set up payroll, and deal with any of the countless HR issues that might crop up at a start-up. He's spent most of his career working in the cannabis industry, and he told me that human resource compliance was an alien concept to many of these cannabis start-ups.

"You have to keep in mind that in the cannabis space, especially in the earlier days, you're dealing with a lot of people who have never had a company before. They've never run anything," he explained. With a shaved head and bottlecap glasses, Bunton comes across as a little hipper than your average HR director. "So it's like, who cares about policies? Who cares about procedures, time off? It's like, meal breaks? What's a meal break?"

For these cannabis start-ups, Bunton kindly but very firmly ushered them into legal compliance so that time off, meal breaks, and employment policies were put in place. And even if working in the cannabis industry has caused him more than a few headaches when it comes to enforcing compliance, he honestly loves it. He told me the community of people drawn to work in the space tends to be more adventurous and more accepting, more open to differences in life. He appreciates the attitude, even if too often he has to be the HR wet blanket to the rollicking anarchy of the early cannabis start-up.

Having spent more than a decade working in HR, Bunton described how disruptions to payroll and banking services create huge headaches for the companies—and for him personally, as he's trying to make sure all the employees get their paychecks on time and for the correct amount. One of the biggest struggles is finding a payroll company to work with; he offered story after story of how different payroll companies dropped his cannabis start-ups, often with only a month or two of notice. All of them knew exactly what the companies did before they started working with Bunton, making it all the more frustrating to get suddenly dropped.

One of his cannabis start-ups had their payroll company disappear entirely—taking all of the money that had been set aside over the year to cover payroll taxes with it. That happened just before Bunton joined the company, and he had to help the company deal with the consequences.

But the biggest hassle is when bank accounts are suddenly shuttered. Bunton explained that for cannabis companies, there are typically multiple business entities: one business that has a name that is listed on the state-issued cannabis license, and a different business name listed with the bank so they can have a bank account. But if someone at the bank identifies the company as part of the cannabis industry, then the company could see its bank account shuttered, sometimes with as little as twenty-four hours' notice.

For Bunton, this resulted in a huge administrative scramble. When payroll was scheduled to come out of a bank account and then the account was suddenly shut off, he needed to make sure payroll happened some way or another. He told me it was stressful: "My people aren't getting paid. There are two main rules that I have, two main rules: Pay your people right and pay your people on time. They are not here because they love you. They're here to make money. Everything else from there, from the HR standpoint, doesn't matter if they're not being paid right and they're not being paid on time." He said that it was hard to find banks that would work with his companies at all. "You're not going to go to a Bank of America; you're not going to go to a Chase. You're not going to go to a big company like that. They're not going to take your money. It's going to be a smaller company."

He said that for many cannabis companies, it's standard to have multiple bank accounts so that if one account gets shuttered, you can quickly switch payroll to the other bank. But every time it happens, it's a scramble. Cash is a way to safeguard against the vagaries of banking policies. As Bunton explained: "All the companies I've worked with have always had a large cash fund."

I asked if he ever had to pay the employees with cash. "Not in a very long time," he said, proudly.

Bunton's story is representative of the experience of so many professionals in the cannabis industry. These companies struggle to access financial services and often find themselves shut off with little notice. The guidance from FinCEN is not enough to ease the financial path for these companies. And often, the people who bear the brunt of these issues are lower-level employees who face payroll disruptions.

THE MATCH LIST

Companies that lose a payment service may find themselves on a secret list that makes it extremely difficult to find another payment processor. That's because financial companies often share information about clients, particularly those clients with merchant accounts.

Most of us are already familiar with one way financial companies share information: credit scores. In the United States, people who interact with the financial system are given a three-digit score between 300 and 850. Paying credit cards on time, never being the victim of identity theft, and keeping credit accounts open for many years can all contribute to you having a higher score. High scores can signal to financial institutions that you are worthy of a loan in the future. This means you might get a high limit on your credit card or qualify for a mortgage to buy a house. Low scores signal the opposite. If you have a low credit score, you might have a hard time accessing a business line of credit, a mortgage, or a credit card.

One of the factors that contributes to your credit score is whether you have closed certain financial accounts. So if you lose your credit card accounts for allegedly violating the terms of service of the credit card companies, that will impact your credit score and make it harder to get an account in the future.

But there are other, lesser-known data sharing practices beyond the credit score. Mastercard maintains a proprietary database of terminated merchant accounts called the Member Alert to Control High-Risk Merchants (MATCH).[7] Although Mastercard operates the database, entries are made by banks under Mastercard's rules, not by government mandate or judicial order. A merchant (such as a website, nonprofit, or an online content creator) who has had her merchant account suspended can be entered into this database if the suspension fits one of the criteria. Mastercard has fourteen "reason codes" for a merchant being added to the MATCH list.[8] Some of these make a lot of sense, such as "excessive fraud," "excessive chargebacks," or "illegal transactions."

But then there's reason code 10: Violation of Standards. Mastercard notes that this refers to a merchant in violation of "one or more Standards that describe procedures to be employed by the Merchant in Transactions in which Cards are used, including, by way of example and not Cardholders, minimum/maximum Transaction amount restrictions, and prohibited Transactions set forth in Chapter 5 of the Mastercard Rules manual."[9] This sentence is difficult for me to follow, almost as if there's some sort of typo. Nonetheless, I tracked down chapter 5 of "Mastercard Rules" and found it was twenty pages of prohibitions.

Unsurprisingly, this chapter of Mastercard's rules includes a prohibition against "illegal or brand-damaging" transactions including "the sale of a product or service, including an image, which is patently offensive and lacks serious artistic value" or "*any other material that the Corporation deems unacceptable to sell in connection with a Mark*" (emphasis added).[10]

Other credit card networks have their own similar lists or rely on the MATCH list to flag high-risk merchant accounts.[11]

Why does this matter? Because a merchant who loses her payment services due to speech that violates a credit card company's sweeping, arbitrary, and censorious brand protection rules might find herself placed in the MATCH database—and repeatedly rejected from other payment services as a result.

As Chargeback Gurus, a company that helps merchants limit chargebacks, explains:

> What Are the Consequences of Being on the MATCH List?
>
> If an acquiring bank terminates your merchant account, it's a big red flag for other financial institutions. Essentially, you will be labeled a high-risk merchant, and many institutions will not do business with you (or will only do so with exorbitant fees).
>
> While losing the ability to open new merchant accounts can pose a problem, a far greater concern is the inability to process credit card payments. Merchants on the MATCH list will have difficulty obtaining payment processing services, and in some cases, they may even be blacklisted by the credit card networks themselves. *As you might imagine, being unable to process card payments can often be a death knell for a business* [emphasis added].[12]

Getting placed in the MATCH database does not trigger any kind of notification. Indeed, many people learn their company is in the MATCH database only after losing a payment service and then being rejected, sometimes repeatedly, from other merchant accounts. At that point, they may start searching the internet to find out what is happening and realize they have been put on the MATCH list. Consumers and merchants cannot query the MATCH list to see who is on it, or if they themselves are on the list. Only financial institutions have the ability to search the list.

And once you're there, you're likely stuck. Most of the time, merchants must wait five years for their names to be removed from the list. That's five years of difficulty finding payment services or possibly being unable to process credit card transactions at all. Notably, five years is itself entirely arbitrary. Mastercard created that policy, so it can also change the rules.

Merchants struggling to get off the MATCH list might seek the services of a law firm that specializes in payment services to attempt to argue that they were placed on the list incorrectly. When I spoke to a lawyer who works to get merchant clients off the MATCH list, they acknowledged that there are few options for their clients. Many don't have the resources to bring a lawsuit, and there's no law preventing Mastercard and other payment processors, credit card companies, and acquiring banks from using these lists.

Who is actually responsible for the MATCH list is up for debate. Mastercard maintains the list and shares it with other financial institutions but says it "does not verify or confirm the accuracy of any of the information that is submitted by acquirers to MATCH."[13]

Unsurprisingly, Mastercard does not consider MATCH to be problematic. When I shared this section with the company over email, their spokesperson wrote back to say, "It's a risk management tool that acquirers use to inform their decision making during their due diligence efforts. To be clear, if a merchant is in MATCH, the acquirer can still conduct business with them."

But having read the stories of many merchants who found themselves losing payment services and struggling to get off the MATCH list, I think it's deeply problematic. Regardless of the marketing of MATCH as a due diligence tool, the end result is that inclusion on the MATCH list often means losing payment processing services and being denied future payment services. The data in this proprietary database is routinely used to deny financial services to solo entrepreneurs, small businesses, and start-ups. There's no transparency and little recourse for someone who finds themselves on the list.

A CANNABIS JOURNALIST CENSORED BY STRIPE

Jackie Bryant has a gold nose ring and cursed fluidly when I spoke to her. The managing editor of *San Diego Magazine*, Bryant first built her career and her reputation as a subculture icon while serving as the marijuana reporter for San Diego's weekly newspaper *CityBeat*. When Arizona-based Times Media Group bought and slowly dismantled *CityBeat*, Bryant moved her popular column, Cannabitch, to Substack, remarking that Times Media Group struck her as "visionless losers who couldn't put out a good paper to save their lives."[14]

On Substack, Bryant could publish her articles for free online, and readers who wanted to could send her financial support via Stripe, Substack's sole payment processor. This style of direct online publication is popular with many freelance journalists as newspapers face cuts and the industry struggles to figure out new ways of making money.

Prior to meeting Bryant, I didn't understand just how much was being written about cannabis. But cannabis is a multibillion-dollar industry with an enthusiastic fan base, so there are dedicated journalists who cover industry happenings, new products, and community issues the same way there are journalists covering cars or video games. Plus, the decades-long political fight for federal legalization means there's never a lack of things to write about. Bryant is among the more prominent of these cannabis reporters.

Bryant's acerbic analysis of the cannabis industry, playful voice, and meticulous research make her articles a delight to read even if you don't normally follow cannabis publications. Her articles span everything from cheeky holiday gift guides to explorations on evolving cannabis medical research. Cannabitch has proven to be a successful solo enterprise since moving to Substack, earning Bryant thousands a year and winning awards like the San Diego Society of Professional Journalists' Best Blog award.

In fall 2023, Bryant learned that her Stripe account had been flagged due to her journalism about marijuana. "I think they hit me first because of the name of the newsletter," she told me, then she pointed out a variety of other newsletters on Substack focused on cannabis. Bryant appealed the decision, then began a monthslong battle with Stripe to save her account. She sent me her email correspondence with Stripe, in which Stripe's coldly bureaucratic responses are met with Bryant's impassioned and expletive-laced replies.

In one message, Bryant was told, "Unfortunately, following an additional review of your account we're still unable to support your business as it falls under one of our restricted businesses categories."

Bryant wrote back immediately: "I wasn't aware journalism is a restricted category."

Stripe's terms prohibit cannabis products, dispensaries, and "related businesses," as well as "courses and information on cultivating marijuana."[15] But it seems a ludicrous over-enforcement to shutter the account of a journalist for merely writing articles about cannabis.

Substack caught wind of the issue and tried to intervene to help Bryant. The newsletter company wasn't able to get her account reinstated but did help gather information on why her account was on the chopping block, and Bryant was able to share copies of this communication with me. Apparently, even though Bryant did not sell cannabis or cannabis paraphernalia, Stripe was concerned because Bryant was linking to websites that did sell those things. In a response to Substack, a representative of Stripe said:

> The users [*sic*] journal links to places to purchase unsupportable items which is why they fall into the Sub Cat 5. For the user to be supportable, they would no longer be able to link to any sites that sell cannabis or cannabis supplies. There is an example on almost every page the user has published. [...] The user would need to audit their own blog and remove links and we would then re-review their page.

Bryant responded swiftly, writing, "I generally link to things in the context of journalism. There's a zillion newsletters that use stripe [*sic*], that aren't focused on cannabis, that link to cannabis related things in the course of whatever storytelling." In the end, Bryant wasn't willing to remove links from her articles. As she told a representative of Substack, "I decided not to. It's censorship, and I'm not selling anything. If that's the terms, then I guess I reject on principle and will just have to have an unpaid newsletter! It sucks but it's a line too far for me. [...] It's too compromising for my ethics and I need to hold the line."

Bryant told me that Stripe benefited from its relationship with Cannabitch: "Stripe made money off of me this whole fucking time, too. They take 10 percent of my sales, which is not an insignificant amount. They've been taking money for four years from me."

After months of circular debates with Stripe, Bryant gave up. She used social media to tell the world what had happened to her. "The long arm of cannabis prohibition has finally come for me," she wrote on LinkedIn. "Stripe, which is a horrible company to deal with, probably the worst customer service I've ever encountered, is closing my account associated with my Substack newsletter, Cannabitch, because they think I'm violating their terms of sale (I'm not.)."[16]

Her posts got a ton of attention, including from Clare Sausen, a journalist for the prominent cannabis magazine *High Times*, who reached out to Stripe for comment before publishing a detailed article about Bryant's account closure.[17]

That media attention was likely the tipping point for Stripe, which suddenly capitulated and reinstated Bryant's account. On the same day that Sausen published her article, Bryant received a notification that her Stripe account was up and running again: "Thank you for providing additional information about your business, Jacqueline Bryant. We have successfully completed our review, and you are welcome to continue processing payments with Stripe."

This pattern is similar to other cases of financial censorship I have seen: publicity precedes a financial company's decision to change its position and reinstate an account that had been blocked due to an alleged terms of service violation. It's a stark reminder that companies like Stripe have an incredible amount of leeway in how they interpret and enforce their terms of service. When it suits them to do so, they shutter accounts. But with enough heat from outside attention, they can often be pressured to change their position—highlighting that it is corporate whim, not legal requirements, behind many financial censorship decisions.

I asked Bryant about the financial exclusion facing any person or organization connected to cannabis, and she pointed to the deep-seated stigma facing the cannabis world: "I think it's less coordinated and more just the result of decades of prohibition and stigma, to be perfectly honest. And misunderstanding."

Stripe's original request that Bryant remove the hyperlinks in her newsletter continues to bother me. It is a level of review so specific that it amounts to Stripe actively suggesting edits to her written work. It's not only that Stripe shouldn't be weighing in on which links can be included in journalistic articles about cannabis (which, to be clear, is really inappropriate). It's also offensive that Stripe is trying to strip away hyperlinks at all.

In our era of online journalism, hyperlinks are accountability. They serve as a tool to empower readers to assess the source material of a writer and make their own conclusions. Links serve as citations for blog posts and other online articles. Removing those links denies readers a simple way to check the facts themselves or learn more about a topic. Especially in an era where so many have lost confidence in online journalism, we need to encourage writers to include more links, not fewer.

Hyperlinks are also a signal to the wider internet. Larry Page and Sergey Brin founded Google on their PageRank algorithm, which used the number of links to a page to determine how important it was.[18] That signal still plays its part in the algorithms that decide what hits the top of your search results or gets preferentially mentioned by an AI. Demanding the removal of links not only hides context from the readers of journalists affected by Stripe's policies; it hides them from everyone else.

This suggestion is also offensive to those of us who live much of our lives online and who intuitively understand hyperlinks as the glue that holds the internet together. That interconnectivity is core to the creative, chaotic, weird nature of the internet itself. Who among us hasn't found ourselves clicking down an internet rabbit hole and arriving on some strange, unexpected new digital territory that might delight or horrify or entertain us, or maybe a bit of all three? It's not for payment processors to start carving censorship culverts around legal websites.

Bryant refused to remove the hyperlinks from her newsletter, and eventually—after pressure from Substack and a widely read news article—Stripe relented and backed down. But this situation raises many more questions. How many other times has Stripe demanded a writer remove hyperlinks from her articles or risk losing her Stripe account?

And how many writers comply without a fight because they feel they have no other choice?

Evidence of censorship is always erasing itself. The examples I'm able to identify and verify will only ever be the tip of the iceberg, and the full scope of the problem is probably immeasurable. That's because website owners and online writers are quick to change their words, censor images, remove articles, or even take down whole websites if that's what it takes to maintain a relationship with a financial company. Bryant and others like her represent just a minuscule percentage of those impacted: those who refused to comply with the censorship demand *and* were willing to speak out publicly against it *and* had enough of an online presence that the story was able to attract public attention.

In the end, Stripe recognized that Bryant wasn't breaking any laws and reinstated her account. I want to acknowledge that Stripe eventually arrived at the right decision in this case, even if it took months of debate and a lot of public and private pressure for the company to get there. But doing the right thing once does not absolve the company of having vague policies and no public accountability for how those policies are enforced.

OPERATION CHOKE POINT

After Keating unveiled the existence of Operation Choke Point in the *Wall Street Journal*, there was a storm of controversy. Congress held emotional hearings and commissioned lengthy reports, which resulted in news coverage and op-eds and even some academic analysis. The program has been seized on as an example of un-American regulatory overreach by some Republican lawmakers. And some, though far from all, Democratic lawmakers have responded dismissively, arguing that financial regulators need to do their jobs.[19]

Sadly, this politicization further muddies water that was already muddy due to the secrecy of this program. Embedded in this debate around Operation Choke Point are important questions about the role of regulators in guiding the banking system away from certain merchants and the role of banks in punishing certain industries. Those questions are difficult to answer when any discussion of the program is warped by political jockeying.

Unhelpful politicization has no doubt influenced what we know about this program and its aftermath. It has also made the topic more difficult to research. Nonetheless, an overview of the program follows.

In the summer of 2011 the FDIC published a list of "high-risk" industries in its quarterly journal about banking supervision, *Supervisory Insights*.[20] It was a list of thirty industries, including drug paraphernalia, pornography, fireworks sales, home-based charities, surveillance equipment, and travel clubs. Two industries became the topic of much of the debate about Operation Choke Point going forward: firearm sales and payday loans. Both of these are controversial and highly politicized industries, and their inclusions fueled the politicization of the debate about Operation Choke Point.

In the fall of 2011, the FDIC worked to incorporate a summary of high-risk merchants in their official guidance documents. In the draft guidance, the FDIC noted that "while some of these activities might be legitimate, financial institutions should be aware of the increased risks associated with payment to such merchants."[21]

Then the Department of Justice got involved. Under the Financial Institutions Reform, Recovery, and Enforcement Act (FIRREA), the DOJ can issue subpoenas to banking institutions.[22] It sent out a slew of subpoenas to banks and payment processors and attached FDIC guidance about payment processor relationships. Within that guidance was a footnote that named a variety of merchants that "pose elevated risk." While formatted differently, this note mirrored many of the high-risk merchant categories outlined in the prior FDIC guidance. A whistleblower provided a copy of one of these subpoenas to a member of Congress, and the assistant attorney general confirmed during a congressional hearing that the DOJ was stapling copies of this guidance with the high-risk merchant lists to their subpoenas.[23] As the House Committee report summarized, "The inclusion of the FDIC guidance in DOJ's subpoenas effectively 'weaponized' the high-risk merchants list. The implication was clear: banks were compelled to remove those clients from their portfolios, or risk a federal investigation by the Department of Justice."[24]

Some have said that the civil liberties concerns about Operation Choke Point are overblown. Professor Dru Stevenson of South Texas College of Law in Houston wrote a detailed examination of the program in his article "Operation Choke Point: Myths and Reality." A defender of the program, Stevenson characterized Operation Choke Point as "a benign effort in the wake of the global financial crisis to tighten enforcement on consumer fraud and exploitative payday lenders."[25]

But many others raised deep concerns. Professor Derek Bambauer of Levin College of Law examined the role of government agencies pressuring financial institutions under Operation Choke Point and argued it was an example of jawboning. He wrote:

> With Choke Point, the Department of Justice threatened banks with liability merely for doing business with high-risk clients, apparently including gun firms—a far more tenuous connection to wrongdoing, if in fact there was any wrongdoing at all. Put simply, the combination of the FDIC's extension of its supervisory role into designating certain types of business as untouchable, and the extension of the Department of Justice's use of investigatory powers under FIRREA to attack not fraud, but relationships with the high-risk clients designated by the FDIC, put the government far afield from its statutory authority. Any one of these leaps might be permissible, but all of them risk asking us to believe six impossible things before breakfast, and may well constitute jawboning.[26]

Astute readers may notice the similarities between Operation Choke Point and the *NRA v. Vullo* and *Backpage v. Dart* cases. All of them show how the government engages in censorship by proxy, and probably all would count as jawboning (and, in some instances, illegal coercion). Indeed, even the pressure on financial companies to shutter WikiLeaks may well be understood as an example of jawboning in retrospect.

Still others suggested that it was not Operation Choke Point itself but the political controversy and publicity surrounding the program that prompted banks to unnecessarily shutter accounts. As Georgetown law professor Adam Levitin wrote:

> The conflation of DOJ action with prudential regulatory guidance may be creating the very problem *Choke Point*'s critics fear.
>
> Bank compliance officers may be hearing what *Choke Point* critics are saying and believing it and acting on it. If compliance officers believe that the DOJ will come after any bank that serves the high-risk industries identified by the FDIC or FinCEN, not just those that knowingly

facilitate or willfully ignore fraud, they will respond accordingly. *The safe thing to do in the compliance world is to follow the herd and avoid risks. The attack on Operation Choke Point may well have spooked banks' compliance officers, who aren't going to parse through the technical distinctions involved* (emphasis added).[27]

In 2017, the Justice Department announced it would be ending the controversial program.[28] In a letter to Senator Bob Goodlatte, Assistant Attorney General Stephen Boyd called Operation Choke Point "a misguided initiative conducted during the previous administration" and promised that "all of the Department's bank investigations conducted as part of Operation Chokepoint are now over, the initiative is no longer in effect, and it will not be undertaken again."[29]

But while the program may be over, the scars of the program live on in the consciousness of bankers across the United States. Frank Keating spoke out again in 2018 after more documents came to light about how the program worked. He warned that Operation Choke Point casts a long shadow, and that even with the program's end there was a regulatory stigma around certain legal industries: "Banks are not convinced they can again serve these businesses without fear of threats or regulatory pressure. Ending the program doesn't return the banking relationships that were terminated, and the stigma associated with Operation Choke Point will follow these businesses for years to come."[30]

BEYOND CANNABIS

Some legislators are trying to change the situation facing marijuana companies. Congress is debating legislation aimed at prompting major banks to provide financial services to the emerging cannabis industry, and there are efforts to loosen federal prohibitions on cannabis. But it is important to remember that legalization alone does not solve this problem; many accounts of entirely legal organizations, like the nonprofit Marijuana Policy Project and journalist Jackie Bryant, are getting caught up in misguided enforcement efforts.

I am particularly struck by how cannabis is a young industry challenging the market position of other powerful industries. It lacks the resources and lobbying power of more established business interests. Seen through this lens, cannabis can serve as a case study to help us understand other instances of financial censorship among start-up industries. For example, there are many stories of the financial exclusion facing cryptocurrency companies, which challenge the power of the large financial incumbents. Similarly, I've heard complaints of financial exclusion from online pharmaceutical companies that provide direct-to-consumer services, an industry that challenges established (and often inadequate) medical corporations.

Some activists embrace financial exclusion as a tactic they would like to inflict on corporations that seem otherwise impervious to public shaming. But denying any legal organization access to basic financial services, like a bank account, payment services, or credit cards, is a dangerous tactic; it's a blunt instrument just as likely to take down a group you agree with as one you find heinous. I also doubt its efficacy as a tool against the most powerful industries. Multinational corporations that savage our environment, like the oil and gas companies, are not having any difficulty getting access to bank accounts, regardless of what some activists might hope.

But financial censorship can be a technique used to create friction and difficulty for upstart industries that have gained the ire of law enforcement and industry titans. Just as we track the impact of financial censorship on community groups and online speakers, we need to resist efforts to debank emerging industries that may benefit consumers and challenge existing corporate power.

SIX

CASH AS CENSORSHIP RESISTANCE

A mile outside the entrance to Denali National Park, there's a small tourist strip in a town called Denali Park. There you'll find a few hotels, a coffee shop that will make you a latte, an ice cream store, some restaurants, and cute stores for buying souvenirs. There's an outfitter selling good quality backpacking gear, and I found myself there in 2023 when it became clear that the rain jacket I'd carried for 2,600 miles of the Pacific Crest Trail wasn't resilient enough to handle the September rains of Alaska.

I loved this little town, especially the moose I'd see drinking from the river when I headed out on my morning run and how, when I stood at the edge of town, the road seemed to just disappear into the Alaskan wilderness.

But I didn't love the tiny town's currency practices. As I wandered from ice cream shop to coffee shop to restaurant along that strip, I was met by small signs at nearly every register: "No cash accepted. Credit or debit card only." Those little signs were all too familiar. I'd seen them popping up more and more frequently at retail stores near my home in San Francisco.

I saw a spike of retail stores rejecting cash during the long tail of the COVID-19 pandemic. Each transfer of a bill from a customer to an employee was seen as another chance to spread the virus. So why not just require customers to swipe a credit card or tap their phones to pay instead? It might even help save lives, the reasoning went.

Individual businesses may have many legitimate reasons for choosing to reject cash. Maybe the bank is too far away, maybe they need to streamline checkout processes, or maybe there were too many errors introduced by counting cash. Or, as many businesses in San Francisco argued, maybe they believed refusing cash would make them less of a target for criminals.

But beyond the choice of any one individual business, there are larger societal issues surrounding the shift toward cashlessness. This shift is not just happening at a few retail stores; cashless merchants are popping up everywhere from big-city tech centers to far-flung small towns. This move away from cash is gift wrapped in efficiency, but what about the serious costs of this shift? And I don't mean the substantial credit card transaction fees we're forking over, but the costs to our society.

Because among its many other attributes, cash is a powerful tool for circumventing financial censorship.

Cash is private in a way the vast majority of digital payments are not. This is very different from, say, credit card transactions, which are broadcast to multiple banking institutions and can be accessed by government agents with the bare minimum process. Plus, each purchase with a credit card becomes part of an indelible digital record associated with you for years to come. For those that are seeking a more private, less controlled way of interacting with the financial system, there's cash.

I've personally seen the impact of cash as a tool for change in the world. My first internship at the age of seventeen was with an advocacy group in northern Virginia called the Virginia Partisans. It was an organization that worked to promote the concerns of the LGBTQ community to Democratic elected officials and candidates in Virginia. The group would fundraise for and endorse Democratic candidates who stood up for lesbian and gay rights, and it brought queer concerns to Democratic Party platforms and policies. My two supervisors, both volunteers, were unfailingly generous in taking time to explain to me how our political system worked. Through their mentorship, I also began to grasp the importance of cash as a vehicle for advocacy.

In Virginia at the time, sexual orientation was not a protected class. This meant, for example, that teachers at my public high school could lose their jobs if their sexual orientation were revealed. One of my supervisors explained to me that we always used discreet envelopes in our mailings to help protect people's confidentiality from nosy neighbors, and that many people who sent back donations to our organization mailed in cash. This cash helped them support a cause they believed in and was key to their community's survival. This cash also protected the donors; it ensured that their contributions wouldn't be captured in the database of a bank or credit card company.

Cash can be especially important for community groups advocating for change who have reason to fear their political work might one day attract dangerous scrutiny. To this day, LGBTQ advocates have plenty of reason to care about privacy and be concerned about records of their transactions being kept in perpetuity. Advocates working on countless other social and environmental issues might have a similar need for privacy, including folks working on immigration, religious freedom, racial justice, policing, women's rights, drug legalization, and countless other topics. As we've seen in recent years, even social movements that seem to be making strides in achieving societal acceptance can face a backlash if there's a shift in political power.

Cash also serves as a vital lifeline for people who struggle to open, maintain, or access traditional banking services. This can include unhoused people who can't provide a physical address to a bank, anyone without appropriate and current government-issued identification, people whose poor credit rating and/or poverty mean they are often getting thrown out of banking services, people whose language skills or technical skills aren't up to the complexity of opening a bank account, and many people who, due to life circumstances, just cannot get to a physical bank or open an online account.

There are massive racial and income disparities in who has access to banking services. The FDIC defines "unbanked" as a situation in which neither you nor your spouse has a checking, savings, or money market account. In a survey examining banking trends in 2022, the FDIC reported that 6 percent of adults in the United States were unbanked. The same report showed that 13 percent of Black adults and 10 percent of Hispanic adults were unbanked, compared to 3 percent of white adults. And in families that had a household income below $25,000 a year, 17 percent were unbanked.[1] Cash serves as a lifeline for these communities.

For so many reasons, cash means freedom and privacy to many people. And today, it helps bridge important gaps that financial companies aren't addressing.

Anyone can hold cash or spend it or give it away directly without asking someone else for permission. There are no terms of service to agree to and no corporations to approve using it. That's exactly what makes it such a powerful tool for circumventing financial censorship.

I remember the first fundraiser I held for WikiLeaks after the banking blockade was put in place against the organization. I had just moved to San Francisco and hadn't met a lot of people yet. Eight people came to my event, which was a potluck dinner in my studio apartment. I collected permissionless, anonymous, untraceable cash from all of the attendees and then sent a donation through the mail to the Wau Holland Foundation, which was the fiscal sponsor of WikiLeaks.

In that moment, I marveled at the simplicity and power of cash. Even when making online donations was impossible, I could still host a fundraiser and collect cash. Given how controversial WikiLeaks was at the time, it seemed important that there was no record of who gave money. There was no public event or invitation for that fundraiser, and I didn't keep any record of attendees. Even in the face of a blockade from the biggest financial companies in the world, cash was a way I could support a nonprofit journalism site publishing documents that I saw were changing the world.

Jerry Brito, the executive director of the cryptocurrency research and advocacy nonprofit Coin Center, argued for the liberating value of cash in his 2019 white paper "The Case for Electronic Cash": "Cash is an open access system in which anyone—banked or unbanked—can participate without having to seek the permission of financial gatekeepers. Because cash is permissionless, it is censorship resistant. You can use cash to contribute to an unpopular cause or to purchase goods or services that are legal but socially or culturally taboo."[2]

My little fundraiser illustrates why cash is both a valuable stopgap for routing around financial censorship and far from the full solution we need to this problem. My fundraiser raised under $1,000 for WikiLeaks. That was a drop in the bucket compared to the enormous amount of money the organization had lost due to the financial blockade. Even though others around the world were probably hosting their own small fundraisers, those would never equate to the loss of online donations.

The physicality of cash makes its usefulness inevitably limited. Cash will never be a substitute for online payments that can be used to seamlessly send money to worthy nonprofits, subscribe to newspapers, buy books, support creators, and send money to people on the other side of the country or the world. The ease and speed of online transactions have changed our expectations about how money moves, and moving back into a cash-first world would be a burden for many people. Even so, we should remember that many people are benefiting tremendously from the availability of cash right now.

IN DEFENSE OF CASH

Beyond individual businesses choosing to eschew cash, there are also societal pushes to literally remove cash from the economy. I find these particularly concerning.

Kenneth Rogoff, celebrated Harvard economics professor and former chief economist of the International Monetary Fund, has been at the forefront of championing a world with nearly no cash. In his book *The Curse of Cash*, Rogoff argues that cash is a tool for criminality. His book lays out a four-part plan for significantly reducing cash from the US economy, which I'm copying here verbatim from his book:

1. PHASING OUT PAPER CURRENCY: All paper currency is gradually phased out, beginning with all notes of $50 and above (or foreign equivalent), then next the $20 bill, leaving only $1, $5, and (perhaps) $10 bills. These small bills could be left in circulation for an indefinite period. In the final phase, small bills would be replaced by equivalent-denomination coins of substantial weight.
2. UNIVERSAL FINANCIAL INCLUSION: The government provides all individuals the option of access to free basic-function debit cards/smartphone accounts, either through banks or through a government option. This can be substantially implemented by making government transfer payments into the debit account after it is created.
3. PRIVACY: Regulatory and legal framework aims to discourage other means of making large-scale payments that can be completely hidden from the government.
4. REAL-TIME CLEARING: This is a technical point, but an important one. Government helps facilitate development of the "rails" of the payment infrastructure to achieve (near) real-time clearing for most transactions.[3]

He notes that phasing out cash might take a long time, but the government could speed things along by setting "a date after which large notes expire" so as to prompt people holding currency to deposit it into digital accounts.[4]

I was at first mildly heartened by the inclusion of privacy in that four-part plan, but that slight optimism was immediately dashed. Rogoff acknowledges but is largely dismissive of privacy concerns, noting that "late twentieth century notions of privacy already seem quaint" and pointing out the many incursions on data privacy by both the government and corporations. He argues that it would be unreasonable for the government to design a system that prevented it from accessing private banking data (he says, "A government is not going to create an encryption system itself without making sure it has the key. And if it has a key, it will eventually be used as the government sees fit"—on this point, Rogoff and I are in complete agreement). Instead, Rogoff says, "One can imagine a government creating a system where transactions are anonymous for private citizens, and one that contains significant restrictions on government access as well."[5]

Notably, we don't have significant restrictions on government access to financial data currently, so this would be something new.

Rogoff is not the only person promoting the idea of moving away from cash. While this book is squarely focused on the United States and its policies, those policies will be influenced by other countries. And some of those countries have already experimented with reducing cash in society. For example, India attempted to eliminate the 500- and 1,000-rupee notes—only to create chaos and hardship for its economy.[6] As journalist Julie McCarthy wrote for NPR, "Removing it from circulation devastated millions of workers paid in cash."[7] The European Central Bank decided to phase out the 500-euro note as a crackdown on illegal activity.[8]

But the quintessential example is Sweden, which intentionally embraced moving away from cash and prioritized digital payments. Their policy resulted in a major dip in the use of cash for purchases over several years. Rogoff points to Sweden as a favorable example in his book, though Sweden has since walked back its position. In 2024, Sweden's central bank called for measures to protect cash. It urged new legislation to ensure merchants would accept cash for purchases of essential goods and services like food, medicine, and fuel.[9]

It would be very dangerous to ignore these efforts to reduce cash in society. This anti-cash movement would further empower financial intermediaries that already have vast control over our financial lives. A move away from cash is a move toward deepening contractual relationships with financial companies that we have no particular reason to trust and several good reasons to distrust. It's a move away from a censorship-resistant, untraceable, permissionless system toward a censored, traceable, centralized system. It's stepping toward a system with an uncountable number of small fees we will accrue over a lifetime and an uncountable number of incursions into our freedom and privacy.

"That guy is the epitome of financial privilege right there," Human Rights Foundation's Alex Gladstein told me when I described Rogoff's proposal. "He's cheerleading us into an Orwellian police state." Gladstein is among many who are critical of Rogoff's proposal.

Economist Pierre LeMieux reviewed Rogoff's proposal and ripped it apart for naively trusting the benevolence of the state, making unsubstantiated assumptions about the consequences of using negative interest rates, dismissing the many legitimate uses of cash, and failing to acknowledge the ways the underground economy serves as a check for government abuses. He warned, "A world where government does not supply cash and prevents anybody else from doing so—which is close to what Rogoff recommends—would be as dangerous as a world where government supplies cash and forces everybody to use it."[10]

There are also advocates stepping in to try to safeguard cash as a payment method. Senior policy analyst Jay Stanley of the ACLU urged people to speak out about cashless businesses, including contacting their elected officials about the issue. As he wrote in 2019: "The bottom line is that the technocratic 'dream' of a cashless society is a vision in which we discard what is left of the anonymity that has characterized urban life since the dawn of modernity, and our freedom from the power of centralized companies like banks. Doing without cash may be convenient at times, but if we lose cash as an option we're going to regret it later."[11]

There are also some promising legislative measures. In the city of San Francisco, Supervisor Vallie Brown introduced legislation that would require most brick-and-mortar stores in the city to accept cash as a means of payment. She said, "A large population of people just didn't have credit cards and they didn't have bank cards. When I started to talk to people about why, they were like, 'We can't afford bank fees. We live paycheck to paycheck and you have to have a certain amount in your bank account. That last $50, we're going to need it for food.'"[12] The San Francisco Board of Supervisors unanimously passed the legislation in 2019.

San Francisco isn't the only place working to ensure that cash continues to be legal tender accepted everywhere. Philadelphia passed a similar measure in 2019, and the state of New Jersey followed suit. Massachusetts already required businesses to accept cash. Many other states are considering similar bills.[13]

As of this writing, there is no federal law requiring businesses to take cash as a form of payment,[14] but some federal legislators are working to change that. The Payment Choice Act would require retail businesses to accept cash as a form of payment for on-site sales of $500 or less.[15]

These legislative efforts would help ensure that most brick-and-mortar businesses continue to allow people to pay in cash, but they will do little to offset the move to a cashless society if bills above (or potentially including) ten dollars are intentionally removed from circulation. Doing that requires a more concerted effort to push back on policy proposals to reduce cash overall, and perhaps a societal movement to preserve the future of cash.

SEVEN

CAN CRYPTOCURRENCY BE A PRACTICAL TOOL AGAINST CENSORSHIP?

I first began investigating Bitcoin in late 2010. It was the early days of the WikiLeaks financial blockade, before I began collecting the censorship stories that would become the first skeleton of this book. The first article I published about Bitcoin, in January 2011 on the EFF *Deeplinks* blog, was squarely focused on whether it could be a tool to resist censorship.[1]

The intervening years have seen a massive amount of innovation in the cryptocurrency space, many upheavals, and a few blockbuster scandals. I have never been interested in cryptocurrency as an investment tool or even as an economic model. Instead, I wondered whether Bitcoin and other cryptocurrencies could be used as a tool to thwart financial censorship.

That curiosity was spurred by pragmatism. Passing legislation is a massive undertaking, convincing companies to do the right thing is an uphill battle, and building advocacy movements takes time and resources. Technological solutions are appealing precisely because they can start working today, without years of lobbying and movement building. And while cash is inherently limited to the physical world, cryptocurrency is a solution appropriate for smartphones and websites, where the humans exchanging money may be in different towns or on different continents.

This chapter won't try to convince anybody that Bitcoin or other cryptocurrencies are good or bad for the world. So many different factors are implicated in that analysis, including environmental impacts, individual privacy, monetary policy, consumer protection, imperialism, and national privilege, that it's beyond the scope of this research. Plus, I find those conversations are rarely productive, since most people are pretty set in their opinions about cryptocurrency, whatever they may be. Instead, let's focus specifically and solely on whether and how cryptocurrency can be a tool against financial censorship.

WHAT CRYPTOCURRENCY IS

Transacting with cash is straightforward and intuitive: one person hands the other cash. In that moment, when the physical bills switch from one hand to another, the transaction is complete. The payer no longer has the cash and the recipient has the cash. People trust in the value of physical bills in part because they are hard to replicate; the average person can't make a bunch of copies of a twenty-dollar bill and pass them around whenever they need to buy something.

How does that translate to the digital world, where payments are virtual and you can't hold the evidence of a transaction in your hand? In particular, when money is represented by computer code, how can you have confidence that the electronic funds you received weren't also digitally sent to other people, like someone trying to send multiple people copies of the same concert ticket? This is called the "double spend problem," and it's one of the inherent challenges of building a digital financial system.

One very popular way to solve the double spend problem is to use financial institutions as intermediaries to keep track of who has what. Traditionally, if I want to send you a bank transfer of five dollars, my bank will update its ledger to subtract five dollars from my account, then communicate with your bank using many-decades-old automated clearinghouse technology, which would in turn update its ledger so that your account has an additional five dollars.

It turns out that banks aren't the only way to accomplish this. In a technical white paper sent to a mailing list on Halloween 2008, the pseudonymous writer Satoshi Nakamoto described a digital system that allowed people to transact directly with one another, no banks or credit card companies required.[2]

Here's what he proposed: Create a single public ledger of who owns what that everyone can see. Maintain the ledger through a network of many computers working together to update it with new transactions. Satoshi Nakamoto called his ledger a "blockchain" and the new digital currency system "Bitcoin." While Bitcoin was new, the proposal built off earlier ideas for digital cash and public ledger technologies.

Anyone can see the Bitcoin ledger, and what you see is all transactions recorded in a pseudonymous way (for example, user 123 sent one bitcoin to user 456 on January 1, 2024). Each "username" (a "public key") automatically has a corresponding "password" (a "private key") that enables the owner to update the ledger to "send" that Bitcoin to someone else (i.e., record on the ledger that they are transferring value to someone else).

How does this work in practice? Imagine a group of friends trading childcare services with one another using a shared notebook to keep track of how much time each person spends watching the kids. Every time one person provides childcare to somebody else, they write the transaction in the notebook, which is left on a table for everyone to see. Nobody owns the notebook, and anybody can add a transaction to it or check prior transactions.

That's similar to how the Bitcoin blockchain works. Instead of picking up a pen to write transactions down in a physical notebook, Bitcoin miners contribute computing power in the process of confirming transactions to the digital public ledger. The ledger keeps track of "Bitcoin" transactions, but there is no separate, physical thing called Bitcoin; Bitcoin is just what is on the ledger.

There are a few features of Bitcoin that contribute to its popularity when prior attempts at electronic cash had not taken off in the same way. First, it's a resilient system. Instead of living on one computer controlled by one company, copies of the Bitcoin blockchain (and pieces of copies of it) exist across a multitude of computers all over the world. This means there's no single point of failure; if one computer goes down, there are others that can continue the network. It's also permissionless. Anyone, anywhere in the world can become a Bitcoin miner without applying for a license or asking for someone for approval. Anyone can generate a Bitcoin address and then anyone, anywhere in the world, can transfer bitcoins to that address without asking permission from someone else or setting up an account with a financial institution.

Additionally, Bitcoin transactions are immutable. To change analogies for a moment: Adding a group of transactions (called a block) to the Bitcoin blockchain is like adding a new floor to a high-rise building. Once a block of transactions has been accepted by the community of miners, it's part of the foundation on which future transactions are built. Just like you can't remove lower floors from a building without causing catastrophe to the upper floors, you can't go back and remove, undo, or alter earlier transactions in the Bitcoin blockchain without messing up all the transactions that came later. This immutability lets people trust that once they've received or sent a transaction on the blockchain, it won't be reversed.

The invention of Bitcoin inspired many other forms of cryptocurrency. While these cryptocurrencies replicate some of the features of physical cash, there are also some fundamental differences, the most obvious being that they can be exchanged electronically and over great distances. While a few governments, including Jamaica and Nigeria, have issued digital currencies through their central banks, the United States has not.[3] (And many have argued that the United States shouldn't.)[4] Without government backing, cryptocurrencies are worth whatever the market will pay for them, and that can fluctuate dramatically compared to, for example, the relative predictability of the US dollar's value.

Bitcoin and many other cryptocurrencies also lack the privacy-preserving features of cash. They naturally create an indelible record of transactions, much like a credit card company does, but that record is public instead of existing in a privately held corporate database. There are some safeguards: Digital addresses are publicly identified by a string of numbers rather than an individual's name, and you can have as many addresses as you would like. But if your address is ever connected to your identity, the privacy of your transactions is compromised, and there are companies that try to make that connection by various means. There are also mixer services that try to bring additional layers of privacy to your transactions as well as some cryptocurrencies that have worked to solve this problem with extra privacy-enhancing steps.[5]

CRYPTOCURRENCY'S CENSORSHIP RESISTANCE

Distributed ledgers at the heart of cryptocurrencies are naturally resistant to censorship. There's no single intermediary to approve or reject transactions, no corporate terms of service to enforce, and generally no legal entity that can be bullied by government agents to reject certain transactions.

That's not to say it's impossible to imagine a way to undermine this censorship resistance. Blockchains are vulnerable to "51 percent attacks" in which a malicious actor controls more than 50 percent of the computing power of a network and uses that to control the transaction history. Someone who controlled (by owning or successfully regulating) that much computing power in the Bitcoin network for the indefinite future could, among other things, block specific transactions or even prevent any new transactions from being recognized at all. The Bitcoin protocol today is widely decentralized and involves so much computing power that executing one of these attacks for the purposes of censorship is honestly hard to imagine. Smaller cryptocurrency networks are more vulnerable to this style of attack, especially ones that prioritize efficiency over decentralization.

It's also worth noting that Bitcoin in particular has faced some serious moments that challenged whether it would continue to be a decentralized, censorship-resistant network. So far, the protocol and the miners who confirm the transactions have stuck to the vision outlined in the original white paper, even when faced with intense pressure, perhaps in part due to a commitment to the philosophy that informs the community. The biggest challenge came to a head in 2017. The Blocksize War saw a community within Bitcoin advocate for increasing the size of the blocks that were included in the Bitcoin blockchain so as to speed up transactions on the network.[6] Critics of the plan warned that adopting this protocol update would mean that only entities with substantial resources, like companies and maybe universities and nonprofits, would be able to act as miners on the network. This would result in more centralized points of control.

In the end, the community split over the issue, and the subset of people who fought for larger block sizes created a different (and ultimately far less popular) version of Bitcoin known as Bitcoin Cash, while those who favored smaller blocks stuck with what would continue to be known as Bitcoin.[7]

Alex Gladstein, chief strategy officer of the Human Rights Foundation, told me in an interview that this showdown informed his opinion of the protocol: "I found it so profound that the David won the fight. The Goliaths didn't win. The people who controlled all of this capital, all of the mining power, all of this Bitcoin, they lost. They were unable to impose their will on the network. And that was very interesting to me. And I was like, okay, so if it could survive this, then maybe it could actually be a robust tool against dictators." Soon after, the Human Rights Foundation began using Bitcoin to support pro-democracy activists and NGOs fighting authoritarian regimes around the world.

Many early blockchain developers and enthusiasts embraced a distinctive worldview and ethical code. The culture, though hardly monolithic, included many of the ideals that are popular in free software communities and the cypherpunk community: resistance to surveillance, a sense that technology should be secure and auditable, a willingness to work in public, a willingness to volunteer personal energy toward a group project that would benefit many, an appreciation for data privacy, and a sort of generalized suspicion of power and authority in all its forms. The Cypherpunk Manifesto, a community-defining document published by Eric Hughes in 1993, expressed this philosophy. As Hughes explained, cypherpunks weren't just united by a common philosophy. They were united by the action of creating computer code that brought that philosophy into being:

> Cypherpunks write code. We know that someone has to write software to defend privacy, and since we can't get privacy unless we all do, we're going to write it. We publish our code so that our fellow Cypherpunks may practice and play with it. Our code is free for all to use, worldwide. We don't much care if you don't approve of the software we write. We know that software can't be destroyed and that a widely dispersed system can't be shut down.[8]

In that same document, Hughes asserted that electronic money was a part of the cypherpunk dream: "We the Cypherpunks are dedicated to building anonymous systems. We are defending our privacy with cryptography, with anonymous mail forwarding systems, with digital signatures, and with electronic money."

I chatted about this idea with Peter Van Valkenburgh, director of research for Coin Center. He told me that Bitcoin was designed to be resistant to censorship: "There's no choke point in the middle that a state actor or a malicious third party could lean on to prevent the transaction from going forward. So censorship resistance is at the very beginning of

Bitcoin, culturally and explicitly, in the way the [Bitcoin] white paper described the technology, in the way the technology was ultimately built."

The cultural aspect is open to interpretation, but Van Valkenburg says he sees two distinct political ideologies mixed up in the community of Bitcoin: "There's a civil-libertarian strain, which is more privacy and censorship resistance, and then there's more of a libertarian-libertarian strain, which is sound money, and preventing debasement, and a return to something more like commodity money like gold. And those two cultural traditions in Bitcoin persist to this day, and sometimes they are somewhat at odds with each other."

DANGERS OF CENTRALIZATION

The censorship-resistant nature of cryptocurrency is inextricably intertwined with its decentralization. And there are threats to that decentralization on the horizon, and they aren't getting the kind of attention they should. The first threat is legal in nature, and the second is connected to market trends among cryptocurrency users.

The first threat is physical centralization of cryptocurrency to certain geographic locations because it is restricted or outright banned by laws in other countries. This includes bans on holding or trading cryptocurrency, bans on software development of cryptocurrency, prohibitions on educating people in a certain region about cryptocurrency, and bans on mining cryptocurrency. We've seen general prohibitions on cryptocurrency in a number of countries, such as China and Pakistan.[9] The United States has not enacted a countrywide ban on cryptocurrency, but US regulators have pressured companies in the cryptocurrency space, the Department of Justice has used economic sanctions to justify prosecuting a cryptocurrency educator, and the US Office of Foreign Assets Control (OFAC) placed TornadoCash, a tool for enhancing privacy while using cryptocurrency, on the sanctions list.[10] It is also unclear how legal regimes may attempt to pressure cryptocurrency miners to enforce economic sanctions, and how threats of prosecution around this issue could have massive, deleterious effects on the space. When a particular jurisdiction is antagonistic toward cryptocurrency, it discourages people from interacting with the technology there and likely results in a drop-off in usage, software development, and mining activity in that area. This results in cryptocurrency use, development, and mining activity moving toward more friendly jurisdictions—and the more networks are pushed toward a few physical locations, the easier it is to target them for shutdown or pressure from a government entity.

Cryptocurrency bans are not widespread yet, but their early use by a few countries is extremely concerning and could portend future threats to the global decentralization of the networks and, ultimately, their utility for circumventing censorship.

The second threat hinges on tendencies toward centralization among cryptocurrency users. While the technology and philosophy of cryptocurrency may be grounded in censorship resistance, the practical reality is that many users' experience of cryptocurrency mimics their experience with traditional financial services. While cryptocurrency users could generate their own wallets to store their cryptocurrency and trade funds directly with one another, many (and quite possibly most) don't do that.

Instead, people are turning to corporations to handle the technical parts of creating a wallet and managing a private key for them. Users must trust that these companies will keep their cryptocurrency secure, but they might also have some guarantees like insurance if those funds are lost or stolen. Companies that hold assets on behalf of users are often called "custodians" or "custodial services." Chainalysis, a company that conducts research on cryptocurrency usage, found that 60 percent of all Bitcoin that hadn't been lost was held by a licensed custodial service in 2020.[11]

Cryptocurrency holders (even those who manage their wallets themselves) often use a custodial cryptocurrency exchange company to buy and sell digital tokens. Importantly, these exchanges are often the only practical way to exchange large sums of cryptocurrency into fiat currency. This makes them into something of a necessity for people who want to invest a serious amount of money in cryptocurrency and still want the flexibility to exchange it into usable forms for non-cryptocurrency transactions, like paying rent or a utility bill.

People who want to set up an account with a custodial service or exchange will need to apply for an account with that company and follow the Know Your Customer requirements described earlier. Just like setting up a bank account, this involves providing extensive details including your legal name, physical address, identification numbers like your Social Security number or business tax identification numbers, and banking information.

Entrusting assets to a cryptocurrency company also means trusting that company's terms of service and policies. Just like a payment processor can freeze your account or refuse transactions, a custodial service can freeze or block your account. An exchange can close your account, and you may never know why. We saw how dangerous trusting custodial services could be for consumers when Tokyo-based exchange Mt. Gox went bankrupt in 2014 and when Bahamian cryptocurrency exchange FTX went belly-up due to massive fraud by the corporate executives in 2022.[12]

In addition to being vulnerable to malicious hacks, inept security practices, and executive fraud, these cryptocurrency companies are just as capable of shuttering or restricting accounts as traditional financial companies. They have no more legal obligations to serve their customers than financial companies like Visa, PayPal, or Chase do.

These companies become weak points. They are just as likely as traditional financial companies to face pressure from government actors and other financial companies to shutter or restrict certain accounts.

So what can be done about this? First, we must ensure that people understand that custodial cryptocurrency companies are replicating the trust model of traditional finance. Users must make their own choices about whether to self-custody their cryptocurrency.

Second, cryptocurrency companies should stand up for the rights of their users. The recommendations for this are identical to the recommendations for traditional financial companies, and readers who are curious can jump ahead to the chapter on best practices for companies.

Both physical cash and cryptocurrency are technologies that by their nature rob financial institutions of their power to punish. Each, in its own way, is a powerful tool against censorship. They serve as necessary safeguards in our world, where financial companies have so much power to close and block accounts and the US government has a track record of pushing these companies to act as censors by proxy. The same way a spare tire is a necessary fail-safe when we are stranded on the side of the highway peering at a flat tire, these technologies provide vital support right now for individuals and institutions that are inappropriately cast out of the centralized financial system.

But it would be a mistake to think that having a technological solution is all we need: first, because the censorship resistance of these technologies is under threat in all the ways I've outlined above, and second, because so much of the world is still likely to use intermediated services for their digital transactions. Many prefer the convenience, consumer protections, and membership perks of credit card systems, even as they pay annual membership fees and sacrifice the privacy of their financial lives with every transaction.

We cannot solve the problem of financial censorship for only those individuals who are willing to live life entirely through cryptocurrency and cash. We must also solve this problem for the hundreds of millions of people who are subject to the vicissitudes of payment processors' terms of service and credit card companies' restrictive rules.

CHAPTER 8

TAKING ON THE BANKING BLOCKADE

Long before he applied for a job with me, I knew Trevor Timm through Twitter.

I didn't know his name at the time. He was using a pseudonymous Twitter account to speak out against widespread misinformation about the WikiLeaks prosecution and explain the historical and legal context for news organizations publishing classified information. Before we ever spoke on the phone, I was reading his posts and agreeing with every word he wrote.

As the WikiLeaks story unfolded, Trevor was studying at New York Law School. He was also working as the research assistant for James Goodale. You may have heard of Goodale: he was the general counsel for the *New York Times* who steered the paper through the Nixon administration's attempt to censor the publication of the Pentagon Papers. The Supreme Court victory in that case helped establish the First Amendment protections that ensure newspapers can publish classified documents they receive without getting permission from the government.

Impressed with his skills as a researcher, Goodale recruited Trevor to help write a book about the Pentagon Papers. Trevor immediately agreed. It was a dream assignment: an opportunity to research a crucial moment in legal history with one of the preeminent media lawyers in the country. Plus, he needed the money.

As Trevor was researching how President Nixon attacked the *New York Times* for publishing classified information, WikiLeaks was dominating the headlines.

"All of a sudden, there is this white-haired Australian who is publishing State Department cables and Afghanistan War logs, which are classified. It's a big batch of documents, and everyone seems to think that this is illegal and that this person should be in jail," Trevor told me when we sat down for an interview for this book in September 2023. "Meanwhile,

I am literally writing a book on the fact that this, of course, is perfectly legal."

Pentagon Papers were a much more serious security breach than WikiLeaks. You can't justify the former & not the latter: http://bit.ly/uOIhE3@WLLegal Dec 22, 2011[1]

As journalists and politicians decried Assange for breaking the law and endangering the country, Trevor felt like he had to do something. He'd spent a year researching and writing about the intricacies of Nixon's efforts to silence the press, and now he was watching a near-identical situation play out in real time. He felt like he had this key information that somehow other so-called experts commenting on the case had forgotten. His boss was one of the few exceptions—a legal expert willing to say that Assange's actions as a publisher were no more illegal than anything the *New York Times* had done in publishing the Pentagon Papers. But Goodale was one of only a few voices speaking out and was nearly drowned out by the op-ed writers, social media commentators, and even public officials calling for Assange's prosecution.

Trevor wanted to change that. But he had only just graduated from law school and hadn't passed the bar yet. Who would even listen to him?

That's when he decided to start a pseudonymous Twitter account. From a desk in his living room in the Lower East Side Manhattan apartment that he shared with another student, Trevor started "WL Legal," a Twitter account that offered a legal analysis of what was happening to WikiLeaks. "Anytime anybody tweeted about WikiLeaks, I would correct them," he told me. "I would amplify people who were actually saying the right things, like Glenn Greenwald, of course. I would respond to people who were just saying something factual or were asking questions. I would call people out who were totally wrong."

Within months, the WL Legal account had thousands of followers and was growing rapidly. It was soon cited in blog posts and news articles about WikiLeaks and began to help define the often-misunderstood issues around WikiLeaks.

And just so the State Dept knows, the Pentagon Papers were 7,000 pages long & leaked to *many* newspapers. Not exactly one doc, one reporter @WLLegal Jan 12, 2011[2]

If I'm honest, I had my reservations when I first saw Trevor's job application. By then, he had graduated law school and was studying for the bar in New York. Did he really want to join the activism team? The legal team at EFF used the court system to effect change in the world. My tiny team was different; we tried to change the world by influencing public opinion. We wrote long-form blog posts, organized coalitions, and used social media to try to galvanize the world to care about civil liberties. I feared that a lawyer wouldn't find this type of work fulfilling and might always secretly wish they were on the other side of EFF—quite literally, since EFF's rambling warehouse office in the Mission was roughly divided into the northern "legal" side and the southern side, which we called the "illegal" side.

I met with Trevor a half dozen times during that interview process and grilled him on this question. Each time, he assured me that he really, truly wanted to change the world through writing and advocacy. He also revealed that he was the writer behind WL Legal. I was shocked and then impressed. I had always assumed the account was run by a lawyer who didn't want to jeopardize her professional reputation by speaking out about WikiLeaks. Or maybe, I thought, a group of lawyers. The account argued so knowledgeably in defense of press freedom that it seemed beyond the skill of a law student. Of course, Trevor was anything but an average law student. To this day, I think of hiring Trevor as one of the best decisions I made in my career.

I took the job as activism director at EFF having already worked for months as an organizer for the Chelsea Manning Support Network. As more leaks were published by WikiLeaks and its partners, I had to shift my thinking beyond what positions the Chelsea Manning Support Network should take to what role EFF should play in the public conversation. After many hours of exploring it with my colleagues, I became increasingly convinced we should be leading the fight in defense of WikiLeaks' right to publish. I knew we could lend a unique voice to the fight—that EFF could bring a values-driven, forceful defense of free expression that covered the publishing activity of WikiLeaks and encompassed many of the actions of WikiLeaks' supporters and associates, a number of whom were also under attack. My colleagues and I had deep conversations about how to frame our messaging, both around EFF's battered conference room table and after hours at Shotwells, a bar down the street. Trevor's arguments connecting to the First Amendment helped us shape those positions.

As the banking blockade against WikiLeaks dragged on for months, I became increasingly concerned. The financial companies didn't seem to care about the concerns from the civil liberties community. While we could—and did—effectively argue that the government couldn't censor WikiLeaks, we didn't have a defense against the payment processors setting up an independent blockade. It was clear our typical tools weren't going to work. We needed something else.

I wasn't the only one worried. I'd made friends with a pair of left-leaning activists named Martin MacKerel and Leez, and we spoke often about the challenges that beset WikiLeaks. Through many late-night conversations over cheap beers, I started to understand the fight around WikiLeaks as part of a larger political struggle about power, government interests in controlling a narrative, and what America stood to gain through ongoing overseas wars.

EFF board members were also concerned about the banking blockade. The most outspoken board member was JP Barlow, a counterculture icon and former lyricist for the Grateful Dead who wore cowboy boots and loved to say outlandish things online. He declared during a live radio interview—without talking to anyone on EFF staff—that EFF was going to be receiving donations on behalf of WikiLeaks to help it survive the blockade.

But we weren't. And attempting to do so seemed risky.

"I was general counsel of EFF at this point in time, and I thought it was a very bad idea, most importantly because EFF could've ended up blockaded," Cindy Cohn, EFF's current executive director, said when we met in September 2023 to reminisce about that time. "We could go down—and with us all the other people we were helping in our cases and advocacy which was much broader than just the WikiLeaks issue—if the blockade extended to us. But Barlow insisted that we think about this."

She told me—as she has told me countless times—that EFF would always rather be in the role of the legal team arguing a case than be a party in the case. She didn't think EFF could long withstand retribution by the financial companies if they shut us down: "We would have been very quickly in a position where we would have had to lay people off or shrink the size of the organization dramatically, even if it just happened for a little while." She also didn't want to jeopardize the other important work EFF was doing—like suing the NSA for mass surveillance and squaring off against copyright maximalists.

I knew all of this; we talked about it at length as the blockade unfolded. So while I was personally thrilled to hear Barlow announce to all the world that EFF was going to be receiving donations on behalf of WikiLeaks, I didn't see how that could even be a possibility.

My newest hire had a plan, one he'd been thinking about even before he joined my team. But it wasn't until others in the organization started to debate the possibility of EFF taking donations to WikiLeaks that he told us about it. Trevor overheard the EFF fundraising team in a deep conversation about what to do about the financial blockade. His shared office was directly across from the conference room—so he could hear pretty much anything the fundraising team was saying. He told me about that moment:

> I could hear them talking about the WikiLeaks financial blockade. I don't remember the exact conversation, but it was something along the lines of board members—probably [JP] Barlow and [John] Gilmore—want EFF to take donations to WikiLeaks, and I think they were talking about how they couldn't do that. But they were torn because they wanted to help. So I literally heard this conversation happening from my office, and I just decided to waltz into the conference room. And I said, "Hey, I heard that you were talking about the financial blockade and you have this problem. I have an idea."

Then Trevor laid out a plan. It was the same pitch he would give me that week: Start a new nonprofit organization—one that isn't connected to EFF, so it won't jeopardize EFF's finances. Then use the new organization to start taking donations for many different, worthwhile, independent news outlets, including WikiLeaks. If the financial companies try to censor the organization, it will look terrible for them because they will be cutting off the funds to a range of worthwhile news organizations in addition to

WikiLeaks. Name the organization "Freedom of the Press Foundation," so that if the financial companies censor it or the government tries to shut it down, the core issue will be front and center in any news coverage of the event. Gather a high-profile, reputable board of directors so that people will trust this organization with donation money, and so that those board members could serve as a public voice for the organization.

Trevor finished his impromptu speech, said "Thank you," and returned to his office.

A few days later, Shari Steele, EFF's executive director and my boss at the time, stopped by Trevor's office. It was perhaps the second or third time they'd spoken since he had started working at EFF, and Shari managed to be both very warm and incredibly intimidating. She told Trevor that everybody liked his idea, and that they were organizing a group dinner to discuss it.

Trevor didn't have to worry about my support; I'd been talking within EFF for months about doing more to fight back against the extralegal banking blockade. I was saying yes before he even finished explaining the idea. It didn't matter that my full-time job as EFF's activism director took up more than forty hours a week or that I was spending my evenings and weekends campaigning in defense of Chelsea Manning. I didn't hesitate for a second to jump headfirst into starting a new nonprofit.

That's not to say I didn't worry about the risks and possible complications. When I had helped organize the Chelsea Manning Support Network, we had chosen to be a project of an existing nonprofit so that we didn't need to deal with all of the complexity of filing paperwork with the IRS (and possibly waiting months or getting rejected) and setting up our own bank accounts, board of directors, accounting system, and mailing address. With Freedom of the Press Foundation, I already knew that it was crucial we do everything separate from EFF so there was no chance of EFF being sideswiped by our efforts. EFF had sued the US government enough times that I suspected they were itchy for a reason to come after us.

The plan also felt bold. I loved the idea of setting up a nonprofit that could take a stand for press freedom in a way other organizations could not.

Trevor, Cindy, Shari, and I went to dinner with EFF board members (and cofounders) John Gilmore and JP Barlow. We were joined by EFF senior staff attorney Kurt Opsahl, who would go on to succeed Cindy as EFF's general counsel and had a strategic and creative approach to the potential risks to EFF, as well as Jillian York, EFF's international director of free expression and one of the world's best advocates for addressing censorship on social media platforms.

We mapped out how we would build the organization and whom we would invite to the board. Trevor and I agreed to join the new board of directors, as did JP Barlow. Cindy and the rest of her team would be our legal counsel—a role that was perfect for EFF and a massive boon to our soon-to-be-launched nonprofit as we tackled some uncharted legal issues.

It's this moment in time that sticks in my mind. This dinner where everything changed.

Up until then, we shared a common concern and a connection through EFF. We each worried about the banking blockade against WikiLeaks, but, more importantly, we were worried about an attempt to stifle a news organization and what that meant for the future of journalism. We were at a precipitous moment in US history where the existence of a free press—which serves as a necessary check on government power abuses and is a hallmark of a free society—was fragile in a way it hadn't been in the last forty years. But sitting in a dim, warm restaurant at a long table over noodle dishes and whiskey drinks, we were no longer just talking about a grave threat to a free press. We were planning our response.

I walked into that restaurant with some skepticism about whether we'd be able to reach any sort of agreement. Other than Trevor, I wasn't sure if the rest of the group would go for the plan. That skepticism stemmed in part from my reaction to the culture of EFF, where it was a common practice to kick the tires on any idea by questioning each angle and pointing out every possible flaw—a practice that made us far stronger as an organization but often left us feeling disconnected from the colleagues who had skewered our ideas. While I understood Trevor's commitment to the project, I didn't yet have that level of certainty with the others.

But over the course of that dinner, that started to change. We began to coalesce around a shared purpose. We became a team working together on something audacious, each of us with a distinct role to play and skills to lend.

It also felt momentous that our group had formed across different generations of EFF. John Gilmore and JP Barlow were the original EFF. Along with Steve Wozniak and Mitch Kapor, they had started EFF in 1990 as a foundation trying to hire lawyers to defend hackers against unconstitutional law enforcement searches. Shari, Kurt, and Cindy had been at EFF for decades, and they were the current leadership steering the entire organization. But Trevor, Jillian, and I? We were still finding our footing at EFF. I was thirty years old and I'd been at EFF less than two years, while Trevor and Jillian were both younger than I was and had even less time at the organization. But nobody treated our opinions as any less valid just because we were newer to the organization.

Sitting at a table in a Thai restaurant, I realized I was surrounded by a whole group of my favorite kind of people—people who were willing to roll up their sleeves and actually do something to change the world. Over the coming weeks and months, I would develop a deep trust and friendship for each of the people working to make this wild idea a reality.

After that dinner, we started to get momentum. Trevor bought a how-to book about starting a nonprofit organization and downloaded a general-purpose nonprofit charter. John Gilmore wrote us a $5,000 check that would be our first donation, writing in the memo line, "For Freedom of the Press Foundation—long may it wave."

For building the website, we turned to Micah Lee, a brilliant software engineer and writer from EFF. He took the role of Freedom of the Press Foundation's chief technology officer, and his small contract for building the website made him the first paid person for the organization. Later, he'd leave his role as CTO and take a place on the board.

From the first stage of designing the website, we theorized that the identity of our donors and site visitors could be alluring to government officials or others. So we built our website with privacy in mind. Micah built software to monitor website traffic without storing the IP addresses of visitors. He also built a tool that helped us anonymize the donations—we knew how much money was donated, and we knew who donated the money, and we even knew how much money was allotted to each of the news organizations we supported. But we did not maintain a record of which specific donors supported which organizations in our crowdfunding campaign. By designing it this way from the beginning, it would be impossible for us to ever turn over a list of people who had donated to support WikiLeaks.

Even as Trevor, a few other volunteers, and I wrote content for the website Micah was building, we also began reaching out to potential board members. The first person we approached was Daniel Ellsberg, the famed whistleblower who had been at the center of the book Trevor had helped write about the Pentagon Papers, and whom I'd gotten to know and admire through our work together on the Chelsea Manning Support Network. While some people may have been worried about joining a new nonprofit that would confront an international banking blockade, Dan didn't hesitate. He immediately agreed to join us, and he became our first board member who wasn't on the staff or board of EFF.

Next, we invited Glenn Greenwald, a civil liberties lawyer and journalist who was one of the most outspoken voices against the surveillance state and the prosecution of WikiLeaks. Glenn and Trevor had exchanged many messages over the prior years. Glenn had more reservations than Dan. He did not yet know the rest of us well, and we needed to convince him of our sincerity—and of the legality of our undertaking. He also insisted that the organization be supportive of more than WikiLeaks and made it a condition of joining. He understood the strategic need for this and also was deeply committed to the broader cause of press freedom, not just the immediate issue with WikiLeaks. Shortly after our first board meeting, he signed on.

Next we asked Laura Poitras. I first met Laura when I attended the Article 32 hearing for Chelsea Manning's court-martial. An Article 32 hearing is normally a quick arraignment accomplished in an hour or two. But Chelsea's had been a circus; I'd spent a week hanging out at a military base in Fort Meade, Maryland, where I took meticulous notes on the proceedings to publish every night on our campaign website. I also got to see many of my fellow Chelsea Manning supporters in person, including heroes of mine like Daniel Ellsberg and Lt. Dan Choi, and I met incredible journalists like Alexis O'Brien and Laura Poitras.

Even from my first meeting with her, Laura had struck me as incisive and principled—an impression that would deepen over the coming years of working together. Laura's early documentaries on America's brutal overseas wars had been met with critical acclaim, but she was perhaps just as well-known for being the target of invasive searches of all of her digital devices every time she crossed the US border. Glenn's reporting on Laura's punitive border searches would help prompt public condemnation and make it so she could cross the border without harassment. EFF would later take Laura on as a client to seek answers about why she was targeted in this way.

We also connected with John Cusack, who readily agreed to join the board before our official launch. I'd long known of John for his work as an actor, but I learned over those weeks that he was a committed advocate for press freedom as well as a global humanitarian activist. No one did more to help raise the profile of our small nonprofit than John.

Not everyone we contacted was able to join us. Journalist Dan Gillmor, whose book *We the Media* argued for the role of grassroots, independent journalism, wasn't able to join the board when we first launched, but he connected us to Josh Stearns, a director at the nonprofit Free Press who worked on issues of community media and digital access. Josh was glad to join us, and we were thankful for his expertise in community journalism grantmaking. Similarly, novelist and EFF friend Cory Doctorow didn't have time to take on a board seat, but he connected us with his fellow BoingBoing founder Xeni Jardin, a prolific writer and defender of free speech. She agreed.

Who wasn't on the board? Anyone from WikiLeaks. That was on purpose. Even as we were launching a crowdfunding campaign that would route around the banking blockade and provide vital support to WikiLeaks, we wanted a separation between our organization and theirs. We didn't want anyone to make the argument that we were directly connected to them—liable for their actions or subject to the same banking blockade that was strangling their organization.

We also knew we needed 501(c)(3) status before we could accept charitable donations. Unfortunately, it would be many months before the IRS granted our 501(c)(3) application—months that would delay our launch. What we needed was an entity that would be willing to serve as our fiscal sponsor, at least for a while until our 501(c)(3) application was approved. But what organization in its right mind would even consider that, knowing we had a high chance of facing our own banking blockade that could likely extend to our fiscal sponsor? We weren't sure we'd ever find anyone who could take on that much risk and resigned ourselves to waiting for IRS approval.

But an organization did step forward: the Foundation for National Progress, Mother Jones's parent organization, which Shari Steele connected us to. Even when we explained the strong possibility that our organization could be blockaded by the major financial companies, and the very real possibilities that such a blockade could extend to any fiscal sponsor, the Foundation for National Progress was unfazed. They offered to serve as our fiscal sponsor and provided much-needed support for our newly formed organization. Even after we received our official 501(c)(3) designation from the IRS more than a year later, the Foundation for National Progress helped provide organizational support and financial services for over a year as we found our footing. The risks that organization shouldered to make Freedom of the Press Foundation a reality have been largely overlooked for the last ten years, but I do not know how we could have gotten started without their support.

We launched in 2012, and the public unveiling itself felt extremely rushed. But by then, the financial blockade against WikiLeaks had been in place for a year and the whistleblower organization was struggling tremendously. Plus, fundraising season was about to peak: in the United States, many nonprofits that rely on donations bring in a huge percentage of their funding in the last six weeks of the calendar year. We had certainly experienced that at EFF, where a majority of the funding came from individual donors. As December loomed, we rushed to get the final pieces in place so we could announce our new nonprofit.

In the end, the timing was dictated by a journalist at the *New York Times*. In addition to planning articles by our prestigious board members, we'd reached out to several journalists. David Carr of the *Times* often used his column to document and analyze journalism's shift to new media outlets. He decided to dedicate his weekly column to our organization. Titled "Group Aims to Be a Conduit for WikiLeaks Donations," the piece described our new organization and its rarified board of directors, as well as our hopes of routing around the banking blockade without being sideswiped by it ourselves.

This is the kind of incredible coverage many nonprofits could only dream of at their launch, and we let the schedule of Carr's publication decide our own launch. When his story went live on December 16, 2012, a half day before we planned to launch the website, Micah quickly published the website and we sent out our first tweet as an organization:

Introducing the Freedom of the Press Foundation, which will crowd-fund for transparency journalism—including WikiLeaks https://pressfreedomfoundation.org[3]

We quickly saw coverage by other news outlets that helped raise awareness of our small organization. Perhaps the most impactful tool for garnering attention was not a news article but a Twitter glitch: shortly after we launched our website and began tweeting about our organization, Twitter suspended our account. This unaccountable suspension created a massive Twitter buzz, as people speculated about why our account had been shut down and whether we were being actively censored by Twitter. Could this be a harbinger of other forms of corporate censorship? Would the financial companies be next to shut us down?

Whatever happened on Twitter's end got resolved in a few hours, and we were soon back to raising awareness about press freedom. But even now, years later, I believe those few hours of censorship, intentional or otherwise, created a drama around our launch that helped us get critical momentum on the first day.

As promised, we weren't just fundraising for WikiLeaks. Our crowdfunding campaign also offered donors a pathway to support MuckRock News, which supported citizen Freedom of Information Act requests; the UpTake, a citizen journalism website; and the National Security Archive, a nonprofit repository for declassified government documents. They were each phenomenal organizations helping fight for press freedom and transparency.

Ten days after our first launch, we had raised nearly $120,000. Of that, $58,000 was earmarked by donors to go to WikiLeaks. That number was staggering on multiple levels: first, because this would be a huge boon to an organization that had been struggling to bring in any funds under the protracted financial blockade, and second, because donors weren't merely choosing to donate to WikiLeaks—the most famous and controversial of our recipients. We also raised tens of thousands of dollars for the other journalistic organizations in our crowdfunding campaign, showing that this effort and public support really did go beyond WikiLeaks.

Freedom of the Press Foundation continued to provide donation pathways for donors to support WikiLeaks for several years, until the financial blockade was lifted and we were able to test that direct donations went through on the WikiLeaks website once more.

Could the success of Freedom of the Press Foundation serve as a blueprint for future advocacy groups attempting to overcome financial censorship?

I've wondered about that. I've thought through some of the factors that I believe contributed to our initial success. The financial censorship of WikiLeaks was so egregious that it inspired many of us to action, and those of us who got involved early were able to effectively recruit others. But I now recognize that a few other factors were key to our early success:

- We had the unofficial institutional support of EFF, a trusted, established nonprofit with a great network and expertise—including phenomenal legal expertise.
- We were able to successfully recruit a respected and eloquent board of directors.
- We were able to capture the attention of mainstream media through a combination of our mission, our spokespeople, and our network.
- We were able to find a risk-tolerant fiscal sponsor to carry us until we received our own 501(c)(3).
- A swirl of controversy around Twitter censorship during our launch drove additional interest in our new nonprofit and helped us gain critical momentum.
- We were able to build a beautiful, functional, privacy-focused website quickly.
- We paired our most controversial donation recipient with other respected organizations.

Are all of those factors required to successfully counter a financial blockade? No, of course not. But it's a useful way to start to understand the careful strategy Freedom of the Press Foundation used to successfully check the financial blockade against WikiLeaks.

Is this a replicable strategy for other activists trying to circumvent financial censorship?

"I would caution people against it," Trevor said when I asked him about it. He pointed to the legal complexity of setting up a foundation that provides grants, something we didn't have a deep understanding of when we were creating Freedom of the Press Foundation. Trevor is a lawyer, but, as he noted, he's not an expert in contract law. We had to rely on pro bono lawyers to navigate grantmaking and contracts, and the area proved more complicated than we expected.

In addition to the legal complexity, starting a wholly new nonprofit organization is a lot of work. That included months leading up to the launch and many years of work since.

That work was worth it. As of this writing, Freedom of the Press Foundation is twelve years old and has nearly thirty staff members. Laura, Trevor, John, and I are still on the board, meeting to talk about press freedom challenges every few months. Cindy and EFF are still our legal counsel. After years of successfully crowdfunding for independent journalism organizations, we retired our crowdfunding platform and focused entirely on new projects to defend press freedom. This included taking over Secure Drop, free software developed by the late engineer Aaron Swartz that allows any news organization to receive classified documents securely, so that any news organization could be the next WikiLeaks. Our security training team works with newsrooms across the country, teaching them how to use encryption and secure communications to fend off malicious snoops, whether governmental or otherwise. We publish the U.S. Press Freedom Tracker, a research project that documents every attack on journalists in the United States since we launched it in 2017. Today we also have an advocacy arm fighting to protect journalists and the First Amendment.

The financial censorship of WikiLeaks may have been the beginning of the work, but it soon became about the larger fight for press freedom. We discovered there were many powerful and novel threats to press freedom unfolding in the United States, and we continually adapted our strategies to meet those changes.

Gathering at that Thai restaurant in San Francisco all those years ago, I never imagined how much our organization would be called to accomplish. In fact, I always felt a lot of relief that we survived the first week without facing a financial blockade ourselves.

ACTIVISTS FOR AND AGAINST FINANCIAL CENSORSHIP

It's awkward for me to write about the need for activists to spend more time working on financial censorship because there are already activists working on this issue. But most of them are on the wrong side.

Financial censorship has become a tool favored by certain advocates to silence the voices of their opponents. While there are a great number of advocates turning to financial intermediaries to do their dirty work, there are far too few advocates working to advance financial access and neutrality. Without sustained pressure from the civil liberties and human rights communities, financial companies will receive only one message: "Censor." They'll continue to face public and private pressure to shutter the accounts of controversial and marginalized speakers, political activists, journalists, and any number of communities that have found themselves targeted by a creative and well-resourced opponent.

Which brings me to one of the most important points of this book. To date, the activist communities that have organized to defeat financial censorship are very few and have limited resources. I know this because I've been in the thick of this fight for years, organizing coalition letters against financial exclusion, writing articles against debanking, directly reaching out to the lawyers of payment intermediaries, and even starting a nonprofit to thwart a financial blockade.

But for every successful intervention, there are an untold number of other account holders who have no one to speak out for them. There simply isn't a large enough movement working on this issue currently.

Imagine what the financial landscape would look like if we had a focused, well-resourced community of advocates working to ensure financial access for all. Imagine the incredible power of an organized community working to hold financial companies to account, ensuring that civil liberties and free expression are upheld in their policies. Just as we've seen grassroots coalitions coalesce around issues from climate justice to health care, we need a movement for a more neutral, accountable financial system.

NINE

BEST PRACTICES FOR FINANCIAL COMPANIES

It's time for financial companies to engage in some deep self-reflection.

What are they, really? Who are they serving? Where do their loyalties lie, and what philosophies guide their policies?

The concept of *infrastructure* is a particularly helpful lens for understanding the role of core financial services. Internet infrastructure refers to the physical and technological systems that enable the internet to function. The internet service provider that brings internet access to your house, the domain name system that allows your computer to locate specific websites, the fiber-optic cables that silently ship data all around the globe—these are all parts of the hidden infrastructure that make the internet work. Just like highways, water treatment facilities, and the postal system in the physical world, digital infrastructure supports the basic functionality and security of our digital experiences.

Internet infrastructure should be neutral. These are services that help the larger internet ecosystem deliver content to users, but these services do not directly host that speech and thus are not positioned to police that speech.

Human rights groups engaged in technology policy have urged infrastructure services to embrace neutrality. In December 2022, an international coalition of renowned human rights organizations published a website and policy paper called Protect the Stack.[1] The coalition argued that internet infrastructure services are under pressure to play a role in policing online content, but these companies should resist that pressure. That's because while platforms have responsibilities to engage in speech moderation, infrastructure services can never tailor their responses with precision to ensure human rights are respected. The coalition specifically spoke about the dangers of payment processors cutting off services.[2]

It's no surprise that human rights groups understand financial services as part of the conversation about internet infrastructure. The financial industry is increasingly a necessity for people and businesses to participate in modern society. This includes both websites that need to process online payments and the growing prevalence of physical stores that are embracing digital payments, such as restaurants that tell customers to order from their phones. Access to financial services like PayPal and Visa isn't a luxury for a few; it's a necessity for countless people and businesses.

After Protect the Stack launched, EFF published a blog post further examining the concept of infrastructure.[3] As my colleagues wrote: "Essential internet infrastructure should be content-neutral. These services should not make editorial decisions that remove content beyond the scope of the law."

My colleagues also described a tier of services just slightly above infrastructure. "Pretty Much Infrastructure" was the term they used, and it refers to other services that are also necessary to the modern internet functioning properly: "Then there's a layer of things that are not necessarily critical internet infrastructure but are essential for most of us to operate businesses and labor online. Because of how the internet functions today, things in this layer have unique chokepoint capabilities." Payment processors and a few other services supportive of the internet were listed in this category.

I think this is exactly the right way to think about many financial services: maybe not technically infrastructure the way fiber-optic cables are, but still *pretty much infrastructure* because these services are a necessity to exist in online society.

When core financial services understand their role as part of the infrastructure of the internet, it can help them make the right choices when it comes to standing up for users and resisting pressures to engage in censorship. In general, this means erring on the side of being neutral and accessible.

That's the overarching idea. But how, specifically, will financial companies step into the role of infrastructure? Here are four specific principles that can help bring that idea into corporate policies:

1. *Publish transparency reports.* Companies should publish a report at least annually that shows how many requests a company receives to surveil, limit, investigate, or shut down accounts, whether those requests come from governments or any other entity. Reports should

include how many of these requests the company complied with and how many user accounts were impacted. These reports should also include how many accounts were frozen or shuttered due to alleged terms of service violations, broken down by which terms of service provision was violated.

Kraken, a financial company in the cryptocurrency space with over ten million customers around the globe, published a transparency report about government data requests in 2022 and 2023,[4] including which countries request user data, which agencies within the United States request user data, and how often Kraken provides the requested data. It's a fantastic step to bring transparency to government access requests. Kraken could improve this report in the coming years by specifying how often they close or restrict accounts for reasons unrelated to fraud or creditworthiness.

2. *Provide meaningful notice to users.* A financial company should tell a user if a negative decision is being made about their account, except when a company is forbidden from doing so by law or in cases of suspected account takeover. This includes telling the customer why an account is getting restricted, rejected, or closed. If the account is suspected of violating the company's terms of service, the company should tell the user what aspect of the terms were violated.

3. *Offer a timely and meaningful appeal process.* I've spoken to person after person who attempted to find someone at a company to talk to when her account was shuttered, to no avail. That's a symptom of a broken system. When a user's account is rejected, restricted, or closed, that user should have the opportunity to appeal the decision. Appeals should be reviewed by an individual or panel of individuals who were not involved in the initial negative decision about the account. And time matters—appeals should be reviewed and processed swiftly.

4. *Enforce existing speech laws without exceeding them.* When building out their terms of service, financial companies should try to mimic the rights afforded to users under the law. We do not need financial companies to police our online speech. Instead of censoring online content, financial companies should enforce existing law and leave

it to courts and lawmakers to decide whether additional restrictions make sense.

We already have an example of how this could work. While today PayPal may have earned a reputation for being quick to shutter accounts, for a time at least they committed to a different path. In March 2012, in response to civil society pressure described earlier in this book, PayPal updated its position on erotic e-books to be far more permissive: text-only books would not be censored, whole categories of books would not be censored, and PayPal used the Supreme Court's Miller test to define what counted as obscenity.[5]

This is practical, low-hanging fruit to be had for financial companies looking to embrace neutrality and accessibility. And companies can embrace these concepts now, without waiting for any change to the law.

These aren't new ideas. In 2021, my EFF colleague Jillian York and I organized a coalition of civil liberties organizations from around the globe to urge PayPal and its subsidiary Venmo to stop wrongfully closing accounts. "We are calling on PayPal and its subsidiary Venmo to provide more transparency and accountability around its policies and practices for account freezes and closures," we wrote, and then listed many of the principles—transparency reports, meaningful appeals, and meaningful notice—that are in these recommendations.[6]

Unfortunately, as of this writing, PayPal has not responded and has continued to refuse to meet with the civil liberties community about these concerns.

The inspiration for all of this work came from the Santa Clara Principles on Transparency and Content Moderation. Originally developed in May 2018 at a conference organized by law professor Eric Goldman and held at Santa Clara Law School, the Santa Clara Principles reflected an agreement among many academics, organizations, and advocates working to bring accountability to internet companies.[7] These principles urged internet companies to bake human rights into their terms of service and policies.

"It wasn't that these ideas had never been discussed at the companies, because there are always good people who are working in trust and safety especially," Jillian explained to me when we met in 2024 to talk about the origin of the Santa Clara Principles. "They would bring these ideas to upper-level folks, executives, and get brushed off, because the cost of doing these things is high. The literal costs, and also the personnel cost."

Thanks to public advocacy and direct outreach by Jillian and others in the coalition, the Santa Clara Principles were adopted by many of the biggest hosts of content online, including the Apple App Store, Facebook, GitHub, the Google Play Store, Instagram, LinkedIn, Medium, Reddit, Snap, Tumblr, Twitter, and YouTube. The companies adopted these practices to stand up for users' speech rights even though they were not required to do so by any laws.

LEARNING FROM OTHER INDUSTRIES

While we are still in the very early days of developing industry-wide agreements about financial companies respecting and upholding free expression concerns for their account holders, we can look to other industries for inspiration. Big Tech's adoption of the Santa Clara Principles is one example. My favorite example of an industry creating a culture of defending free expression is the newspaper industry.

The newspaper industry faced intense public and legal pressure from the Nixon administration in the 1970s to stop the publication of the Pentagon Papers, a massive trove of classified documents that were leaked by whistleblower Daniel Ellsberg to reporter Neil Sheehan of the *New York Times* as well as to other reporters. The documents were a damning indictment of America's ineptitude, brutality, and failures in the war in Vietnam, and the Nixon administration helped draw even more attention to the many-thousands-page report by trying to sue the *New York Times* and *Washington Post* to stop them from publishing. This resulted in a whirlwind Supreme Court case that created strong protections for a free press in the United States, further humiliated the Nixon administration, and catapulted the policy issues of the Pentagon Papers into the forefront of the public conversation.

Many people know that side of it; I was grateful to spend years working with Daniel Ellsberg on the board of the Freedom of the Press Foundation, and I always appreciated hearing him recount the details of that wild fight. But there's another piece to that story that's perhaps more useful to the financial industry thinking about content issues today.

After a resounding victory in the Supreme Court, *New York Times* general counsel James Goodale created the First Amendment Bar to organize commercial lawyers to understand and defend the First Amendment. For thirty-five years he trained lawyers to understand and strategically defend their clients through his annual Communications Law Seminar. Goodale wrote about it in his memoir *Fighting for the Press: The Inside Story of the Pentagon Papers and Other Battles*: "The organization of the First Amendment Bar had been a great success. The attendance of the seminar grew until it averaged over 300 participants every year. The lawyers and the press who attended the seminar, which I ran annually, exceeded 9,000 (without discounting the same lawyers who attend it annually) in that period of time."[8]

The First Amendment Bar and the annual conference helped connect, inspire, and train lawyers across the press and related industries. It armed them to spot and fight back against inappropriate government requests, and to understand their legal work as part of a larger battle for free expression rights.

When we think about how the financial industry should respond to growing pressure (internally and especially externally) to police the speech of account holders and shutter accounts for perceived reputation risk, the organization and training of media lawyers serves as an inspiration.

All of these best practices exist against the backdrop of government regulation and government scrutiny. It is difficult for financial companies to push back against government pressure, as it was difficult for media companies to push back against the Nixon administration's efforts to censor the news. Just as media lawyers have been doing for thirty years, the financial industry should come together and work strategically to push back against inappropriate government pressure to shutter law-abiding accounts—ideally, as a united front.

FINANCIAL COMPANIES CHARTING A NEW COURSE

Financial companies are under pressure to act as censors of online content, but they don't have to give in to that pressure. There's an opportunity for financial companies to chart a new course. Standing up for the expressive rights of their customers can become a part of the larger conversation about corporate responsibility.

I was particularly inspired after meeting Cathy Beardsley, the CEO of Segpay, a payment facilitator that focuses on adult content. For twenty years, Beardsley has been working to help bring financial access to content that is often barred from traditional financial systems. Even though she's an executive at a financial company, she understands the value of creators expressing themselves. When I described the type of account shutdowns that True Naked Yoga faced, she was quick to speak out against it, telling me, "I don't believe financial companies should be policing online speech in that way."

Even though Segpay has faced its own challenges getting access to financial services, Beardsley told me she's worked hard over two decades to develop relationships with banks and with Visa and Mastercard so that they will confirm transactions for her company. She hopes regulators will come to appreciate that financial companies shouldn't be policing speech. "If it's legal, we should have the opportunity [to process it], just as any other business."

Beardsley flew to Washington with members of the Free Speech Coalition to educate elected officials about this issue. She met with lawmakers and explained how damaging it was to her company to face barriers to financial access. This work of educating lawmakers about the importance of neutral, accessible financial systems is key to paving a future where financial companies don't face pressure to act as censors. Financial companies committed to neutrality should join Beardsley and the Free Speech Coalition in these efforts.

This fight also extends beyond Washington. Experts within the financial space who understand that their services are a form of basic infrastructure must present the issue to the press, law enforcement, and the public. Educating the public is the only way to stave off calls for financial companies to act as censors.

Finally, financial companies can begin to organize themselves to safeguard human rights in the way other industries have. By supporting one another and engaging directly with the civil liberties community, financial companies can stand up to censorship requests that should never involve them.

TEN

WHAT THE GOVERNMENT CAN DO ABOUT FINANCIAL CENSORSHIP

Government intervention is the most important and most delicate tool for reining in financial censorship. It's notable that government intervention isn't always helpful for this problem. As I've documented in numerous examples throughout this book, government officials are too often leaning on financial companies to shutter accounts as a form of censorship by proxy. Plus, the legislative process is messy. Regardless of the noble intentions behind it, a bill can be picked apart by special interests and negotiated into a shadow of its former self before it's ever signed into law. That's especially true at the federal level where the stakes are so high.

Writing any law to end financial censorship would also mean wading into an area that implicates evolving technology *and* state surveillance interests that are not aligned with consumer concerns. That is often a recipe for terrible law.

Nonetheless, government rules are the single most powerful antidote we have against this problem. That's because if we don't fix the underlying laws and regulations, financial censorship will be a persistent issue. Even if a financial company commits to neutrality and adopts the best practices suggested in this book, those practices can be abandoned in a changing political moment or with any leadership transition at the company. And the problem will likely snowball in the coming years as our financial companies increasingly morph into technology companies.

Right now, we don't have a robust, functioning financial marketplace in which consumers have ample choices. Brian Knight and Trace Mitchell, respectively the director of innovation and governance and research associate with George Mason University's Mercatus Center at the time, wrote a 2019 paper describing the unique benefits that banks face as a "regime of privilege."

> Given the barriers to entry that face would-be competition, the regulatory advantages banks enjoy over nonbanks, and the broad use of government-provided bank-exclusive services, it is reasonable to assume that banks receive considerable government support. This support constitutes a major difference between banking and most other industries, and it should perhaps give us pause when banks seek to de facto regulate by cutting off access to the services for which they have received government benefit.[1]

In short, banks enjoy special privileges and benefits (like government-backed insurance), and there are a lot of barriers to entry for start-up companies wanting to enter the financial space. The financial industry today has a handful of powerful companies who can set policies that smaller companies must adopt if they want to participate in the ecosystem. So we can't expect a robust, competitive market to fix this problem. We've got to fix the soft areas of the law that allow financial censorship to occur.

Before we dig into the legislative strategies, it's worth remembering that the government bears a lot of blame for the current state of affairs. Indeed, many cases of financial censorship have been *directly caused* by the government getting involved. US government agents have a history of leaning on financial institutions as an extralegal means to police speech, or of setting regulatory priorities that focus on enforcement and account shutdowns while ignoring civil liberties.

So to kick off this series of recommendations, I will talk about how the government can *do less*, meaning exerting less pressure on financial institutions to engage in censorship. Then I will turn to other policy mechanisms that will ensure neutrality, improve transparency, and align incentives so that financial companies won't be inclined to act as censors. I have organized these principles as follows:

1. End government pressure around financial censorship
2. Codify neutrality into our financial system

3. Protect financial institutions from inappropriate liability
4. Align conflicting laws
5. Require transparency
6. Require notice and appeal processes
7. Enforce protections from financial censorship

These principles have interdependencies. A law prohibiting financial censorship will be most effective if we also put in place mechanisms for transparency (to ensure transgressions are identifiable) and tools for enforcement (so that violators are held accountable). So while each of these ideas would be a massive leap forward in protecting our rights if adopted individually, the most effective way to truly end financial censorship is to adopt all of these concepts as a package.

End Government Pressure Around Financial Censorship

The first and most necessary step to ending financial censorship is for the government to adopt a policy of neutrality for itself. This means that government agents, including law enforcement, elected officials, and regulators, must not pressure financial institutions to shutter the accounts of law-abiding individuals and institutions.

Of course, heavy-handed government coercion of financial institutions was found unconstitutional by the Supreme Court.[2] While the law in this area is still evolving, there are currently many forms of government pressure that don't rise to the legal definition of coercion. Those types of pressure on financial intermediaries must also stop if we are to see a neutral and accessible financial system.

This does not stop the government from working with the banking industry to investigate illegal activity or freeze the funds of people it suspects are engaged in illegal activity. If the government would like to see certain accounts frozen or shuttered, it can go to a judge and get a court order.

Codify Neutrality into Our Financial System

We should also change the law to make it illegal for financial institutions to deny services to or end services for people because they are exercising their rights under the First Amendment.[3] We can see inspiration for this in California's Leonard Law, which prohibits private, nonreligious universities in California from disciplining students for engaging in activities and speech that are protected by the First Amendment.[4] Students shouldn't face academic probation or other penalties for attending a public protest or writing a fiery op-ed against the school administration—and none of us should lose our bank accounts or credit cards for doing those things.

Protect Financial Institutions from Inappropriate Liability

It may seem counterintuitive that a book that contains so much criticism of the financial industry would also argue for any additional liability protections for financial companies. But ending this form of censorship is going to require extending some liability protection to financial companies in order to allow them to act as neutral conduits.

As we saw in the lawsuit trying to hold Visa accountable for illegal activity on Pornhub, there is currently a risk that financial institutions may face legal action for merely providing payment services to a website that is later accused of violating the law.[5] Even when a case is later dismissed, the fear of getting dragged in front of the court on liability charges can motivate financial institutions to be extremely conservative in their business practices. After all, a financial company would need to pay lawyers to get themselves extracted from a lawsuit.

Thus, we need legislation to make it clear that payment intermediaries, banks, and credit card companies are not liable for the activities of the people and institutions who use their services. By amending the law, we could ensure that financial companies are only liable when they fail to follow existing banking regulations or a court order or when they knowingly contribute to illegal activity. This is in line with how platforms that merely host user speech (like many social media companies) are generally shielded from liability for that speech by Section 230 of the Communications Decency Act—an oft-misunderstood bit of law that has been integral to the United States becoming an innovation powerhouse.[6]

Align Conflicting Laws

There are currently financial laws that are specifically designed to make financial companies liable for the activities of the people using their services—such as our approach to economic sanctions, which holds financial institutions liable if a sanctions-violating transaction slips through their network, even if the financial institution was unaware at the time of the transaction. Any law trying to provide liability protection to financial institutions would need to preempt conflicting state financial laws and take precedence over other federal laws.

This would also be an opportunity to address preemption and conflicts in other laws, including how IEEPA currently overrides the antidiscrimination protections of the Equal Credit Opportunity Act and other antidiscrimination laws. We could align these conflicts to ensure that banks can be held liable for discriminatory policies that deny services to people and organizations.

In general, aligning conflicting laws is about incentivizing financial companies to offer basic services to all law-abiding account holders by default while ending penalties against financial companies that keep accounts open. This would be an absolute sea change from our existing approach, which encourages financial companies to shutter accounts both directly and subtly.

Require Transparency

Public accountability is one of the best tools we have for holding the banking industry accountable. By creating reporting requirements for financial institutions and making those reports public, we can spur public conversations about financial censorship, measure the scale of financial censorship, and check to see whether other regulatory interventions are effective.

Financial institutions should be required to report how many accounts are closed or denied due to reasons unrelated to fraud or credit worthiness as well as when particular transactions are blocked due to content. Reports should go to government regulators who can look for patterns and report to Congress. To go a step further, financial institutions could be required or in other ways incentivized to publicly post these numbers at least annually. As part of this reporting, the financial institution could also report whether it received any form of request regarding the accounts in question and provide information on who made that request (whether it was a banking partner, an advocacy group, or a government official). Providing aggregate annual numbers won't endanger the privacy of individual account holders or jeopardize any investigations.

Another key part of transparency is ensuring that there is transparency toward the account holder about why an account was frozen, closed, or denied, unless doing so would violate the law or a court order. This gives account holders insight into why they were targeted and forces financial institutions to explain their decisions.

In some cases, the government may seek to prohibit disclosure of the reasons, claiming risks to national security or criminal investigations. Regulation should require a strong showing to the court before any gag order is issued and should otherwise require financial institutions to provide an explicit reason to the account holder promptly.[7]

Require Notice and Appeal Processes

One of the patterns we see in cases of financial censorship is account holders feeling helpless, unable to speak to anyone at the company that is shutting them down. Often account closures happen quickly—in some instances, with no notice at all—and account holders spend hours attempting to navigate useless customer service help lines to try to get accounts restored, often to no avail.

In general, account holders should be notified before accounts are closed or transactions blocked. The account holder should be able to appeal a decision swiftly after an account is closed or frozen, before someone in the company who has the authority to reverse the decision. This tracks with the rights outlined in New York's proposed Banking Bill of Rights.[8]

This in no way prevents financial institutions from closing or refusing accounts in cases of suspected fraud or identity theft, or where the account holder's credit worthiness drops below the financial institution's acceptable risk margins.

Enforce Protections from Financial Censorship

No regulation, no matter how perfectly and artfully constructed, will prompt change unless there's an appropriate method for enforcing that regulation. When thinking about how to enforce the regulatory approaches above, policymakers should consider:

- Creating substantial penalties to ensure the rights described above are enforced
- Creating a private right of action, so that individual account holders whose rights are violated have an opportunity to hold financial institutions accountable
- Ensuring a regulatory body has the specific task of investigating and enforcing instances of financial censorship

BEYOND ENDING CENSORSHIP

Adopting any of the above principles into law could make a substantial difference in undoing the damage of financial censorship.

But censorship isn't the only problem facing our financial system. We've also seen incursion after incursion on financial privacy rights. At this point, it's pretty much impossible to use our financial system without sacrificing data privacy to numerous companies as well as to the government.

Addressing the problems of financial privacy is a connected but far more complicated topic, and beyond the scope of this book. But if we are talking about fixing financial laws, I must at least mention it. Financial surveillance is the bedrock of financial censorship. In addition to providing fair and neutral access to the financial system, we should remove the invasive surveillance of our financial lives.

We must also recognize the unique roles of cash and cryptocurrency, which have shown themselves to operate as powerful anti-censorship technologies that can serve consumers who are debanked inappropriately. In our financial system, which too often gravitates toward centralization and corporate control, cryptocurrency and cash offer decentralized, censorship-resistant alternatives. Lawmakers should reject efforts to ban these technologies and ensure these tools will be available to future generations.

FROM PRINCIPLES TO LAWS

Lawmakers and regulators have already attempted to craft legislative language that reflects some of these principles. In New York,

Assemblymember Zohran Mamdani introduced a Banking Bill of Rights that would require financial institutions to explain to customers why negative decisions were made about their accounts and provide them with a way of appealing those decisions.[9]

Former comptroller of the currency Brian Brooks put forth the Fair Access to Banking Rule, which would require banks to make decisions about individual accounts rather than reject whole categories of customers.[10] While the rule was later abandoned, lawmakers on the federal level have attempted to advance the same idea.[11] US senator Kevin Cramer (R-ND) introduced a Fair Access to Banking Act, which tries to bring Brooks's access rule into federal law.[12] Also on the federal level, Senator Jeff Merkley is promoting the SAFER Banking Act to prompt federally regulated financial companies to provide services to cannabis organizations allowed by state law.[13]

Right now, these efforts are largely disconnected. But we can understand them across the backdrop of financial censorship and see how each of these proposals might have made a difference for some of the people profiled in this book. While the backers of these proposals may not consider themselves working together, all of these efforts are part of a movement to make the financial system more accessible and accountable. Each of these concrete proposals offers a pathway to make our system more fair, available, and neutral.

As the public becomes increasingly aware of the dangers of financial censorship, we can hope more lawmakers and regulators will take up this cause. These proposals can serve as the beginning of a larger effort to realign the financial system so that it stands with its users, not just the banks and government agencies.

CONCLUSION

DISRUPTING THE POWER TO PUNISH

This is a book about speech and finance. But through the course of writing it, I've come to appreciate that it's about something else: power.

Financial companies have incredible power to punish speakers. These companies use perceived terms of service violations, automated filtering for "reputational risk," flagging of "high-risk" businesses, and blunt, inaccurate screening for economic sanctions to restrict and close accounts. Through these policies, financial companies don't only have power over individual accounts; they have the power to punish or disrupt communities, movements, and whole swaths of online speech.

Account holders, by contrast, are almost powerless. Faced with these denials and restrictions, they face an uphill battle even trying to get answers about why their accounts were shuttered. Appealing those decisions is more often than not a losing proposition. Only garnering substantial publicity is likely to make a difference in reinstating accounts.

But there's another, murkier power at play: government pressure. Financial companies are heavily influenced by government priorities for restricting certain accounts. We see elements of this in programs like Operation Choke Point, a government campaign that pressured financial companies to shutter the accounts of certain industries. There are also specific cases that illustrate the pressure government officials place on financial institutions, including Sheriff Dart pressuring credit card companies to stop payments for Backpage.com, New York State Department of Financial Services superintendent Maria Vullo coercing financial institutions to end services to the National Rifle Association, and Senator Lieberman pressuring companies to cut off services to WikiLeaks.

Those are examples we can point to. We can only wonder at how many other examples are never made public, and how many of the account closures we are tracking are actually government censorship by proxy.

The impact of this financial exclusion is punishing people and organizations who are exercising rights that would otherwise be protected under the First Amendment. We've heard the stories of creators, activists, journalists, small business entrepreneurs, and nonprofit leaders who are losing access to the financial system because of who they are and what they do. And as we've seen, those most likely to be impacted are often from communities that are denied power in our society.

Nonetheless, there are still those who try to justify financial discrimination as a useful policy tool that could, theoretically, be wielded to achieve specific outcomes. So let's talk directly about the most common justifications for supporting financial censorship.

JUSTIFICATION 1: Criminals shouldn't have access to banking services because they'll use those services to break the law.

Financial censorship refers to shuttering the accounts of people and organizations engaged in legal speech or activity. It's not about criminals at all. None of the recommendations in this book would in any way stop financial companies from shuttering or restricting the accounts of criminals. In instances of illegal activity, law enforcement officials can ask a court to freeze accounts.

JUSTIFICATION 2: People I don't agree with shouldn't have access to financial services.

Confronted with the stories of many people who have lost their financial services through no fault of their own, it can be tempting to try to carve out an argument that favors only people you agree with. Some might argue that the people you like and agree with should have financial services, but other people, especially people you strongly disagree with or even find abhorrent, shouldn't, even if they are not breaking any laws.

This is a dangerous and short-sighted approach because the systems of financial exclusion that are turned against our foes today can be turned back on us tomorrow. This means that even if you trust the folks who have power currently to agree with your impression of who shouldn't have access to banking services, you should be ready for the tide to shift when a different group of people has the power to make those decisions. After all, it is always a bad idea to expect that current power structures will never change.

One thing should be abundantly clear if you have gotten this far into the book: Financial companies don't do a good job of policing online speech. They don't have the expertise to make those decisions, and they don't have the right incentives to do the job carefully. In story after story, we see them shuttering the accounts of people who should never have had their accounts singled out and then making any form of appeal nearly impossible. Given all this, we can't expect financial services to police speech—even for people we don't personally like.

A widely available, neutral financial system is part of a fair and open society. Just as we expect our court system and voting system to be fair and neutral, just as we expect utilities and communications systems to not discriminate against certain customers, so we should also expect basic financial services to be available and nondiscriminatory.

JUSTIFICATION 3: There's no other way to punish bad people because existing laws aren't strong enough.

It is true that restricting the accounts of disfavored people and organizations is unbelievably efficient. It can happen in the blink of an eye with hardly any oversight. By comparison, a criminal or civil prosecution is ponderously slow and complicated, and there are some types of speech that are distasteful but don't rise to the level of breaking the law.

Nonetheless, financial companies are uniquely bad at making content decisions and shouldn't be trusted to police the speech of account holders. Financial companies don't have the guidance of the prior precedents and due process protections embedded in our court system. While I wouldn't argue that social media companies and search engines are doing a great job on these topics, those companies built up teams and developed policies around allowable speech over many years, and many of those companies worked closely with the civil liberties community to refine those policies. Plus, they host individual user accounts and user-generated speech. These tech companies are far better suited to create policies about allowable speech than distant financial companies.

A helpful lens for thinking about content moderation issues: The closer a company is to hosting speech or guiding users to accessing speech, the more appropriate it is for that company to be developing policies about policing that speech. The more distant a company is, including any company providing infrastructure services, the less appropriate it is for those companies to be weighing in on specific speech choices. That's why it's appropriate for a newspaper to make detailed editorial decisions about what it prints, but it would be inappropriate for an internet service provider to have policies about which legal websites customers should access.

JUSTIFICATION 4: People losing their financial services probably did something to deserve it.

People lose their financial services all the time even when they have done nothing wrong. This book includes story after story of people who wrongly lost their accounts. We must stop assuming that the punishment of financial exclusion is indicative of some underlying wrongdoing.

JUSTIFICATION 5: Financial companies are private corporations; they shouldn't be forced to provide services to anyone.

Our existing financial system is not a robust, functional market. Banks enjoy a "regime of privilege" provided by the government that makes it easier for incumbents to persist while creating barriers for newcomers to enter the market.[1] Consumers don't have abundant choices. The choices they do have are deeply enmeshed with one another; getting cut off from one financial service often leads to getting dropped by other financial services. Payment processors are beholden to banks and credit card companies, and all of the financial services are skittish about regulatory scrutiny.

Given the broken marketplace, we can't expect the ship to right itself. We need to help guide the financial system toward more neutrality. The vast majority of that work can be accomplished by realigning incentives and changing public perception around the role of financial intermediaries. But truly ending the abuses of the financial system will mean going the final step and requiring financial neutrality in our laws.

GROUNDED IN FAIRNESS AND TOLERANCE

Beyond the specific proposals discussed in this book is an appeal to understand financial access as a necessity, not a privilege that can be revoked when it suits the agenda of those who have power.

What's really at stake here is the ideals of our democratic society. Just like free and fair elections, an independent judiciary, access to knowledge, travel freedom, and political tolerance, neutrality in the financial system is part of creating a fair society that is governed by rule of law.

Financial censorship, by contrast, is taking a chapter from the playbook of repressive regimes. Under the guise of promoting national security or upholding financial regulations, financial companies are closing the accounts of people who have done nothing wrong. As we've seen throughout this book, the people who suffer the most are often those already marginalized: immigrant communities, activists, journalists, those engaged in controversial but legal speech, and those working in start-up industries that challenge existing power structures. Financial censorship is a powerful tool for punishing otherwise legal speakers, and it's a tool often wielded in secret.

The debate over financial censorship is a debate over the kind of society we want to be. We cannot purport to be a democracy that safeguards free expression while handing financial companies the power to punish those speakers that challenge the status quo.

RECOMMENDED READING

Secrets: A Memoir of Vietnam and the Pentagon Papers by Daniel Ellsberg

A Century of Repression: The Espionage Act and the Freedom of the Press by Ralph Engelman and Carey Shenkman

Chokepoint Capitalism: How Big Tech and Big Content Captured Creative Labor Markets and How We'll Win Them Back by Rebecca Giblin and Cory Doctorow

Check Your Financial Privilege: Inside the Global Bitcoin Revolution by Alex Gladstein

Fighting for the Free Press: The Inside Story of the Pentagon Papers and Other Battles by James Goodale

Guilty of Journalism: The Political Case Against Julian Assange by Kevin Gosztola

This Machine Kills Secrets: How Wikileakers, Cypherpunks, and Hacktivists Aim to Free the World's Information by Andy Greenberg

No Place to Hide: Edward Snowden, the NSA, and the U.S. Surveillance State by Glenn Greenwald

Police and the Empire City: Race and the Origins of Modern Policing in New York by Matthew Guariglia

Bottoms Up and the Devil Laughs: A Journey Through the Deep State by Kerry Howley

Hacks, Leaks, and Revelations: The Art of Analyzing Hacked and Leaked Data by Micah Lee

Code: And Other Laws of Cyberspace, Version 2.0 by Lawrence Lessig

README.txt: A Memoir by Chelsea Manning

Bitcoin and Cryptocurrency Technologies: A Comprehensive Introduction by Arvind Narayanan, Joseph Bonneau, Edward Felten, Andrew Miller, and Steven Goldfeder

Permanent Record by Edward Snowden

The Master Switch: The Rise and Fall of Information Empires by Tim Wu

Silicon Values: The Future of Free Speech Under Surveillance Capitalism by Jillian York

ACKNOWLEDGMENTS

This book was created with the support and generosity of many people from my community and the larger digital rights movement. While there are more people than I could possibly name, I want to offer my appreciation to a few who were instrumental in the book's creation:

Marta Belcher, my longtime collaborator who has cowritten so many blog posts with me and who helped me think through countless technology policy issues, especially around cryptocurrency. I truly could not have written this book without her partnership every step of the way.

Cindy Cohn, my former boss at EFF and longtime inspiration. She offered guidance and frank feedback at many key moments in the writing process. She also trusted me to help her edit her book—and through that process, I learned many of the lessons that were key to writing this one.

My former colleagues and ongoing friends Seth Schoen and Parker Higgins. They spent countless hours reading early drafts of this book and offering me feedback over long phone calls, ultimately helping me shape my arguments and the structure of the book.

My partner and most steadfast supporter, Anton Fulmen, who probably had no idea on our first date all those years ago that I'd ask him to read hundreds and hundreds of pages of early-draft text. Anton was unfailingly generous and thoughtful in his feedback, and his faith in me helped me believe in myself.

Several close friends and family members read early drafts and provided detailed feedback that ensured the book was far stronger, including my parents Jan and Judi Reitman, Harry Pottash, and John Stanley.

I owe gratitude to Ola Tucker, an exceptional financial attorney, and Jim Wheaton, an incredible First Amendment attorney, who both reviewed early drafts of this book. Their expertise challenged and refined many of my points, and the book was much stronger for their feedback.

My superb agent, Madison Smartt Bell of Ayesha Pande Literary Agency, believed in this book from day one and skillfully guided me through placing this at a publishing company aligned with my values.

I was deeply lucky to work with one of the foremost literary editors in the field today, Joanna Green of Beacon Press. My book is far better thanks to her deft hand. Deepest thanks also to Beacon managing editor Susan Lumenello, whose meticulous eye and steady guidance polished the manuscript to its finest form.

This book relied heavily on the personal stories of individuals who struggled with financial censorship or challenged the power of financial institutions. Those stories are the crux of this book. I literally could not have written this book without their courageous choice to share their stories. Thank you to Debra Cleaver, Marty Stolar, Ambassador Sam Brownback and Matt Goddard, Mnar Adley, Kristinn Hrafnsson, Trevor Timm, Mark Coker, Sinclair Sexsmith, Gabriel Bienczycki, Tom Severini, Allie Eve Knox, John Gilmore, Matthew Schweich, Justin Bunton, Jackie Bryant, Muhammad Ali Mojaradi, Shahroo Yazdani, Council Member Shahana Hanif, and Amany Killawi.

A number of people shared their personal stories, but I was unable to name them in the book, either because their story did not end up in the final draft or because they had to speak off the record. I am grateful for the time you spent with me and your courage in sharing your story.

My former colleagues Jillian York, Kurt Opsahl, Joe Bonneau, Dave Maass, Marcia Hofmann, Cory Doctorow, Micah Lee, and David Greene offered guidance, interviews, and much-needed reality checks at various points throughout this process.

There were also a range of experts I turned to, both for their understanding of the policy issues and/or for their understanding of various aspects of the book-writing process. I offer deepest gratitude to Lia Holland, John Bergmayer, Vinhcent Le, Mike Stabile, Dr. Val Webber, Cathy Beardsley, Art Neil, Erika Lee, Alex Gladstein, Peter Van Valkenburgh, Albert Fox Cahn, Carey Shenkman, Burhan Carroll, Anthony Arnove, Brett Soloman, Rebecca MacKinnon, Daniel Ellsberg, Moira Meltzer-Cohen, Laura Harper, Lamya Agarwala, Mark Graham, and Margaret Flowers.

NOTES

Notes and background are based on interviews with the following: Mnar Adley, November 8, 2023 (Zoom); Lamya Agarwala, July 23, 2024 (Zoom); Cathy Beardsley, August 22, 2024 (Zoom); John Bergmayer, May 29, 2024 (Zoom); Gabriel Bienczycki, December 23, 2022–January 4, 2023 (email); Eliana Bisgaard-Church, August 14, 2024 (Zoom); Ambassador Sam Brownback, March 22, 2023 (Zoom); Jackie Bryant, April 12, 2024 (Zoom); Justin Bunton, November 8, 2023 (Zoom); Albert Fox Cahn, December 5, 2022 (Zoom); Burhan Carroll, July 23, 2024 (Zoom); Josephine Chew, January 5–11, 2024 (email); Debra Cleaver, March 9, 2023 (Zoom); Cindy Cohn, September 19, 2023 (Zoom); Mark Coker, April 13, 2023 (Zoom); Seth Eisen, September 3–November 8, 2024 (email); John Gilmore, November 13, 2023 (in person); Alex Gladstein, February 20, 2024 (Zoom); Matt Goddard, March 15, 2023 (Zoom); Council Member Shahana Hanif, July 9, 2024 (Zoom); Lia Holland, December 14, 2022 (Zoom); Kristinn Hrafnsson, October 12, 2023 (Zoom); Amany Killawi, August 16, 2024 (Zoom); Allie Eve Knox, April 19, 2023 (Zoom); Vinhcent Le, December 19, 2022 (Zoom); Muhammad Ali Mojaradi, June 6, 2024 (Zoom); Matthew Schweich, January 16, 2024 (Zoom); Tom Severini, December 23, 2022–January 4, 2023 (email); Sinclair Sexsmith, May 2, 2023 (Zoom); Carey Shenkman, July 13, 2024 (in person); Mike Stabile, April 28, 2023 (Zoom); Martin "Marty" Stolar, November 2, 2023 (Zoom); Trevor Timm, August 2, September 11, and September 20, 2023 (Zoom); Peter Van Valkenburg, August 12, 2024 (Zoom); Dr. Val Webber, May 3, 2023 (Zoom); Shahroo Yazdani, June 26, 2024 (Zoom); and Jillian York, February 23, 2034 (Zoom).

INTRODUCTION: FINANCIAL EXCLUSION AS PUNISHMENT

1. Financial Crimes Enforcement Network, "Financial Institution Definition," https://www.fincen.gov/financial-institution-definition, accessed October 29, 2024.

2. Margaret Atwood, *The Handmaid's Tale* (Boston: Houghton Mifflin, 1986), 174–79.

CHAPTER 1: SILENCING POLITICAL SPEECH AND ACTIVISTS

1. Debra Cleaver (@debracleaver), "Today I went to buy something mundane on Amazon. Card rejected. Tried another card. Also rejected. Logged into @ChaseSupport. Saw that all 4 of my accounts are closed. No explanation why," Twitter, June 8, 2021, https://x.com/debracleaver/status/1402426559391174659.

2. Debra Cleaver (@debracleaver), "have i mentioned yet that they told me over the phone that they closed my accounts because a 'wholly owned chase subsidiary' terminated its relationship with me, so chase followed suit? they won't tell me the name of the affiliate, due to 'consumer privacy laws,'" Twitter, June 8, 2021, https://x.com/debracleaver/status/1402483421574688774.

3. Debra Cleaver (@debracleaver), "i pointed out that i am the consumer in question, and that i am waiving my own privacy, but the woman was unmoved. so apparently 'consumer privacy laws' now exist to protect me from my own financial information. fascinating," Twitter, June 8, 2021, https://x.com/debracleaver/status/1402483422895902721.

4. Federal Deposit Insurance Corporation (FDIC), "Joint Statement on Bank Secrecy Act Due Diligence Requirements for Customers Who May Be Considered Politically Exposed Persons," news release, August 21, 2020, https://www.fdic.gov/news/press-releases/2020/pr20092a.pdf.

5. Transparency International, "Wolfsberg Group Issues Statement on Corruption," news release, March 12, 2007, https://www.transparency.org/en/press/20070312-wolfsberg-group-issues-statement-on-corruption.

6. "Wolfsberg Guidance on Politically Exposed Persons (PEPs)," Wolfsberg Group, 2017, https://db.wolfsberg-group.org/assets/9c6630de-69a8-4f55-9289-4db938938e34/Wolfsberg%20Guidance%20on%20PEPs.pdf.

7. Nic Sanford Belgard, "The Land at the Center of Cop City and Why We Must Defend It," Indigenous Peoples Powers Project, March 8, 2023, https://www.ip3action.org/the-land-at-the-center-of-cop-city-and-why-we-must-defend-it/.

8. Sean Keenan and Joseph Goldstein, "A New Front Line in the Debate over Policing: A Forest near Atlanta," *New York Times*, March 4, 2023, https://www.nytimes.com/2023/03/04/us/cop-city-atlanta-police-training.html.

9. Atlanta Public Training Center, "About," https://www.atltrainingcenter.com/about, accessed October 29, 2024.

10. Atlanta Public Training Center, "Impact on Surrounding Neighborhoods," https://www.atltrainingcenter.com/about, accessed October 29, 2024.

11. Micah Herskind, "This Is the Atlanta Way: A Primer on Cop City," *Scalawag*, May 1, 2023, https://scalawagmagazine.org/2023/05/cop-city-atlanta-history-timeline/; Keenan and Goldstein, "New Front Line."

12. Chloe Kim, "'Cop City' Activist Manuel Paez Terán Shot 57 Times in Atlanta, Autopsy Says," BBC News, April 20, 2023, https://www.bbc.com/news/world-us-canada-65340456.

13. Cara Tabachnik, "What We Know About Atlanta's 'Cop City' and the Standoff Between Police and Protestors," CBS News, March 6, 2023, https://www.cbsnews.com/news/atlanta-protests-cop-city-georgia-state-of-emergency-forest-defenders/.

14. Sarah Taitz and Shaiba Rather, "How Officials in Georgia Are Suppressing Political Protest as 'Domestic Terrorism,'" ACLU, March 24, 2023, https://www.aclu.org/news/national-security/how-officials-in-georgia-are-suppressing-political-protest-as-domestic-terrorism.

15. Emma James, "EXCLUSIVE—REVEALED: Atlanta Antifa Terror Suspect Worked as a Production Assistant for CNN and Is Daughter of UK Foreign Office Consultant and New Jersey-Based Chinese Media Tycoon," *Daily Mail*, January 23, 2023, archived by the Wayback Machine of the Internet Archive, January 23, 2023, https://web.archive.org

/web/20230123222323/https://www.dailymail.co.uk/news/article-11667905/Antifa-terror-suspect-daughter-Pharma-China-giant-British-Foreign-Office-consultant.html.

16. Nick Pinto, "Why Did Chase Bank Cancel This NYC Cop City Protestor's Accounts?" *Hell Gate NYC*, April 8, 2023, https://hellgatenyc.com/chase-bank-cancels-cop-city-protesters-accounts/.

17. Sanction Scanner, "Adverse Media Screening for Banks," September 16, 2024, https://www.sanctionscanner.com/blog/importance-of-adverse-media-screening-690.

18. Jenna Lee, "Why Automated Adverse Media Screening Is Essential for AML," *Persona*, last modified October 18, 2024, https://withpersona.com/blog/why-automated-adverse-media-screening-is-essential-for-aml.

19. Office of the Comptroller of the Currency, *Comptroller's Handbook: Bank Supervision Process* (Washington, DC: Office of the Comptroller of the Currency, 2019), archived by the Wayback Machine of the Internet Archive, October 20, 2020, https://web.archive.org/web/20201020005406/https://www.occ.gov/publications-and-resources/publications/comptrollers-handbook/files/bank-supervision-process/pub-ch-bank-supervision-process.pdf.

20. Greg Baer, "How and Why Are Regulators Protecting the Reputation of Banks?" Bank Policy Institute, January 10, 2020, https://bpi.com/how-and-why-are-regulators-protecting-the-reputations-of-banks/#:~:text=%E2%80%9CThe%20nature%20of%20reputation%20risk,reputation%20risk.%E2%80%9D%5B9%5D; Lewis Gaul and Jonathan Jones, "CAMELS Ratings and Their Information Content," Office of the Comptroller of the Currency, January 6, 2021, archived by the Wayback Machine of the Internet Archive, July 6, 2024, https://web.archive.org/web/20240706045211/https://occ.treas.gov/publications-and-resources/publications/economics/working-papers-banking-perf-reg/pub-econ-working-paper-camels-ratings.pdf.

21. Wolfsberg Group, "The Wolfsberg Group Frequently Asked Questions (FAQs) on Negative News Screening," https://db.wolfsberg-group.org/assets/b3652a98-4bc6-4b42-9f05-e378a4adbd95/Negative%20News%20Screening%20FAQs%20(2022).pdf, accessed October 29, 2024.

22. Wolfsberg Group, "The Wolfsberg Group Frequently Asked Questions (FAQs) on Negative News Screening."

23. Wolfsberg Group, "The Wolfsberg Group Frequently Asked Questions (FAQs) on Negative News Screening."

24. Maria T. Vullo, "Guidance on Risk Management Relating to the NRA and Similar Gun Promotion Organizations," Industry Guidance, New York Department of Financial Services, April 19, 2018, https://web.archive.org/web/20240102223520/https://www.dfs.ny.gov/industry_guidance/industry_letters/il20180419_guidance_risk_mgmt_nra_NRA_similar_gun_promotion_orgs_banking_industry.

25. On Petition for Writ of Certiorari at 10, National Rifle Association of America v. Vullo, No. 22-842 (Sup. Ct. July 7, 2023), https://www.supremecourt.gov/DocketPDF/22/22-842/254241/20230207165502328_NRA%20Vullo%20Cert%20Petition%20File.pdf.

26. Governor Andrew Cuomo (@NYGovCuomo), "The NRA is an extremist organization. I urge companies in New York State to revisit any ties they have to the NRA and consider their reputations, and responsibility to the public," Twitter, April 20, 2018, https://x.com/NYGovCuomo/status/987359763825614848.

27. National Rifle Association of America v. Vullo, 602 U.S. 175 (2024), https://supreme.justia.com/cases/federal/us/602/22-842/.

28. Anthony D. Romero, "Why Is the ACLU Representing the NRA Before the US Supreme Court?" ACLU, March 18, 2024, https://www.aclu.org/news/free-speech/why-is-the-aclu-representing-the-nra-before-the-us-supreme-court.

29. Bantam Books, Inc. v. Sullivan, 372 U.S. 58 (1963), https://supreme.justia.com/cases/federal/us/372/58/.

30. *National Rifle Association of America v. Vullo*, 175, 197.

31. John Vecchione, "Courthouse Steps Decision: *NRA v. Vullo*," virtual panel, moderated by Casey Mattox, posted June 10, 2024, Federalist Society, available on YouTube, 1 hr., 34 sec., https://www.youtube.com/watch?v=iC1VIow3EMM&t=2919s.

32. ACLU, "Supreme Court Unanimously Rules in Favor of NRA in Free Speech Case, Upholds First Amendment Rights of All Advocacy Groups," news release, May 30, 2024,

https://www.aclu.org/press-releases/supreme-court-unanimously-rules-in-favor-of-nra-in-free-speech-case-upholds-first-amendment-rights-of-all-advocacy-groups.

CHAPTER 2: JOURNALISM IN THE CROSSHAIRS

1. Matt Taibbi, "PayPal's IndyMedia Wipeout," *Racket News*, May 3, 2022, https://taibbi.substack.com/p/paypals-indymedia-wipeout.

2. *Consortium News*, "About," https://consortiumnews.com/about/, accessed November 11, 2024.

3. Robert Scheer, "No Such Thing as Dissent in the Age of Big Tech," *Scheer Intelligence*, KCRW, May 6, 2022, https://www.kcrw.com/culture/shows/scheer-intelligence/no-such-thing-as-dissent-in-the-age-of-big-tech.

4. Natylie Baldwin, "Ukraine: The Real Zelensky," *Consortium News*, April 29, 2022, https://consortiumnews.com/2022/04/29/ukraine-the-real-zelensky/.

5. Joe Lauria, "Curfew for Anniversary of Odessa Massacre That Sparked Rebellion," *Consortium News*, April 30, 2022, https://consortiumnews.com/2022/04/30/curfew-for-anniversary-of-odessa-massacre-that-sparked-rebellion/.

6. Caitlin Johnstone, "Being Anti-War Isn't Easy," *Consortium News*, April 28, 2022, https://consortiumnews.com/2022/04/28/caitlin-johnstone-being-anti-war-isnt-easy/.

7. Scheer, "No Such Thing as Dissent in the Age of Big Tech."

8. Taibbi, "PayPal's IndyMedia Wipeout"; "PayPal Freezes Funds for Consortium News, an Outlet Critical of U.S. Policy on Ukraine," *Democracy Now!*, May 4, 2022, https://www.democracynow.org/2022/5/4/headlines/paypal_freezes_funds_for_consortium_news_independent_outlet_critical_of_us_policy_on_ukraine; Kim Iversen, "PayPal BANS Independent Anti-War Journalists," *The Hill*, posted May 3, 2022, available on YouTube, https://www.youtube.com/watch?v=joHW1GDn91E; Joe Lauria, "PayPal Backs Down After Outpouring of Support for CN," *Consortium News*, May 4, 2022, https://consortiumnews.com/2022/05/04/paypal-backs-down-after-outpouring-of-support-for-cn/.

9. Lauria, "PayPal Backs Down After Outpouring of Support for CN."

10. Joe Lauria, "'Mistaken' PayPal Email Means CN Is Permanently Banned," *Consortium News*, May 6, 2022, https://consortiumnews.com/2022/05/06/mistaken-paypal-email-means-cn-is-permanently-banned/.

11. Mnar Adley (@MnarMuh), "My official statement on Paypal banning myself, @MintPressNews & our senior staff writer @AlanRMacLeod," Twitter, April 29, 2022, https://x.com/MnarMuh/status/1520113881959522304; Alan MacLeod (@AlanRMacLeod), "On a personal note, there's strong circumstantial evidence that both Mason's nat sec contact and the much-mocked US Disinfo Czar Nina Jankowicz were personally involved in shutting down my own PayPal account in April. Mason proposes doing this to other left-wing journalists," Twitter, June 8, 2022, https://x.com/AlanRMacLeod/status/1534513971344064513.

12. David Z. Morris, "Deplatformed by PayPal, Antiwar Journalists Speak Out," *CoinDesk*, May 23, 2022, https://www.coindesk.com/layer2/2022/05/23/deplatformed-by-paypal-antiwar-journalists-speak-out/.

13. Rosie Gray and Jessica Testa, "The Inside Story of One Website's Defense of Assad," *BuzzFeed News*, October 1, 2013, https://www.buzzfeednews.com/article/rosiegray/the-inside-story-of-one-websites-defense-of-assad.

14. Office of the Press Secretary, "Remarks by the President to the White House Press Corps," news release, August 20, 2012, https://obamawhitehouse.archives.gov/the-press-office/2012/08/20/remarks-president-white-house-press-corps/.

15. Robert Mackey, "Reporter Denies Writing Article That Linked Syrian Rebels to Chemical Attack," *The Lede* (blog), *New York Times*, September 21, 2013, https://archive.nytimes.com/thelede.blogs.nytimes.com/2013/09/21/reporter-denies-writing-article-that-linked-syrian-rebels-to-chemical-attack/.

16. Dale Gavlak and Yahya Ababneh, "Syrians in Ghouta Claim Saudi-Supplied Rebels Behind Chemical Attack," *MintPress News*, August 29, 2013, https://www.mintpressnews.com/syria-ghouta-claim-saudi-supplied-rebels-chemical-attack/168135/.

17. Caleb Howe, "PayPal Blames 'Error' for Policy Change with $2500 'Misinformation' Fines After Elon Musk Calls Them Out," *Mediaite*, October 8, 2022, https://www

.mediaite.com/tech/paypal-blames-error-for-policy-change-with-2500-misinformation-fines-after-elon-musk-calls-them-out/.

18. David Marcus (@davidmarcus), "It's hard for me to openly criticize a company I used to love and gave so much to. But @PayPal's new AUP goes against everything I believe in. A private company now gets to decide to take your money if you say something they disagree with. Insanity. https://paypalobjects.com/marketing/ua/pdf/US/en/acceptableuse-full-110322.pdf," Twitter, October 8, 2022, https://x.com/davidmarcus/status/1578795041719750663.

19. Howe, "PayPal Blames 'Error' for Policy Change with $2500 'Misinformation' Fines After Elon Musk Calls Them Out"; "Top Financial Services, Energy & Commerce Republicans Seek Answers Regarding PayPal's Anti-Free Speech Policy," Financial Services Committee, US House of Representatives, October 18, 2022, https://financialservices.house.gov/news/documentsingle.aspx?documentid=408456.

20. Ben Zeisloft, "New PayPal Policy Lets Company Pull $2,500 from Users' Accounts If They Promote 'Misinformation,'" *Daily Wire*, October 7, 2022, https://www.dailywire.com/news/new-paypal-policy-lets-company-pull-2500-from-users-accounts-if-they-promote-misinformation.

21. Ivana Saric, "PayPal Won't Fine Users for Misinformation Posts, Policy Posted 'in Error,'" *Axios*, October 9, 2022, https://www.axios.com/2022/10/09/paypal-misinformation-fines.

22. Valur Gunnarsson and Mark Tran, "Icelandic PM Becomes World's First Leader to Step Down over Banking System Crisis," *The Guardian*, January 26, 2009, https://www.theguardian.com/world/2009/jan/27/iceland-prime-minister-resignation.

23. Andy Greenberg, "Meet the New Public Face of WikiLeaks: Kristinn Hrafnsson," *Forbes*, December 7, 2010, https://www.forbes.com/sites/andygreenberg/2010/12/07/meet-the-new-public-face-of-wikileaks-kristinn-hrafnsson/.

24. Andie Sophia Fontaine, "Information Is Never Neutral: The Editor of WikiLeaks Breaks His Silence," March 22, 2019, *Reykjavík Grapevine*, https://grapevine.is/mag/feature/2019/03/22/information-is-never-neutral-the-editor-of-wikileaks-breaks-his-silence/.

25. Rachel Slajda, "How Lieberman Got Amazon to Drop WikiLeaks," December 1, 2010, *Talking Points Memo*, https://talkingpointsmemo.com/muckraker/how-lieberman-got-amazon-to-drop-wikileaks.

26. Committee on Homeland Security and Government Affairs, "Amazon Severs Ties with WikiLeaks," news release, US Senate, December 1, 2010, https://www.hsgac.senate.gov/media/dems/amazon-wikileaks/.

27. New York Times Co. v. United States, 403 U.S. 713 (1971), https://supreme.justia.com/cases/federal/us/403/713/.

28. Bartnicki v. Vopper, 532 U.S. 514 (2001), https://supreme.justia.com/cases/federal/us/532/514/.

29. Freedom of the Press Foundation, "Law Professors to DOJ: Drop Assange Prosecution," news release, February 14, 2024, https://freedom.press/issues/law-professors-to-doj-drop-assange-prosecution/.

30. Andrea O'Sullivan, "The Government Is Treating Assange Like a Hacker to Punish His Journalism," *Reason*, April 23, 2019, https://reason.com/2019/04/23/the-government-is-treating-assange-like-a-hacker-to-punish-his-journalism/; Freedom of the Press Foundation, "Law Professors to DOJ."

31. Greg Myre, "How Much Did WikiLeaks Damage U.S. National Security?" NPR, April 12, 2019, https://www.npr.org/2019/04/12/712659290/how-much-did-wikileaks-damage-u-s-national-security; "US Informants Not Harmed by WikiLeaks Releases, Assange Extradition Trial Told," *Press Gazette*, last updated September 30, 2020, https://pressgazette.co.uk/news/us-informants-not-harmed-by-wikileaks-releases-assange-extradition-trial-told/.

32. Parker Higgins, "Press Freedom Coalition Calls on Biden's Justice Dept. to Drop the Assange Prosecution," Freedom of the Press Foundation, February 8, 2021, https://freedom.press/issues/biden-justice-end-assange-prosecution-coalition-letter/.

33. "An Open Letter from Editors and Publishers: Publishing Is Not a Crime," *New York Times*, November 28, 2022, https://www.nytco.com/press/an-open-letter-from-editors-and-publishers-publishing-is-not-a-crime/.

34. Wau Holland Stiftung, "Press Release About the Freezing of the WHS PayPal Account," December 7, 2010, https://wauland.de/en/news/2010/12/press-release-paypal/.

35. Andy Greenberg, "Visa, MasterCard Move to Choke WikiLeaks," *Forbes*, December 7, 2010, https://www.forbes.com/sites/andygreenberg/2010/12/07/visa-mastercard-move-to-choke-wikileaks/?sh=636fa7dc2cad.

36. Joe Rauch, "Bank of America Cuts Off WikiLeaks Payments," Reuters, December 18, 2010, https://www.reuters.com/article/idUSN18133210/.

37. "Updated Statement about WikiLeaks from PayPal General Counsel, John Muller," *PayPal* (blog), December 8, 2010, archived by the Wayback Machine of the Internet Archive December 11, 2010, https://web.archive.org/web/20101211104352/https://www.thepaypalblog.com/2010/12/updated-statement-about-wikileaks-from-paypal-general-counsel-john-muller/. Note this is in contrast to rumors of a statement made by PayPal VP of Platform Osama Bedier, per Dan Goodin: "PayPal Banned WikiLeaks after US Gov Intervention," *The Register*, December 8, 2010, https://www.theregister.com/2010/12/08/paypal_state_dept_wikileaks/.

38. "On August 25, 2011 MasterCard admitted in a letter from its counsel to the European Commission that Lieberman's and King's staffs contacted it regarding Sunshine Press." *DataCell EHF v. Visa Inc.*, Complaint, No. 1:14-cv-01658-GBL-TCB (E.D. Va. Dec. 8, 2014) at 4.

39. WikiLeaks, *WikiLeaks: Banking Blockade and Donations Campaign*, report, October 24, 2011, https://wikileaks.org/IMG/pdf/WikiLeaks-Banking-Blockade-Information-Pack.pdf.

40. WikiLeaks, *WikiLeaks: Banking Blockade and Donations Campaign*.

41. Committee on Homeland Security and Government Affairs, "Bipartisan Legislation Goes After WikiLeaks by Amending Espionage Act," news release, US Senate, December 2, 2010, https://www.hsgac.senate.gov/media/wikileaks.

42. Andy Greenberg, "An Interview with WikiLeaks' Julian Assange," *Forbes*, November 29, 2010, https://www.forbes.com/sites/andygreenberg/2010/11/29/an-interview-with-wikileaks-julian-assange/?sh=72e087522c27.

43. Andy Greenberg, *This Machine Kills Secrets: How WikiLeakers, Cypherpunks, and Hacktivists Aim to Free the World's Information* (New York: Dutton, 2012), 179.

44. Eric Lipton and Charlie Savage, "Hackers Reveal Offer to Spy on Corporate Rivals," *New York Times*, February 11, 2011, https://www.nytimes.com/2011/02/12/us/politics/12hackers.html.

45. John Bergmayer, "Free Speech and Common Carriage: Unpacking the Supreme Court's Examination of the Texas and Florida Social Media Laws," *Public Knowledge*, February 29, 2024, https://publicknowledge.org/free-speech-and-common-carriage-netchoice/.

46. John Bergmayer, "What Makes a Common Carrier, and What Doesn't," *Public Knowledge*, January 14, 2021, https://publicknowledge.org/what-makes-a-common-carrier-and-what-doesnt/.

47. David Greene, "Victory! Supreme Court Rules Platforms Have First Amendment Right to Decide What Speech to Carry, Free of State Mandates," Electric Frontier Foundation, July 1, 2024, https://www.eff.org/deeplinks/2024/07/effs-statement-netchoice-decisions.

48. Moody v. NetChoice, LLC, 603 U.S. 707 (2024), https://www.supremecourt.gov/opinions/23pdf/22-277_d18f.pdf; Evelyn Douek, "The Supreme Court's Netchoice Ruling," *Moderated Content* (podcast), episode 81, Stanford Law School, July 8, 2024, 52 min., 37 sec., https://law.stanford.edu/podcasts/the-supreme-courts-netchoice-ruling/.

49. Equal Credit Opportunity Act, Pub. L. No. 93-495, 88 Stat. 1521 (1974), codified at 15 U.S.C. § 1691, et seq, https://uscode.house.gov/view.xhtml?req=granuleid%3AUSC-prelim-title15-chapter41-subchapter4&edition=prelim.

CHAPTER 3: BANKING WHILE MUSLIM

1. Muhammad Ali Mojaradi, "Debunking Fake Rumi #1: 'We Extracted the Message of the Qur'an . . . ,'" virtual talk, posted March 4, 2021, by sharghzadeh, YouTube, 16:41, https://youtu.be/OwkZP2wu3CU?si=os_Dt2CUnBKYmsVq.

2. Clayton Thomas, "U.S. Sanctions on Iran," Congressional Research Service, August 7, 2024, https://crsreports.congress.gov/product/pdf/IF/IF12452.

3. Youssef Chouhoud, "Banking While Muslim: From Closed Accounts and Denied Transactions to Investigations, Muslims Are the Most Likely Faith Group to Report Challenges with Financial Institutions," Institute for Social Policy and Understanding, March 14, 2023, https://ispu.org/banking-while-muslim/.

4. Edited for grammar and typos. Rowaida Abdelaziz, "Payments Denied, Flagged and Scrutinized: The Harrowing Experience of Banking While Muslim," *HuffPost*, March 24, 2023, https://www.huffpost.com/entry/muslims-banking-challenges_n_641c9ef9e4b0bc5cb6557b6a?hp_auth_done=1#comments.

5. Abdelaziz, "Payments Denied, Flagged and Scrutinized."

6. Christopher A. Casey, Jennifer K. Elsea, and Dianne E. Rennack, "The International Emergency Economic Powers Act: Origins, Evolution, and Use," Congressional Research Service, January 30, 2024, https://sgp.fas.org/crs/natsec/R45618.pdf.

7. Rachel Lyngaas, "Sanctions and Russia's War: Limiting Putin's Capabilities," US Department of the Treasury, December 14, 2023, https://home.treasury.gov/news/featured-stories/sanctions-and-russias-war-limiting-putins-capabilities.

8. Jacob Weisberg, "Thanks for the Sanctions," *Slate*, August 2, 2006, https://slate.com/news-and-politics/2006/08/why-do-we-keep-imposing-sanctions-that-help-dictators.html.

9. Shahana Hanif (@ShahanaFromBK), "#EatingWhileMuslim #VenmoingWhileMuslim means @venmo will block transactions that are Muslim phrases or reference Islam. i was just tryna pay @RimaBegumji. reminded me of #PersianShenanigans[.] anyways, this Bangladeshi meal was in the Bronx at Al-Aqsa Restaurant. pls eat there [Bangladeshi flag emoji]," Twitter, December 23, 2019, https://x.com/ShahanaFromBK/status/1209291962966261760.

10. Sydney Pereira, "Brooklyn Woman Accuses Venmo of 'Singling Out Muslims' When Blocking Transactions," *Gothamist*, December 24, 2019, https://gothamist.com/food/brooklyn-woman-accuses-venmo-singling-out-muslims-when-blocking-transactions.

11. Verified Complaint of Shahana Hanif against Venmo, LLC, at 6, City of New York Commission of Human Rights, July 21, 2020, https://static1.squarespace.com/static/57db6af7f7e0abec41695d80/t/5f16f317a6fe1d6238b67db1/1595339543750/Hanif+v.+Venmo+Complaint1.pdf.

12. US Department of Justice, "Title VI Legal Manual (Updated)," https://www.justice.gov/crt/fcs/T6Manual7#C, accessed November 1, 2024.

13. Rep. Ilhan Omar et al. to Secretary of US Department of the Treasury Janet Yellen et al., December 2, 2022, https://omar.house.gov/sites/evo-subsites/omar.house.gov/files/evo-media-document/POC%20Banking%20Discrimination%20FINAL%20Letter%20w.%20signatures.pdf.

14. Order, Nia v. Bank of America, N.A., 21-cv-1799-BAS-BGS (S.D. Cal. Mar. 26, 2024), https://casetext.com/case/nia-v-bank-of-am-3.

15. Rep. Rashida Tlaib et al. to Secretary of US Department of the Treasury Steven Mnuchin, April 22, 2020, https://cleaver.house.gov/sites/evo-subsites/cleaver-evo.house.gov/files/Final_BWM_Regulators.pdf.

16. David Graeber, *The Utopia of Rules: On Technology, Stupidity, and the Secret Joys of Bureaucracy* (Brooklyn, NY: Melville House, 2015), 89.

CHAPTER 4: CONTROLLING BODIES AND SEXUALITY

1. Mark Coker, "Smashwords Year in Review 2012: The Power in Publishing Is Shifting to Authors," Smashwords, December 31, 2012, https://blog.smashwords.com/2012/12/smashwords-year-in-review-2012-power-in.html.

2. Smashwords, "Q&A with Mark Coker Smashwords Founder and Former CEO Draft2Digital CSO," updated March 2023, https://www.smashwords.com/about.

3. Mark Coker, "The Following Email Was Sent to All Smashwords Authors/Publishers/Agents Monday, February 27 Who Have Published Erotica at Smashwords," Smashwords, February 27, 2012, https://www.smashwords.com/press/release/28.

4. Selena Kitt, "Slippery Slope: Erotic Censorship," *Self Publishing Revolution*, February 19, 2012, http://theselfpublishingrevolution.blogspot.com/2012/02/slippery-slope-erotica-censorship.html.

5. Roth v. United States, 354 U.S. 476 (1957), https://supreme.justia.com/cases/federal/us/354/476/.

6. *Roth v. United States*, 477.

7. Miller v. California, 413 U.S. 15 (1973), https://supreme.justia.com/cases/federal/us/413/15/.

8. American Civil Liberties Union v. Reno, 929 F. Supp. 824 (E.D. Pa. 1996), https://law.justia.com/cases/federal/district-courts/FSupp/929/824/1812782/.

9. Reno v. American Civil Liberties Union, 521 U.S. 844, 849 (1997), https://supreme.justia.com/cases/federal/us/521/844/. As this quotation from the opinion indicates, this was not the typical US district court but a special three-judge panel combining the role of a trial court and an appellate court.

10. Lee Tien, "After 10 Years, an Infamous Internet-Censorship Act Is Finally Dead," Electronic Frontier Foundation, January 21, 2009, https://www.eff.org/deeplinks/2009/01/copa.

11. Mike Masnick, "Internet Association Sells Out the Internet: Caves In and Will Now Support Revised SESTA," *Techdirt*, November 3, 2017, https://www.techdirt.com/2017/11/03/internet-association-sells-out-internet-caves-will-now-support-revised-sesta/.

12. Elliot Harmon, "How Congress Censored the Internet," Electronic Frontier Foundation, March 21, 2018, https://www.eff.org/deeplinks/2018/03/how-congress-censored-internet; "New Lawsuit Challenges FOSTA—The Federal Law Sparking Website Shutdowns," Electronic Frontier Foundation, June 28, 2018, https://www.eff.org/press/releases/new-lawsuit-challenges-fosta-federal-law-sparking-website-shutdowns.

13. David Greene, "DC Circuit FOSTA Ruling Lets a Bad Law Stay on the Books, but Offers Meaningful Protection for Some Sex Work Forums and Sex Workers Using Online Services," Electronic Frontier Foundation, July 22, 2023, https://www.eff.org/deeplinks/2023/07/dc-circuit-fosta-ruling-lets-bad-law-stay-books-offers-meaningful-protection-some.

14. The Supreme Court has separately addressed the issue of child pornography. In *New York v. Ferber*, the Supreme Court decided that the Miller test for obscenity did not apply when it came to the exploitation of children (New York v. Ferber, 458 U.S. 747 [1982], https://supreme.justia.com/cases/federal/us/458/747/). Instead, this was a matter of child safety and did not merit First Amendment protections. The court defined child pornography as works "that visually depict sexual conduct by children below a specified age." In 2002, the Supreme Court clarified its position by striking down portions of the Child Pornography Prevention Act in *Ashcroft v. Free Speech Coalition*, noting that any attempt to ban images that convey the impression of or appear to be a minor engaging in sexually explicit conduct are not actual child pornography because no children are harmed. In writing the majority opinion for that case, Justice Anthony Kennedy pointed out how even films like the 1996 *Romeo + Juliet* could be banned under the Child Pornography Protection Act if the law were not struck down (Ashcroft v. Free Speech Coalition, 535 U.S. 234, 247 [2002], https://supreme.justia.com/cases/federal/us/535/234/.) In the case of Smashwords, it's clear that written fiction which does not include visual renderings would not be considered child pornography.

15. Mark Coker, "Smashwords Author/Publisher Update," news release, Smashwords, March 2, 2012, https://www.smashwords.com/press/release/30.

16. Visa, "Visa Core Rules and Visa Product and Service Rules," October 19, 2024, accessed November 23, 2024, p. 93, https://usa.visa.com/dam/VCOM/download/about-visa/visa-rules-public.pdf. Note that this is the current version of the Visa rules and not what would have been in place in 2012. However, archival versions of these rules show similar language over many years. See "1.3.3.4 Brand Protection and Use of the Visa-Owned Marks" from an archival version of Visa's rules dated October 15, 2016, archived through the Wayback Machine of the Internet Archive January 3, 2017, https://web.archive.org/web/20170103114159mp_/https://usa.visa.com/dam/VCOM/download/about-visa/visa-rules-public.pdf.

17. Mastercard, "Mastercard Rules," June 4, 2024, https://www.mastercard.us/content/dam/public/mastercardcom/na/global-site/documents/mastercard-rules.pdf. Note that this is the current version of the Mastercard rules and not what would have been in place in 2012. However, archival versions of these rules show similar language over a number of years. See "5.11.7 Illegal or Brand-Damaging Transactions" from an archival version of "MasterCard Rules" dated December 7, 2011, archived by the Wayback Machine of the Internet Archive, January 3, 2012, https://web.archive.org/web/20120103220335/http://www.mastercard.com/us/merchant/pdf/BM-Entire_Manual_public.pdf.

18. Mastercard, "Human Rights Statements," https://www.mastercard.com/global/en/vision/corp-responsibility/human-rights-statement.html, accessed November 24, 2024.

19. National Coalition Against Censorship Staff, "NCAC, ABFFE Protest PayPal Ban on Erotic Material," news release, March 2, 2012, https://ncac.org/incident/ncac-abffe-protest-paypal-ban-on-erotic-material.

20. Chris Conley, "Tell PayPal: Stop the Digital Book Bonfire," ACLU of Northern California, March 7, 2012, https://www.aclunc.org/blog/tell-paypal-stop-digital-book-bonfire.

21. Remittance Girl, "Pragmatic Compromises & the Moral Hazard of Expediency," *Remittance Girl Erotic Fiction*, https://remittancegirl.com/discussions/pragmatic-compromises-the-moral-hazard-of-expediency/, accessed August 15, 2024.

22. Anuj Nayar, "PayPal's Acceptable Use Policy on Sale of Certain 'Erotica,'" *PayPal* (blog), March 8, 2012, archived by the Wayback Machine of the Internet Archive, May 11, 2012, https://web.archive.org/web/20120511080303/https://www.thepaypalblog.com/2012/03/paypals-acceptable-use-policy-on-sale-of-certain-erotica/.

23. Remittance Girl, "Visa Writes Us Back! 'This Is Not Our Doing,'" BannedWriters, March 10, 2012, archived by the Wayback Machine of the Internet Archive, April 13, 2012, https://web.archive.org/web/20120413131511/http://www.bannedwriters.com/2012/03/10/visa-writes-us-back-this-is-not-our-doing-paypal-censorship-erotica/; Remittance Girl, "MasterCard's Letter to Banned Writers: No Involvement," Banned Writers, March 13, 2012, archived by the Wayback Machine of the Internet Archive, April 16, 2012, https://web.archive.org/web/20120416010134/http://www.bannedwriters.com/2012/03/13/mastercards-letter-to-banned-writers-no-involvement-censorship-paypal-erotica.

24. Anuj Nayar, "Update: PayPal's Acceptable Use Policy," *PayPal* (blog), March 13, 2012, archived by the Wayback Machine of the Internet Archive, May 15, 2012, https://web.archive.org/web/20120515040327/https://www.thepaypalblog.com/2012/03/update-paypal%E2%80%99s-acceptable-use-policy/.

25. Mark Coker, "PayPal Revises Policies to Allow Legal Fiction," Smashwords, March 13, 2012, https://blog.smashwords.com/2012/03/paypal-revises-policies-to-allow-legal.html.

26. National Coalition Against Censorship, "PayPal Lifts Ban on Erotic Books," news release, March 13, 2012, archived by the Wayback Machine of the Internet Archive, May 20, 2012, https://web.archive.org/web/20120520132835/https://ncac.org/PayPal-Lifts-Ban-on-Erotic-Books.

27. Kurt Opsahl and Rainey Reitman, "Payment Provider Stripe Upholds Free Speech, Reactivates Nifty Archives," Electronic Frontier Foundation, November 2, 2012, https://www.eff.org/deeplinks/2012/11/payment-provider-stripe-upholds-free-speech-reactivates-nifty-archives.

28. Justin Hendrix, "Long Before OnlyFans Bowed to the Banks, Cindy Gallop Took Them On," *Tech Policy Press*, August 25, 2021, https://www.techpolicy.press/long-before-onlyfans-bowed-to-the-banks-cindy-gallop-took-them-on/.

29. "The 47th Academy Awards: 1975," Oscars.org, https://www.oscars.org/oscars/ceremonies/1975.

30. 31 C.F.R. Part 14, Right to Financial Privacy Act, eCFR, https://www.ecfr.gov/current/title-31/subtitle-A/part-14; Nicholas Anthony, "The Right to Financial Privacy: Crafting a Better Framework for Financial Privacy in the Digital Age," Policy Analysis no. 945, Cato Institute, May 2, 2023, https://www.cato.org/policy-analysis/right-financial-privacy#legislative-expansions.

31. 31 C.F.R. § 1020.220, Customer Identification Programs for Banks, Savings Associations, Credit Unions, and Certain Non-Federally Regulated Banks, eCFR, https://www.ecfr.gov/current/title-31/subtitle-B/chapter-X/part-1020.

32. Financial Crimes Enforcement Network, *Notice to Customers: A CTR Reference Guide*, informational pamphlet, https://www.fincen.gov/sites/default/files/shared/CTRPamphlet.pdf, accessed November 12, 2024.

33. ACLU, "Testimony of Legislative Counsel Gregory Nojeim on 'Know Your Customer' Banking Regulations Before the House Judiciary Subcommittee on Commercial and Administrative Law," March 4, 1999, https://www.aclu.org/documents/testimony-legislative-counsel-gregory-nojeim-know-your-customer-banking-regulations-house.

34. Financial Crimes Enforcement Network, *Reporting Suspicious Activity: A Quick Reference Guide for Money Services Business*, informational pamphlet, https://www.fincen.gov/sites/default/files/shared/report_reference.pdf, accessed November 12, 2024.

35. EBANX, "Payment Gateway," https://www.ebanx.com/en/resources/payments-explained/payment-gateway/, accessed November 24, 2024; NerdWallet, "What Is Credit Card Processing and How Does It Work?" https://www.nerdwallet.com/article/small-business/credit-card-processing, accessed November 24, 2024.

36. "Exhibit B: Letter to Mr. Charles W. Scharf, Chief Executive Officer, Visa Incorporated and Members of the Board of Directors, Visa Incorporated," June 29, 2015, archived at https://www.courtlistener.com/docket/4263036/2/backpagecom-llc-v-dart/; "Exhibit C: Letter to Mr. Ajaypal Banga, President and Chief Executive Officer, MasterCard and Members of the Board of Directors, MasterCard Incorporated," June 29, 2015, archived at https://www.courtlistener.com/docket/4263036/2/backpagecom-llc-v-dart/.

37. Amicus Curiae Brief of the Center for Democracy & Technology, Electronic Frontier Foundation, and Association of Alternative Newsmedia in Support of Plaintiff-Appellant and Reversal, Backpage.com, LLC v. Thomas J. Dart, 807 F.3d 229 (7th Cir. 2015), https://cdt.org/wp-content/uploads/2015/11/Backpage.com-v.-Dart-7th-Circuit-amicus-brief-CDT-EFF-AAN-FINAL.pdf. Specifically: "Government coercion of technological and financial intermediaries in order to suppress lawful speech and to shut down hosts of third-party content is a major threat to free expression in the digital age. It is a particularly insidious form of government censorship, as it occurs through informal channels that circumvent due process protections and judicial oversight. Any judicial decision affirmatively allowing government actors to use their official position to suppress disfavored speech via extralegal threats will be a devastating blow to online speakers who rely on technological and financial intermediaries in order to express their opinions and ideas and to access information online."

38. Backpage.com, LLC v. Thomas Dart, 807 F.3d 229, 231 (7th Cir. 2015), https://dockets.justia.com/docket/circuit-courts/ca7/15-3047.

39. Violet Blue, "PayPal, Square, and Big Banking's War on the Sex Industry," Engadget, December 2, 2015, https://www.engadget.com/2015-12-02-paypal-square-and-big-bankings-war-on-the-sex-industry.html.

40. Zahra Stardust, Danielle Blunt, Gabriella Garcia, Lorelei Lee, Kate D'Adamo, and Rachel Kuo, "High Risk Hustling: Payment Processors, Sexual Proxies, and Discrimination by Design," *CUNY Law Review* 26, no. 1 (Winter 2023): 57, https://academicworks.cuny.edu/clr/vol26/iss1/4/.

41. Natasha Tusikov, "Censoring Sex: Payment Platforms' Regulations on Sexual Expression," in *Media and Law: Between Free Speech and Censorship*, Sociology of Crime, Law and Deviance, vol. 26, ed. Mathieu Deflem and Derek M. D. Silva (Leeds: Emerald, 2021), 66.

42. Tusikov, "Censoring Sex."

43. Nicholas Kristof, "The Children of Pornhub," *New York Times*, December 4, 2020, https://www.nytimes.com/2020/12/04/opinion/sunday/pornhub-rape-trafficking.html.

44. Michelle Celarier, "Bill Ackman Sent a Text to the CEO of Mastercard. What Happened Next Is a Parable of ESG," *Institutional Investor*, June 16, 2021, https://www.institutionalinvestor.com/article/2bswuu1nfc040h07ghudc/culture/bill-ackman-sent-a-text-to-the-ceo-of-mastercard-what-happened-next-is-a-parable-for-esg.

45. Jay Peters, "PayPal Abruptly Cuts Off Pornhub's Payroll, Leaving Performers with Few Payment Options," *Verge*, November 14, 2019, https://www.theverge.com/2019/11/14/20965167/paypal-pornhub-payroll-model-program-payment-options-paxum-verge-performers.

46. Adi Robertson, "Visa and Mastercard Cut Off Pornhub After Report of Unlawful Videos," *The Verge*, December 10, 2020, https://www.theverge.com/2020/12/10/22168240/mastercard-ending-pornhub-payment-processing-unlawful-videos.

47. Visa, Inc., "Memorandum of Law in Support of Motion to Dismiss," Fleites v. MindGeek S.A.R.L., No. 2:21-CV-04920-CJC-ADS (C.D. Cal. Oct. 18, 2021), at 2, 11, https://www.courtlistener.com/docket/59992265/55/1/serena-fleites-v-mindgeek-sarl/.

48. Brief of the International Center for Law & Economics and Scholars of Law & Economics as Amici Curiae Supporting Defendant Visa Inc., Fleites v. MindGeek S.A.R.L., No.

2:21-CV-04920-CJC-ADS (C.D. Cal. Jan. 17, 2022), https://laweconcenter.org/wp-content/uploads/2022/02/2022-01-17-Fleites-Amicus-Br-FILED.pdf.

49. "Order Granting in Part and Denying in Part Visa's Motion to Dismiss, Demanding a More Definite Statement with Respect to Plaintiff's Civil Conspiracy Claim, and Granting the International Center for Law & Economics' Motion to File an Amicus Brief," Fleites v. MindGeek S.A.R.L., No. 2:21-CV-04920-CJC-ADS (C.D. Cal. July 29, 2022), https://pershingsquarefoundation.org/wp-content/uploads/2022/07/031138281455.pdf.

50. "Order Granting in Part and Denying in Part Visa's Motion to Dismiss, Demanding a More Definite Statement with Respect to Plaintiff's Civil Conspiracy Claim, and Granting the International Center for Law & Economics' Motion to File an Amicus Brief."

51. Free Speech Coalition, "Financial Discrimination and the Adult Industry," March 2023, https://action.freespeechcoalition.com/files/FinancialDiscriminationandtheAdultIndustry.pdf.

52. Kate Rooney and Yun Li, "Visa and Mastercard Suspend Payments for Ad Purchases on Pornhub and MindGeek amid Controversy," CNBC, August 4, 2022, https://www.cnbc.com/2022/08/04/visa-suspends-card-payments-for-ad-purchases-on-pornhub-and-mindgeek-amid-controversy.html.

53. Alfred F. Kelly Jr., "We Do Not Tolerate the Use of Our Network for Illegal Activity," *Visa* (blog), August 4, 2022, archived by the Wayback Machine of the Internet Archive, August 4, 2022, https://web.archive.org/web/20220804175238/https://usa.visa.com/visa-everywhere/blog/bdp/2022/08/03/we-do-not-1659542369610.html.

54. Eric Griffith, "Pornhub Reveals Explicit Traffic Numbers," *PC Magazine*, December 20, 2019, https://www.pcmag.com/news/pornhub-reveals-explicit-traffic-numbers.

55. Mike Masnick, "Campaigners for SESTA See It as a First Step to Stomping Out Porn," *Techdirt*, October 2, 2017, https://www.techdirt.com/2017/10/02/campaigners-sesta-see-it-as-first-step-to-stomping-out-porn/.

56. Haley McNamara et al. to Chief Executive Officer of Mastercard Ajaypal Singh Banga, "RE: International Concern Over Your Company's Involvement in Sexual Exploitation," National Center on Sexual Exploitation, coalition letter, May 5, 2020, archived by the Wayback Machine of the Internet Archive, June 2, 2020, https://web.archive.org/web/20200602093112/https://endsexualexploitation.org/wp-content/uploads/ICOSE_Mastercard_JointInternationalLetter_CreditCardCompanies_mail_final.pdf.

CHAPTER 5: CANNABIS AND INDUSTRY CENSORSHIP

1. Frank Keating, "Justice Puts Banks in a Choke Hold," *Wall Street Journal*, April 24, 2014, https://www.wsj.com/articles/SB10001424052702304810904579511911684102106.

2. Lee Fang, "Police and Prison Guard Groups Fight Marijuana Legalization in California," *Intercept*, May 18, 2016, https://theintercept.com/2016/05/18/ca-marijuana-measure/; Ryan Grim, "California Pot Initiative Opposed by Beer Industry," *HuffPost*, September 21, 2010, https://www.huffpost.com/entry/this-buds-not-for-you-bee_n_732901; Christopher Ingraham, "One Striking Chart Shows Why Pharma Companies Are Fighting Legal Marijuana," *Washington Post*, July 13, 2016, https://www.washingtonpost.com/news/wonk/wp/2016/07/13/one-striking-chart-shows-why-pharma-companies-are-fighting-legal-marijuana/; Ziemowit Bednarek, Jacqueline M. Doremus, and Sarah S. Stith, "U.S. Cannabis Laws Projected to Cost Generic and Brand Pharmaceutical Firms Billions," *PLOS One* 17, no. 8 (2022): 1–19, https://doi.org/10.1371/journal.pone.0272492.

3. Financial Crimes Enforcement Network, "BSA Expectations Regarding Marijuana-Related Businesses," February 14, 2014, https://www.fincen.gov/resources/statutes-regulations/guidance/bsa-expectations-regarding-marijuana-related-businesses#.

4. Gene Marks, "Cannabis Firms Are Cut Off from the US Financial System, but Relief Is in Sight," *The Guardian*, October 8, 2023, https://www.theguardian.com/business/2023/oct/08/cannabis-companies-us-financial-system-banking-safer-act.

5. Nate Lipton, "Cannabis Industry Can't Use Banks. That Hurts a Lot More Than Dispensaries," *Arizona Republic*, November 8, 2023, https://www.azcentral.com/story/opinion/op-ed/2023/11/08/cannabis-industry-access-banking-pass-safer-act/71476380007/.

6. Sen. Jeff Merkley, "Challenges for Cannabis and Banking: Outside Perspectives: Hearing Before the Comm. on Banking, Housing, and Urban Affairs of the Senate," 116th

Cong., 1st sess., 2019, 6–8, https://www.congress.gov/event/116th-congress/senate-event/LC64544/text?s=2&r=249.

7. Mastercard, "Customer Compliance Program: Member Alert to Control High-Risk Merchants," posted March 29, 2018, YouTube, 12 min. 20 sec., https://www.youtube.com/watch?v=Wi-UV6zidmo&list=PLjw9YryPdJoaXsXMHD6d7SM5XoNe1pFhZ&index=5.

8. Jessica Velasco, "What Is the MATCH List and the Terminated Merchant File (TMF)?" Kount, February 1, 2024, https://kount.com/blog/what-is-match-list-terminated-merchant-file-tmf.

9. MATCH Documentation, "MATCH," Mastercard as archived by Wayback Machine of the Internet Archive, July 14, 2024, https://web.archive.org/web/20240714213706/https://developer.mastercard.com/match/documentation/.

10. Mastercard, "Mastercard Rules," June 4, 2024, https://www.mastercard.us/content/dam/public/mastercardcom/na/global-site/documents/mastercard-rules.pdf, p. 117.

11. "American Express Merchant Operating Guide," October 2024, archived by the Wayback Machine of the Internet Archive, December 23, 2024, https://web.archive.org/web/20241223171322/https://icm.aexp-static.com/content/dam/gms/en_us/optblue/us-mog.pdf; "High Risk Merchant Lists," Stripe, archived by the Wayback Machine of the Internet Archive, November 7, 2024, https://web.archive.org/web/20241107205132/https://docs.stripe.com/disputes/match.

12. Chargeback Gurus, "MATCH List and Terminated Merchant File (TMF)," December 5, 2021, https://www.chargebackgurus.com/blog/mastercard-match-list-are-you-on-it.

13. Mastercard, "MasterCard MATCH Module 1," posted September 28, 2015, YouTube, 14 min. 56 sec., https://www.youtube.com/watch?v=KjAwqMfeDA4.

14. Thomas Larson, "Jackie Bryant Builds a Platform: The News Will Never Be the Same," *San Diego Reader*, January 26, 2022, archived by ThomasLarson.com at https://www.thomaslarson.com/publications/san-diego-reader/413-jackie-bryant-builds-a-platform.html.

15. Stripe, "Prohibited and Restricted Businesses," last modified November 2024, https://stripe.com/legal/restricted-businesses.

16. Jackie Bryant, "LinkedIn! The long arm of cannabis prohibition has finally come for me. Stripe, which is a horrible company to deal with, probably the worst customer service I've ever encountered, is closing my account associated with my Substack newsletter...," LinkedIn, March 2024, https://www.linkedin.com/posts/jacquelineannebryant_linkedin-the-long-arm-of-cannabis-prohibition-activity-7175854756689575936-aDfv?utm_source=share&utm_medium=member_desktop.

17. Clare Sausen, "Stripe Says No to Funding Cannabis Journalism, Backs Down After a Fight," *High Times*, March 25, 2024, https://hightimes.com/culture/stripe-says-no-to-funding-cannabis-journalism-backs-down-after-a-fight/.

18. Google, "About Search," Facts About Google and Competition, archived by the Wayback Machine of the Internet Archive, August 26, 2011, https://web.archive.org/web/20110826063413/http://www.google.com/competition/howgooglesearchworks.html.

19. Maxine Waters, Ranking Member, H. Comm. on Financial Services, "The Department of Justice's 'Operation Choke Point': Hearing Before the Subcomm. on Oversight and Investigations of the H. Comm. on Financial Services," 113th Cong., 2nd sess., 2014, pp. 15–16. Representative Maxine Waters (D-CA) says: "Let me thank our witnesses here today for doing your job. This is exactly what some of us expect you to do. I want you to know that many of us are aware of activities that are fraudulent that are being perpetrated on the most vulnerable in our society. Oftentimes, you have the poorest of communities who are the victims of many of these schemes and fraudulent activity. So I am very, very pleased about 'Operation Choke Point.' I want you to be as aggressive as you can possibly be."

20. Darrell Issa (CA-49), Chairman, and Jim Jordan (OH-04), Chairman, Subcommittee on Economic Growth, Job Creation and Regulatory Affairs, *Federal Deposit Insurance Corporation's Involvement in "Operation Choke Point,"* Staff Report, US House of Representatives, Committee on Oversight and Government Reform, 113th Cong., December 8, 2014, https://oversight.house.gov/wp-content/uploads/2014/12/Staff-Report-FDIC-and-Operation-Choke-Point-12-8-2014.pdf.

21. Issa and Jordan, *Federal Deposit Insurance Corporation's Involvement in "Operation Choke Point."*

22. Alex P. McBride, Lawrence K. Nesbitt, and Courtney L. Snyder, "FIRREA Civil Money Penalties: The Government's Newfound Weapon Against Financial Fraud," Jones Day, May 8, 2013, https://www.jonesday.com/en/insights/2013/05/firrea-civil-money-penalties-the-governments-newfound-weapon-against-financial-fraud.

23. Stuart F. Delery, Assistant Attorney General, Civil Division, US Department of Justice, *Guilty Until Proven Innocent? A Study of the Propriety and Legal Authority for the Justice Department's Operation Choke Point: Hearing Before the Subcomm. on Regulatory Reform, Commercial, and Antitrust Law of the H. Comm. on the Judiciary*, 113th Cong., 2nd sess., 2014, pp. 17–20 (testimony of), July 17, 2014, citing 1:56:00 in video: https://judiciary.house.gov/committee-activity/hearings/guilty-until-proven-innocent-study-propriety-legal-authority-justice-0, https://www.congress.gov/113/chrg/CHRG-113hhrg88724/CHRG-113hhrg88724.pdf.

24. Issa and Jordan, *Federal Deposit Insurance Corporation's Involvement*.

25. Dru Stevenson, "Operation Choke Point: Myths and Reality," *Administrative Law Review* 75, no. 2 (2023): 317–61, https://administrativelawreview.org/wp-content/uploads/sites/2/2023/07/ALR-75.2_Stevenson.pdf.

26. Derek E. Bambauer, "Against Jawboning," *Minnesota Law Review* 100, no. 1 (2015): 52–126, https://www.minnesotalawreview.org/wp-content/uploads/2015/11/Bambauer_ONLINE.pdf.

27. Adam Levitin, "Operation Choke Point Hysteria: Are Choke Point's Critics Responsible for the Account Closings?" *Credit Slips*, July 17, 2014, https://www.creditslips.org/creditslips/2014/07/operation-choke-point-hysteria-are-choke-points-critics-responsible-for-the-account-closings.html.

28. Victoria Guida, "Justice Department to End Obama-Era 'Operation Choke Point,'" *Politico*, August 17, 2017, https://www.politico.com/story/2017/08/17/trump-reverses-obama-operation-chokepoint-241767.

29. Asst. Att. Gen. Stephen E. Boyd to Chairman, H. Comm. on Judiciary Bob Goodlatte (August 16, 2017), archived by the Wayback Machine of the Internet Archive, September 20, 2017, https://web.archive.org/web/20170920102558/https://alliedprogress.org/wp-content/uploads/2017/08/2017-8-16-Operation-Chokepoint-Goodlatte.pdf.

30. Frank Keating, "Operation Choke Point Reveals True Injustices of Obama's Justice Department," *The Hill*, November 7, 2018, https://thehill.com/blogs/congress-blog/politics/415478-operation-choke-point-reveals-true-injustices-of-obamas-justice/.

CHAPTER 6: CASH AS CENSORSHIP RESISTANCE

1. Board of Governors, US Federal Reserve System, *Report on the Economic Well-Being of U.S. Households in 2022*, May 2023, https://www.federalreserve.gov/publications/2023-economic-well-being-of-us-households-in-2022-banking-credit.htm.

2. Jerry Brito, "The Case for Electronic Cash," Coin Center, February 2019, https://www.coincenter.org/the-case-for-electronic-cash/.

3. Kenneth S. Rogoff, *The Curse of Cash: How Large-Denomination Bills Aid Crime and Tax Evasion and Constrain Monetary Policy* (Princeton, NJ: Princeton University Press, 2017), 94.

4. Rogoff, *The Curse of Cash*, 95.

5. Rogoff, *The Curse of Cash*, 102.

6. BBC News, "India Rupees: Chaos at Banks After 'Black Money' Ban," November 10, 2016, https://www.bbc.com/news/world-asia-india-37933233#.

7. Julie McCarthy, "What Can India Teach Us About Abolishing High-Value Currency?" NPR, February 9, 2017, https://www.npr.org/sections/parallels/2017/02/09/513736356/what-can-india-tell-us-about-the-worth-of-abolishing-high-value-banknotes.

8. Ethan Wolff-Mann, "The 500 Euro-Note Phaseout Could Have an Unintended Consequence," *Yahoo Finance*, September 9, 2019, https://finance.yahoo.com/news/500-euro-bill-cash-negative-interest-rates-135948574.html.

9. Sveriges Riksbank, *Further Measures Are Required to Preserve Cash*, March 14, 2024, https://www.riksbank.se/en-gb/payments--cash/payments-in-sweden/payments-report--2024/the-riksbanks-work-and-policy/more-measures-needed-to-protect-cash/further-measures-are-required-to-preserve-cash-/.

10. Pierre Lemieux, "Banning Cash: This Time Is Not Different," *Regulation* 39, no. 4 (Winter 2016–17): 50–53, https://www.cato.org/regulation/winter-2016-2017/curse-cash.

11. Jay Stanley, "Say No to the 'Cashless Future'—and to Cashless Stores," ACLU, August 12, 2019, https://www.aclu.org/news/privacy-technology/say-no-cashless-future-and-cashless-stores.

12. Erika D. Smith, "As Coronavirus Surges, More Stores Are Going Cashless. The Price Tag Is Racism," *Los Angeles Times*, June 27, 2020, https://www.latimes.com/california/story/2020-06-27/coronavirus-cashless-business-racism-inequity-square; Joshua Sabatini, "SF Approves Ban on Cashless Stores," *San Francisco Examiner*, May 7, 2019, https://www.sfexaminer.com/archives/sf-approves-ban-on-cashless-stores/article_fdb5311f-c1e2-567f-970a-d9f216057912.html

13. Alexandra Olson and Ken Sweet, "As Cashless Stores Grow, So Does the Backlash," Associated Press, last modified April 12, 2019, https://apnews.com/domestic-news-domestic-news-general-news-98613f20d0254b8bacd908ef12107fef; Amy Phillips, "AG: Cash Has to Be Accepted Everywhere," WWLP, December 13, 2023, https://www.wwlp.com/news/state-politics/ag-cash-has-to-be-accepted-everywhere/; David Tente, "Bans on Cashless Retail Establishments—April 2023 Update," ATM Industrial Association, April 20, 2023, https://www.atmia.com/news/bans-on-cashless-retail-establishments-april-2023-update/19584/.

14. McKenzie Sadeghi, "Fact Check: No US Law Requires Businesses to Take Cash, but Local Laws May Mandate It," *USA Today*, September 16, 2020, https://www.usatoday.com/story/news/factcheck/2020/09/16/fact-check-cashless-businesses-banned-only-some-local-state-laws/3330804001/.

15. Payment Choice Act of 2023, S.1984, 118th Cong. (2023), June 14, 2023, https://www.congress.gov/bill/118th-congress/senate-bill/1984.

CHAPTER 7: CAN CRYPTOCURRENCY BE A PRACTICAL TOOL AGAINST CENSORSHIP?

1. Rainey Reitman, "Bitcoin—a Step Toward Censorship-Resistant Digital Currency," Electronic Frontier Foundation, January 20, 2011, https://www.eff.org/deeplinks/2011/01/bitcoin-step-toward-censorship-resistant.

2. Satoshi Nakamoto, "Bitcoin: A Peer-to-Peer Electronic Cash System," white paper, Bitcoin.org, October 31, 2008, https://bitcoin.org/bitcoin.pdf.

3. Human Rights Foundation, "Central Bank Digital Currency Tracker," https://cbdctracker.hrf.org/home, accessed November 12, 2024.

4. Edward Snowden, "Your Money AND Your Life," *Continuing Ed—with Edward Snowden*, October 8, 2021, https://edwardsnowden.substack.com/p/cbdcs.

5. For example, ZCash and Monero each use a public ledger for confirming transactions but use encryption that can mask the amount of the transaction, the destination wallet, and the originating wallet from the public ledger.

6. There are different perspectives on how this unfolded. Curious readers would benefit from reading Vitalik Buterin, "Some Reflections on the Bitcoin Block Size War," personal website, May 31, 2024, https://vitalik.eth.limo/general/2024/05/31/blocksize.html, as well as Jonathan Bier, *The Blocksize War: The Battle over Who Controls Bitcoin's Protocol Rules* (self-published, 2021).

7. Leigh Cuen, "Why Some People Love Bitcoin Cash," *International Business Times*, August 22, 2017, https://www.ibtimes.com/why-some-people-love-bitcoin-cash-2581403.

8. Eric Hughes, "A Cypherpunk's Manifesto," Satoshi Nakamoto Institute, March 9, 1993, https://nakamotoinstitute.org/library/cypherpunk-manifesto/.

9. Atlantic Council, "Cryptocurrency Regulation Tracker," last modified July 2024, https://www.atlanticcouncil.org/programs/geoeconomics-center/cryptoregulationtracker/.

10. Dave Michaels, "Big Battles Loom in SEC's War on Crypto," *Wall Street Journal*, December 28, 2023, https://www.wsj.com/finance/regulation/big-battles-loom-in-secs-war-on-crypto-aeffod78; "U.S. Citizen Who Conspired to Assist North Korea in Evading Sanctions Sentenced to Over Five Years and Fined $100,000," US Department of Justice, April 12, 2022, https://www.justice.gov/opa/pr/us-citizen-who-conspired-assist-north-korea-evading-sanctions-sentenced-over-five-years-and; Kurt Opsahl, "Code, Speech, and the Tornado Cash Mixer," Electronic Frontier Foundation, August 22, 2022, https://www.eff.org/deeplinks/2022/08/code-speech-and-tornado-cash-mixer/.

11. Chainalysis, "60% of Bitcoin Is Held Long Term as Digital Gold. What About the Rest?" June 18, 2020, https://www.chainalysis.com/blog/bitcoin-market-data-exchanges-trading/.

12. Joel Khalili, "After a 10-Year Wait, Mt. Gox Bitcoin Is Finally Being Returned," *Wired*, July 5, 2024, https://www.wired.com/story/after-a-10-year-wait-mt-gox-bitcoin-is-finally-being-returned/; David Yaffe-Bellany, "How Sam Bankman-Fried's Crypto Empire Collapsed," *New York Times*, November 14, 2022, https://www.nytimes.com/2022/11/14/technology/ftx-sam-bankman-fried-crypto-bankruptcy.html.

CHAPTER 8: TAKING ON THE BANKING BLOCKADE

1. Trevor Timm (@WLLegal), "Pentagon Papers were a much more serious security breach than WikiLeaks. You can't justify the former & not the latter: http://bit.ly/u01hE3," Twitter, December 22, 2011.

2. Trevor Timm (@WLLegal), "And just so the State Dept knows, the Pentagon Papers were 7,000 pages long & leaked to *many* newspapers. Not exactly one doc, one reporter," Twitter, January 12, 2011.

3. Freedom of the Press (@FreedomofPress), "Introducing the Freedom of the Press Foundation, which will crowd-fund for transparency journalism—including WikiLeaks https://pressfreedomfoundation.org," Twitter, December 16, 2012, https://x.com/FreedomofPress/status/280432436490403840.

CHAPTER 9: BEST PRACTICES FOR FINANCIAL COMPANIES

1. Electronic Frontier Foundation, "International Coalition of Rights Groups Call on Internet Infrastructure Providers to Avoid Content Policing," news release, December 1, 2022, https://www.eff.org/press/releases/international-coalition-rights-groups-call-internet-infrastructure-providers-avoid.

2. Protect the Stack Coalition, "Protect the Stack: Why Infrastructure Providers Should Not Police Content," December 1, 2022, https://protectthestack.org/.

3. Electronic Frontier Foundation, "We Need to Talk About Infrastructure," December 20, 2022, https://www.eff.org/deeplinks/2022/12/we-need-talk-about-infrastructure.

4. "Announcing the 2022 Kraken Transparency Report," *Kraken*, February 1, 2023, https://blog.kraken.com/news/announcing-the-2022-kraken-transparency-report.

5. Anuj Nayar, "Update: PayPal's Acceptable Use Policy," *PayPal* (blog), March 13, 2012, archived by the Wayback Machine of the Internet Archive, May 15, 2012, https://web.archive.org/web/20120515040327/https://www.thepaypalblog.com/2012/03/update-paypal%E2%80%99s-acceptable-use-policy/.

6. Electronic Frontier Foundation, "22 Rights Groups Tell PayPal and Venmo to Shape Up Policies on Account Closures," news release, June 15, 2021, https://www.eff.org/press/releases/22-rights-groups-tell-paypal-and-venmo-shape-account-freezes-and-closures.

7. Santa Clara Principles are not the first time we have seen these tech companies proactively standing up for free expression. Notably, the Global Network Initiative, launched in 2008, is a coalition of corporations, academics, investors, and civil society members working to ensure that freedom of expression, privacy, and other human rights are upheld by technology companies. https://globalnetworkinitiative.org/.

8. James C. Goodale, *Fighting for the Press: The Inside Story of the Pentagon Papers and Other Battles* (New York: CUNY Journalism Press, 2013), 193, quotation on 194.

CHAPTER 10: WHAT THE GOVERNMENT CAN DO ABOUT FINANCIAL CENSORSHIP

1. Brian Knight and Trace Mitchell, "Private Policies and Public Power: When Banks Act as Regulators Within a Regime of Privilege," *New York University Journal of Law and Liberty* 13, no. 1 (October 9, 2019): 74, https://ssrn.com/abstract=3466854.

2. National Rifle Association of America v. Vullo, 602 U.S. 175 (2024), https://supreme.justia.com/cases/federal/us/602/22-842/.

3. There are a range of other financial products and institutions that also have been leveraged to censor certain people and institutions, including insurance services, online advertising, crowdfunding sites, investments, and corporate loans. It would be interesting

to consider whether those tools are also being used as a blunt instrument for shuttering dissenting speech, but that is beyond the scope of this research and not included in these recommendations. This research and these recommendations are specific to bank accounts, credit card accounts, and payment services.

4. Foundation for Individual Rights and Expression, "Enacted Campus Free Speech Statutes—California," https://www.thefire.org/research-learn/enacted-campus-free-speech-statutes-california, accessed November 1, 2024.

5. Fleites v. MindGeek S.A.R.L., No. 2:21-CV-04920-CJC-ADS (C.D. Cal. Jan. 17, 2022), https://laweconcenter.org/wp-content/uploads/2022/02/2022-01-17-Fleites-Amicus-Br-FILED.pdf.

6. Electronic Frontier Foundation, "Section 230," https://www.eff.org/issues/cda230, accessed November 11, 2024.

7. This information should be given promptly if the financial institution is permitted to do so, or otherwise as soon as any gag order expires.

8. New York State Assembly, Assembly Bill AO7794, 2023–2024 Leg., Regular Session, proposed June 15, 2023, https://assembly.state.ny.us/leg/?term=2023&bn=A07794.

9. N.Y. State Assembly Bill AO7794.

10. Office of the Comptroller of the Currency, "OCC Finalizes Rule Requiring Large Banks to Provide Fair Access to Bank Services, Capital, and Credit," news release, January 14, 2021, https://occ.gov/news-issuances/news-releases/2021/nr-occ-2021-8.html.

11. Office of the Comptroller of the Currency, "OCC Puts Hold on Fair Access Rule," news release, January 28, 2021, https://www.occ.gov/news-issuances/news-releases/2021/nr-occ-2021-14.html.

12. US Senate, *Fair Access to Banking Act*, S.293, 118th Cong., 1st sess., introduced February 7, 2023, https://www.congress.gov/bill/118th-congress/senate-bill/293.

13. US Senate, *SAFER Banking Act*, S.2860, 118th Cong., 1st sess., introduced September 20, 2023, https://www.congress.gov/bill/118th-congress/senate-bill/2860.

CONCLUSION: DISRUPTING THE POWER TO PUNISH

1. Brian Knight and Trace Mitchell, "Private Policies and Public Power: When Banks Act as Regulators Within a Regime of Privilege," *New York University Journal of Law and Liberty* 13, no. 1 (October 9, 2019), https://ssrn.com/abstract=3466854.

INDEX